POSTCARD HISTORY SERIES

Delaware

IN VINTAGE POSTCARDS

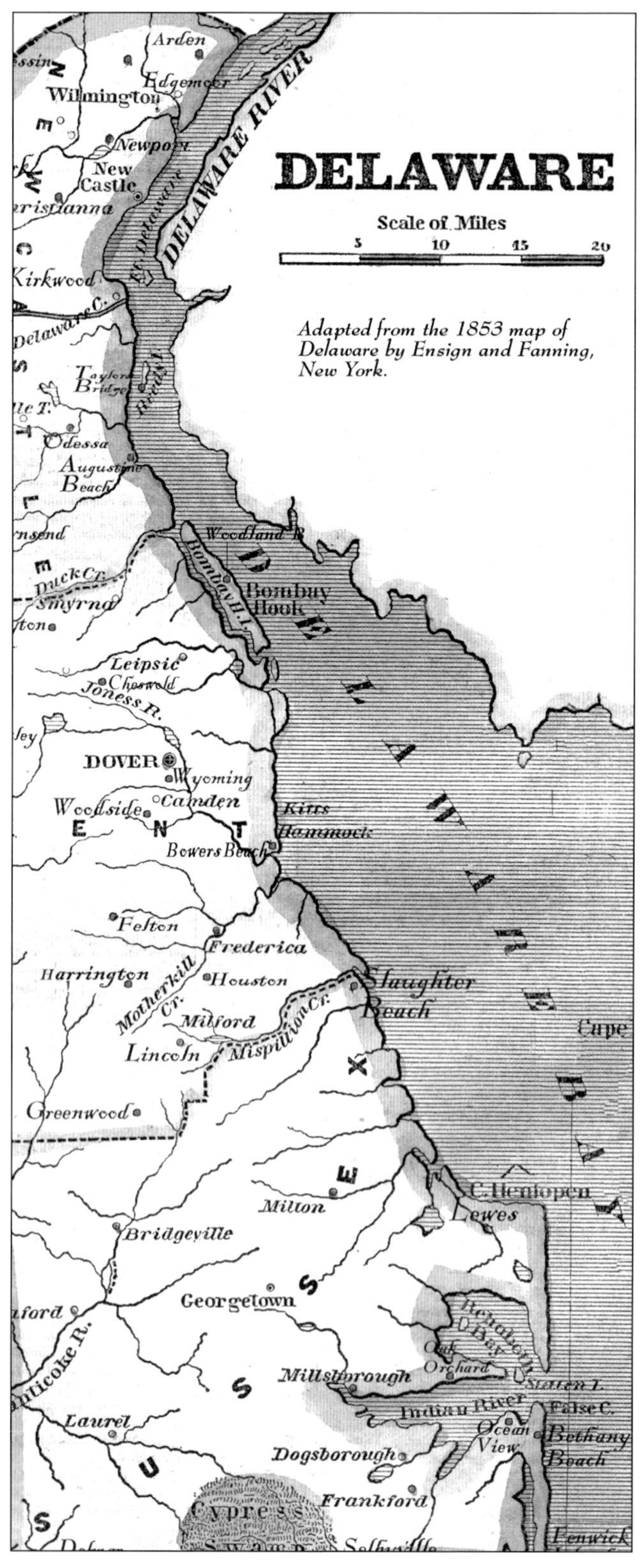

Adapted from the 1853 map of Delaware by Ensign and Fanning, New York.

POSTCARD HISTORY SERIES

Delaware

IN VINTAGE POSTCARDS

Ellen Rendle and Constance J. Cooper

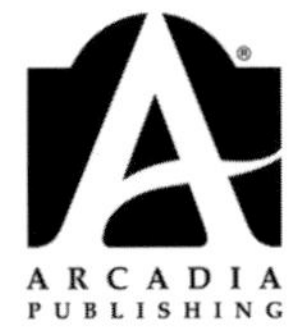

ISBN 978-0-7385-1380-5

Published by Arcadia Publishing
Charleston, South Carolina

Printed in the United States of America

Library of Congress Catalog Card Number: 2001091921

For all general information contact Arcadia Publishing at:
Telephone 843-853-2070
Fax 843-853-0044
E-Mail sales@arcadiapublishing.com
For customer service and orders:
Toll-Free 1-888-313-2665

Visit us on the Internet at www.arcadiapublishing.com

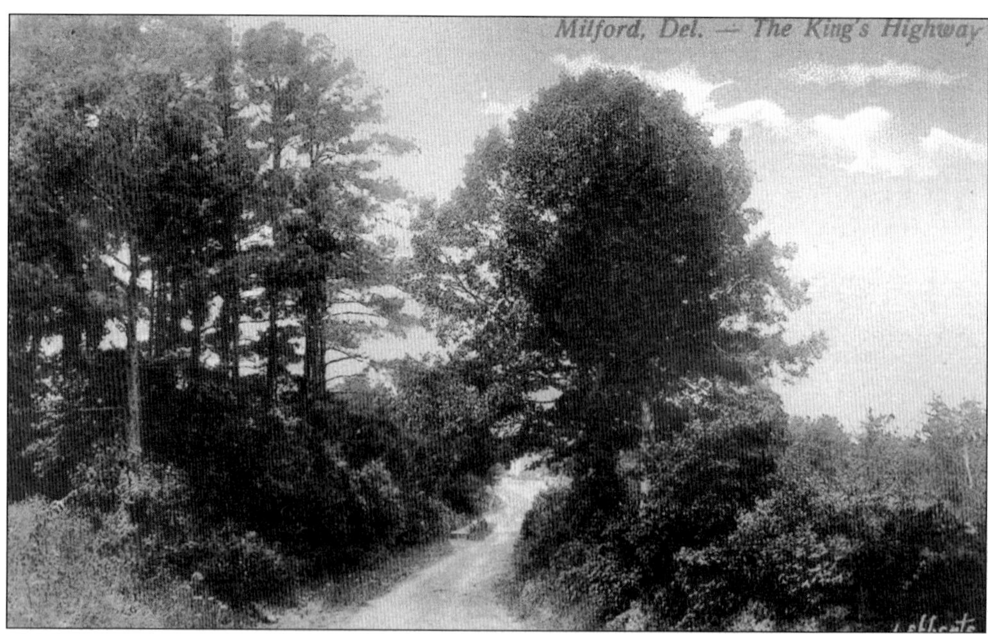

THE KING'S HIGHWAY, MILFORD, 1910S. The present Route 13 closely follows the King's Highway route, which may have been laid out before 1700. George B. Hynson, a lawyer, publisher, and author of the state song, "Our Delaware," wrote a poem entitled "From New Castle to Lewes: The King's Highway." Part of that poem follows.

Riding down to Lewes
On the King's highway,
Skirting creeks and riverlets,
Winding to the Bay;

Through the somber forest shades—
Thickets wild with bloom
Where the sweet magnolia
Revels in perfume,

While the thrush and mocking bird
Carol all the day—
Riding down to Lewes
On the King's highway . . .

Contents

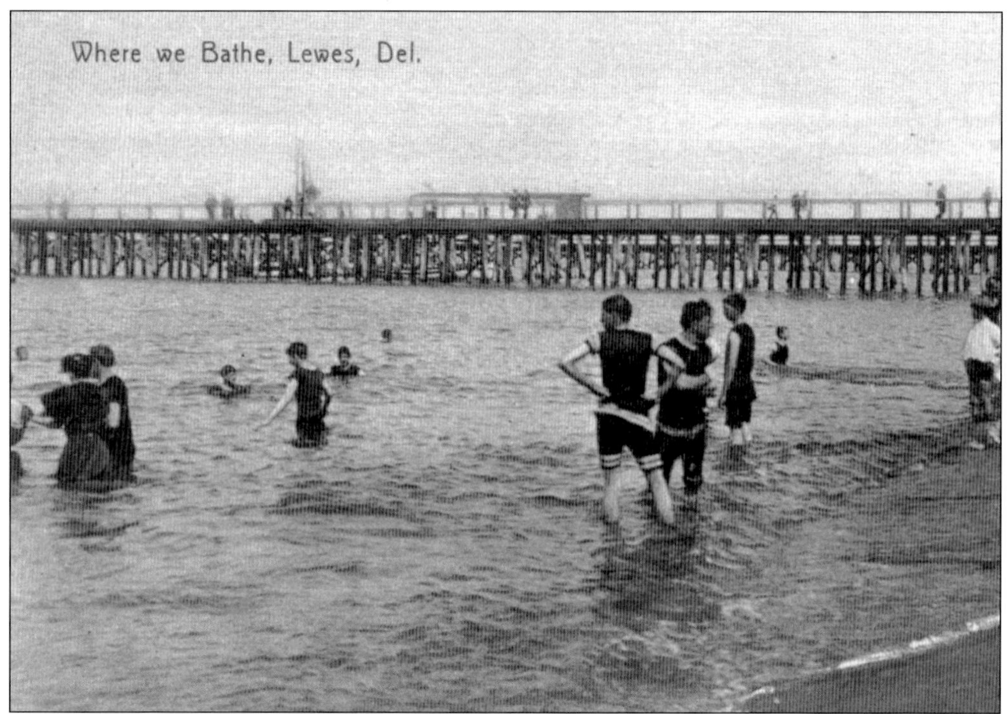

WHERE WE BATHE, LEWES, c. 1910. Here, bathers relax in the ocean. The Iron Pier visible in the background was built by the federal government and was originally used as a light station and life-saving station. It was later used by the Queen Anne's Railroad for shipping produce, freight, and passengers. Lewes served as southern Delaware's connection to eastern inland Delmarva ports.

ACKNOWLEDGMENTS

Compiling *Delaware* has been a great opportunity for the authors to rediscover the First State's back roads and small towns. We hope that you enjoy the trip as much as we have.

We would like to thank the following individuals for their assistance: Gordon Pfeiffer, president of the Historical Society of Delaware for his enthusiasm and generosity; Dr. Barbara E. Benson, executive director of the Historical Society of Delaware for her support and guidance; Annette Bristow for her patience, enthusiasm, scanning, and typing and typing and typing; Jim Sekcienski of the Whitecaps Café for his help with Oak Orchard postcards; Morgan Heinen for help with Milford views; Mrs. Dorothy Downs, who generously lent cards for the Society's use; and finally, to all the people who have donated postcards to the Society's collection over the years.

We are delighted to be able to share such a large number of our cards with you.

INTRODUCTION

Postcards weren't just souvenirs for travelers in the early 1900s. One of the nation's first crazes in the early years of the 20th century, postcards were used by many people to send quick messages and greetings, much as we use the telephone and e-mail today. Unlike our modern means of communication, however, these early postcards left a paper trail that can inform, amuse, and delight us today. Many cards were commercially produced. They depicted main streets, residential neighborhoods, schools, churches, public buildings, historic sites, beautiful scenery, and even farms and factories. The format proved to be so popular that private individuals had unique photographic images of themselves, or their homes, farms, and businesses printed as postcards to send to friends and family. Although many of the towns and scenes may now seem quaint or even obscure, they were not in their own time. Today these cards provide a rich visual record of the past.

Not only did people send postcards, they also saved and collected them. Today, many have found their way into the collections of libraries and historical societies. The Historical Society of Delaware has approximately 1,800 postcards of scenes in the First State dating from the early 1900s to the present. *Delaware* presents over 200 cards dating from 1905 to 1925, a fraction of the society's collection. They were selected to present highlights of the landscape and built environment of Delaware in the early 20th century. The society's entire postcard collection may be viewed during the library's regular hours.

Homes, main streets, schools, steamers carrying passengers along the Chesapeake and Delaware Canal, a yard full of yams at a Seaford packing plant, shad nets and boats in New Castle—all teach us about ways of life long vanished. Looking at cards, we witness first hand the pride of Georgetown residents as they decorated their downtown for Homecoming. We see busy resorts at Bowers, Oak Orchard, and Augustine Beach, places that today serve as private havens compared to their busy past. We see the pride invested in churches, schools, and courthouses, and the bright business and economic prospects symbolized in the postcard of a small town's railroad station.

The early 20th century was a transitional era for Delawareans. People traveled by buggy, steamer, railway, or automobile. During the 20 years depicted in this book, the state's landscape was undergoing important changes. Small southern towns like Laurel, Milton, and Milford experienced a decline in shipbuilding and the use of ships for transporting produce to market. The railroad, which laid its tracks down the state during the late 1850s and 1860s, both made and broke small towns. Some, like Delmar, used the railroad to grow. This community did not exist until a station was build in the middle of a forest and businesses and homes grew around it. Others, like Cantwell's Bridge (Odessa), shunned the railroad to cling to shipping by water, only to find their economic base migrating to the nearest railroad station.

During this era, miles of roads were paved for automobile traffic, providing yet another avenue for commerce and travel. Opening ceremonies for the Du Pont Highway in 1924 signaled a new era. Newly paved roads across Sussex County brought countless out-of-state tourists to the beach.

It is not surprising then that postcards seem to be akin to badges of pride for small communities. New school buildings, hospitals, parades, and business concerns were all sources of this pride. Who wouldn't want to send a distant friend or relative the latest card showing a beautiful new residential street in town, or the latest view of the main business intersection?

In the end, we are the recipients of these postcards. They were not made for us or sent to us. But they tell us the story of their era, one of hope and pride. *Delaware* is a delightful trip around the 1,982 square miles that First Staters call home, through the marshlands and farmlands, along the shorelines of creeks, rivers, and bays, and down city streets. These images allow us to travel on the best mode of transportation for a trip back to the early 1900s—the postcard.

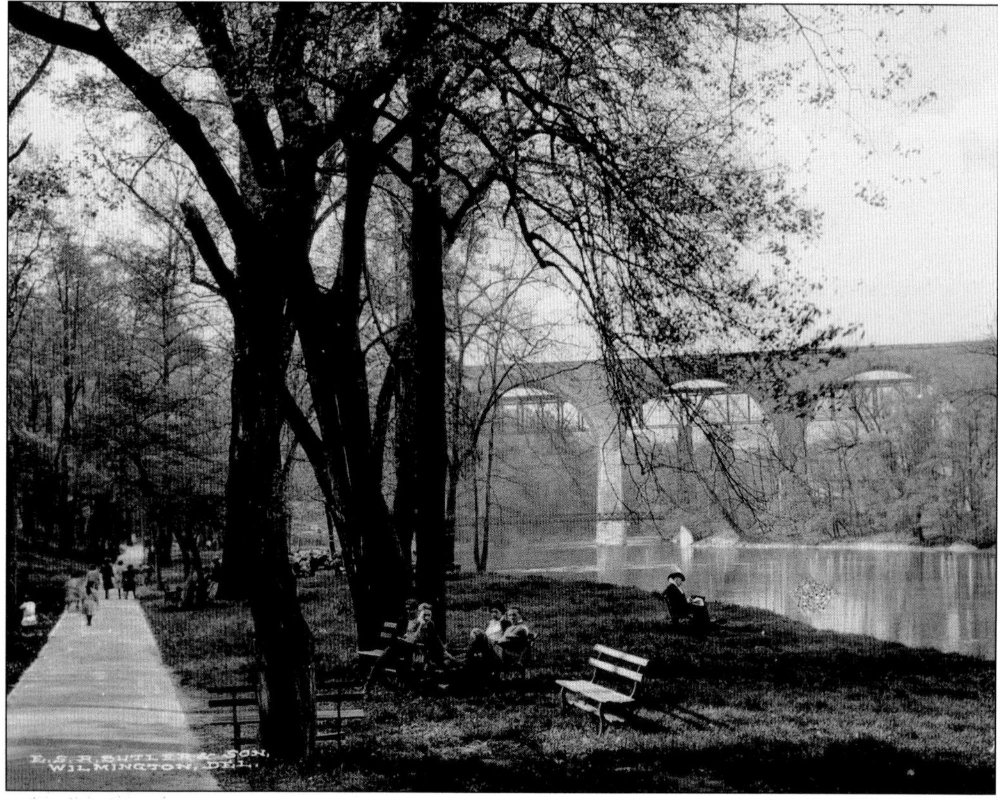

BRANDYWINE PARK, 1910–1930. A scene familiar to Wilmington residents, this view looks west in Brandywine Park. The Baltimore and Ohio (B&O) Railroad stone bridge, built in 1909, is seen with the older, steel-truss B&O bridge, built in 1884, behind it.

One

Sussex County Beaches

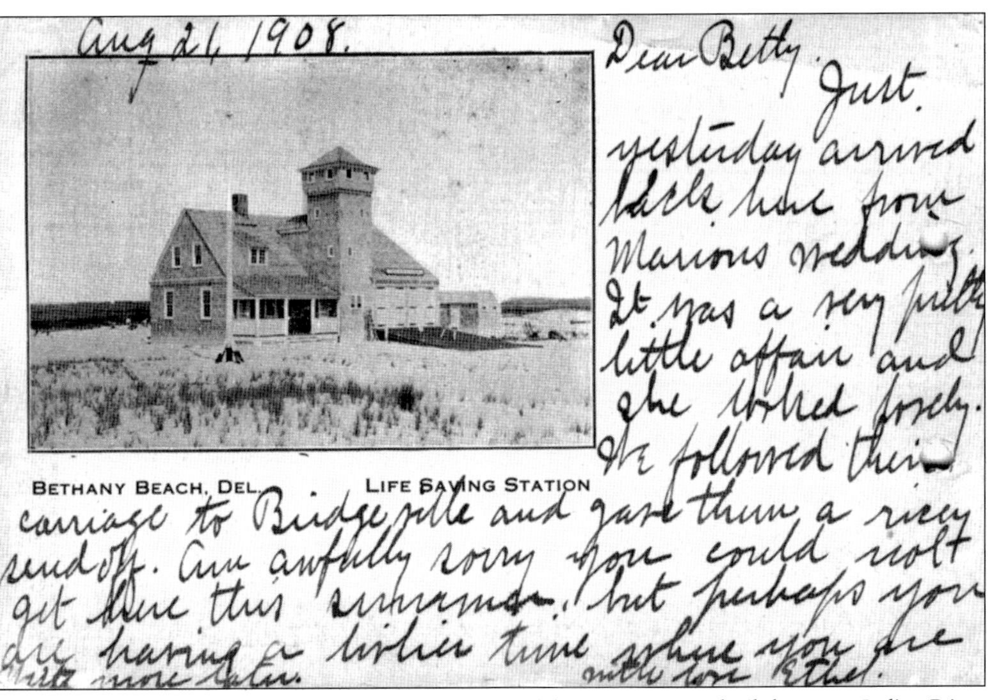

Life-Saving Station, Bethany Beach, 1908. This life-saving station, built between Indian River and Fenwick Island in 1907, was taken over by the Coast Guard in 1909. A chain of life-saving stations every five miles along the coastline rescued sailors from wrecked or marooned ships and prevented the looting of stranded ships.

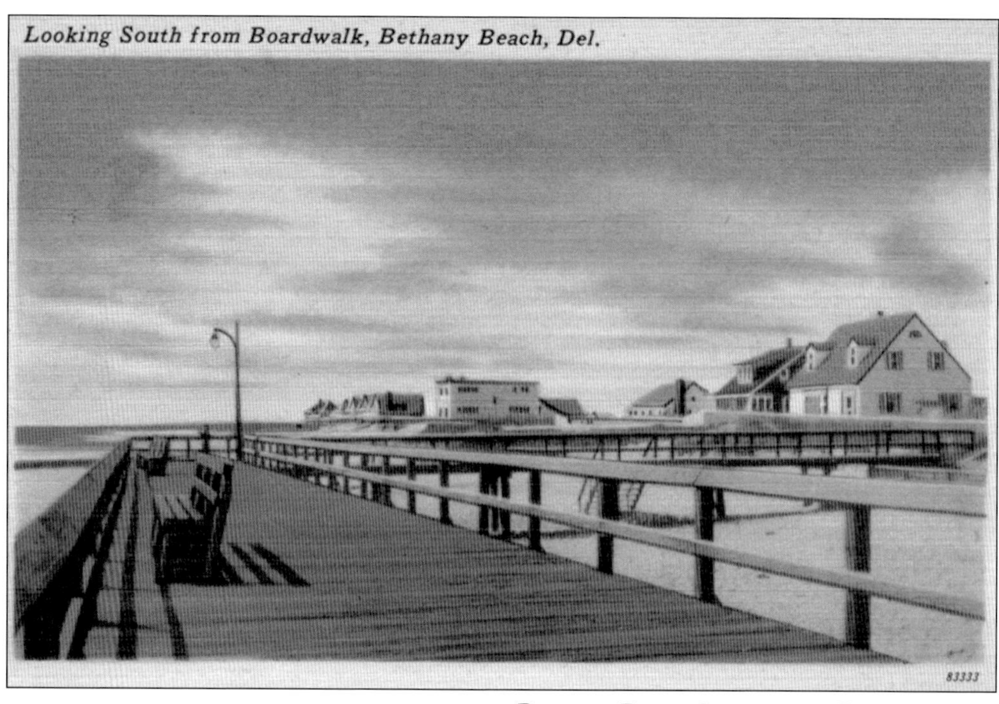

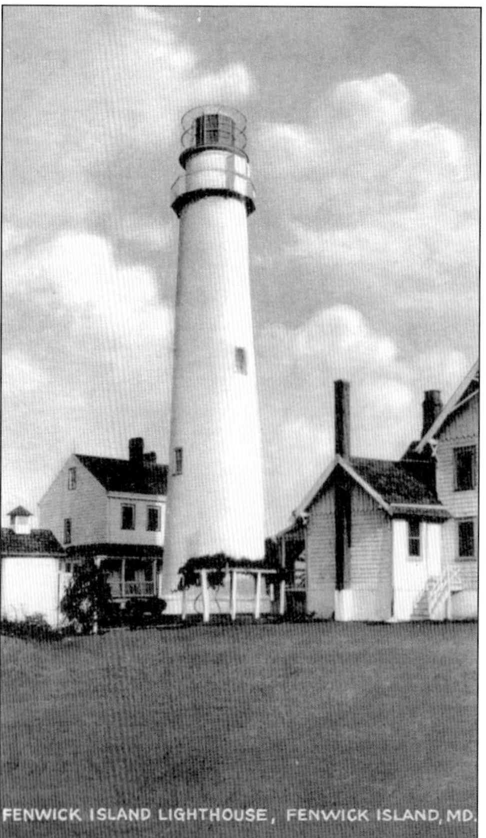

BETHANY BEACH SOUTH FROM BOARDWALK, AFTER 1925. Bethany Beach was described in 1983 in the *Chicago Tribune* as "the quintessential American beach, upright, without being dull." The Disciples' Christian Missionary Church founded the town in 1898 and named it Bethany Beach in 1901. The first boardwalk, laid in 1907, was destroyed by a storm in 1920. Delaware's second largest beach town retains a quiet atmosphere today.

FENWICK ISLAND LIGHTHOUSE, FENWICK ISLAND. Made of brick and standing 85 feet tall, this lighthouse was in use from August 1, 1859, until it was deactivated on December 14, 1978. It is currently owned by the State of Delaware. A local friends group opens it for tourists.

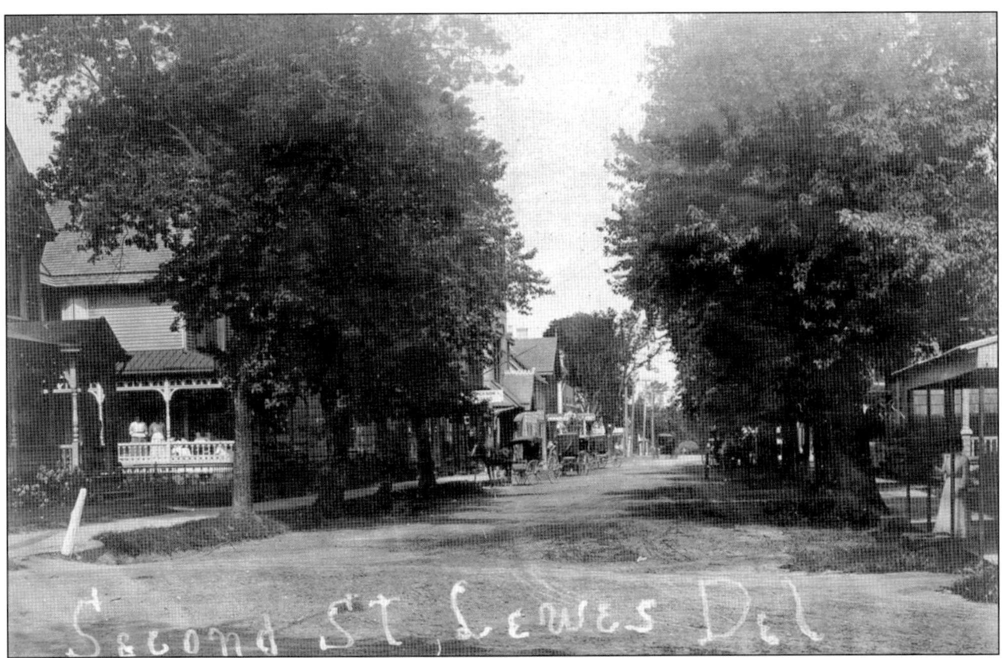

SECOND STREET, LEWES, *C.* 1910. This card, along with the cards on pages 12 and 13, all include detailed descriptions written by the sender; the backs of the cards are shown on the lower-half of each page. This beautiful tree-lined block was home to a Dr. Joseph B. Lyons and Dr. Hiram R. Burton, two of the town's doctors. Just one block away are businesses with horses and buggies parked along the street.

POST CARD

AZO
PLACE
STAMP
HERE
AZO

CORRESPONDENCE HERE

This street starts from
Dr Lyons and runs to
Dr. Burton. The house
on the left, where you see
the porch is Fred Burtons.
Mrs Wallace, Lib, Maggie
Fred and Edith. The
end of the street is Drs
Burtons.

1998.53

NAME AND ADDRESS HERE

You can tell the
other places. This
is a very good
picture, things will
look familiar.

From
Dollie

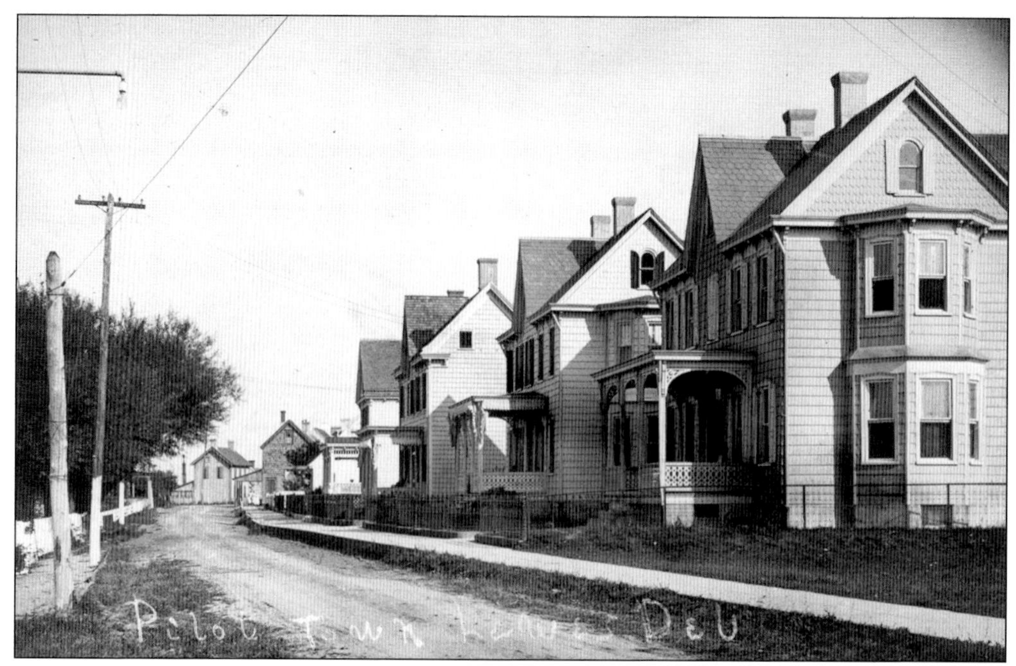

Pilot Town, Lewes, c. 1910. Pilot Town got its name from the river pilots who lived along the road that fronted the canal. The first two homes from the right were owned by pilots John and Jim Kelly, respectively.

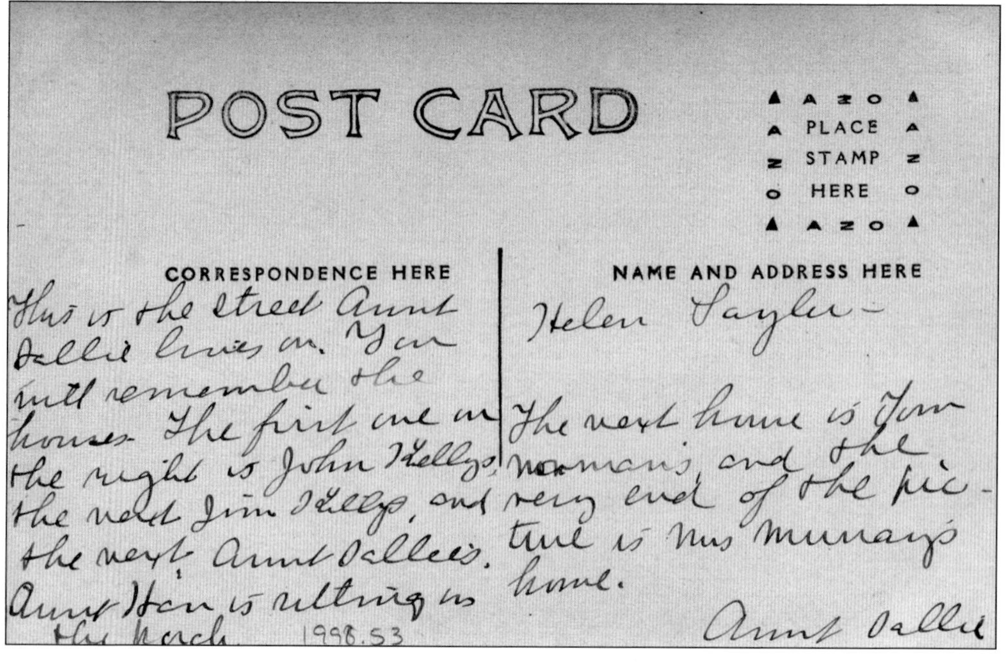

POST CARD

AZO
PLACE
STAMP
HERE
AZO

CORRESPONDENCE HERE

This is the street Aunt Sallie lives on. You will remember the houses. The first one on the right is John Kelly's, the next Jim Kelly's, and the next Aunt Sallie's. Aunt Han is sitting in the porch

1998.53

NAME AND ADDRESS HERE

Helen Sayler –

The next home is Tom Norman's and the very end of the picture is Mrs Murray's home.

Aunt Sallie

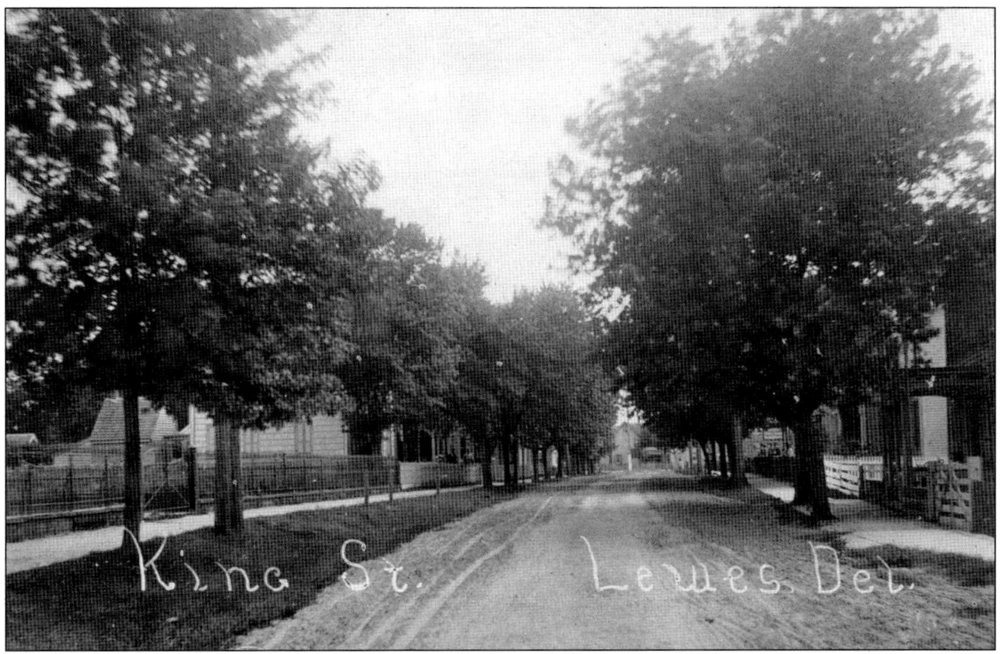

King Street, Lewes, c. 1910. Looking along King Street toward the railroad depot, the fence to the far right surrounds the Presbyterian churchyard.

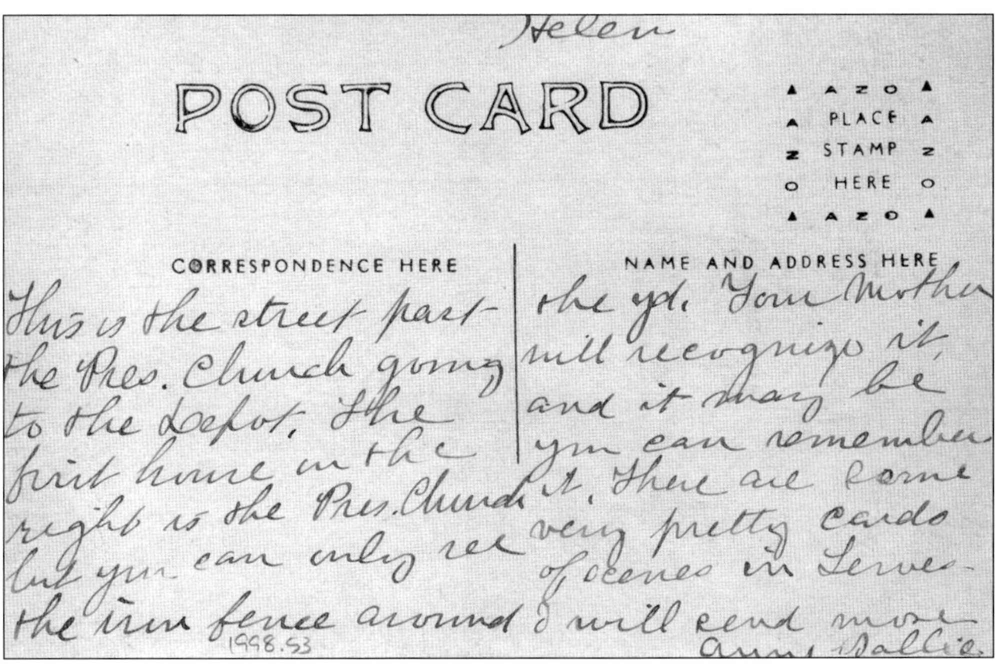

Helen

POST CARD

AZO
PLACE
STAMP
HERE
AZO

CORRESPONDENCE HERE

This is the street past
the Pres. Church going
to the Depot. The
first house on the
right is the Pres. Church
but you can only see
the iron fence around

NAME AND ADDRESS HERE

the yd. Your Mother
will recognize it,
and it may be
you can remember
it. There are some
very pretty cards
of scenes in Lewes.
I will send more
Aunt Sallie.

1998.53

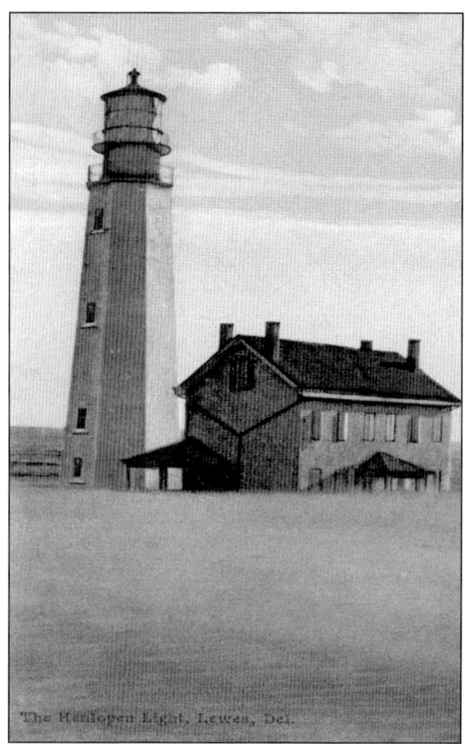

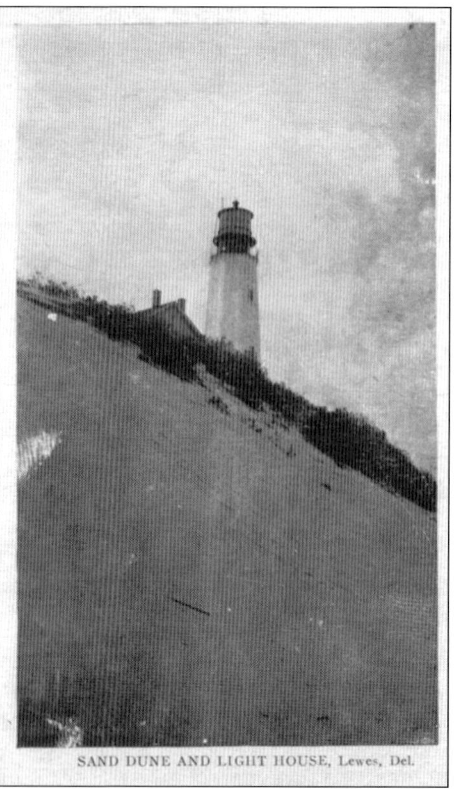

Above: **THE HENLOPEN LIGHT, LEWES, 1909.**
Below: **SAND DUNE AND LIGHT HOUSE, LEWES, 1910S.**
This most famous ghost of Lewes, built in 1765, was only the sixth lighthouse to be built in the colonies. It was among a dozen lighthouses turned over to the federal government according to the peace treaty with Britain after the Revolutionary War. Drifting sands continually presented problems for the light and its keepers. Some estimate that the lighthouse was built one mile inland, and by the 1860s, the rate of drift was calculated at 11 feet per year. In April 1926, the sand had shifted so much that the entire structure toppled.

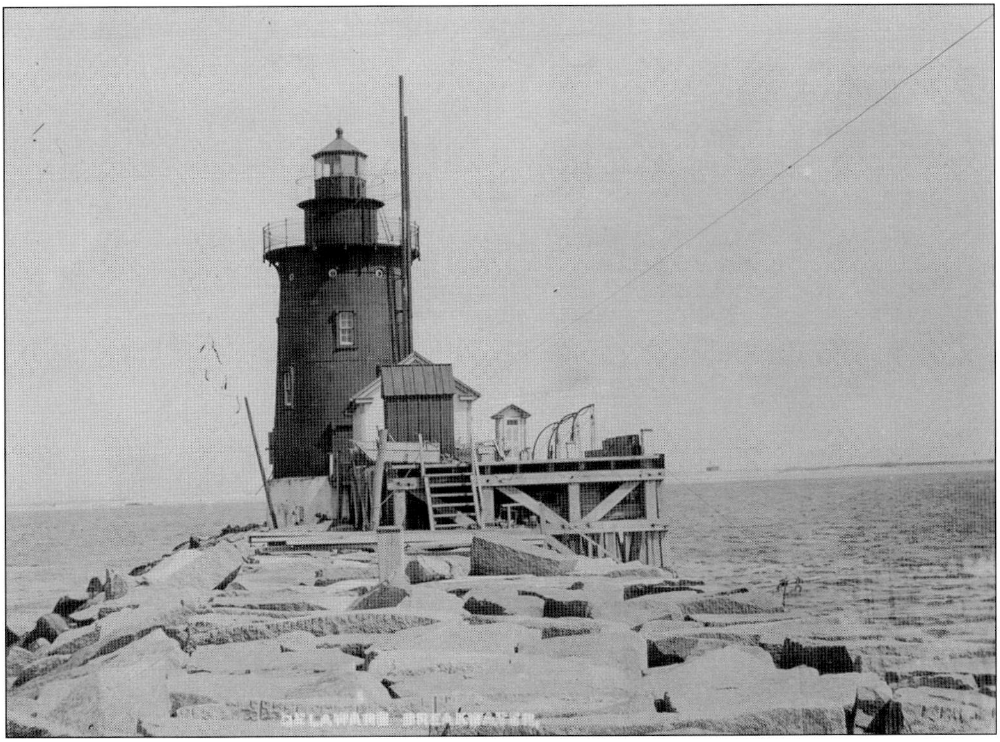

DELAWARE BREAKWATER, 1898–1900. Pictured here is an early view of the Delaware Breakwater east end lighthouse.

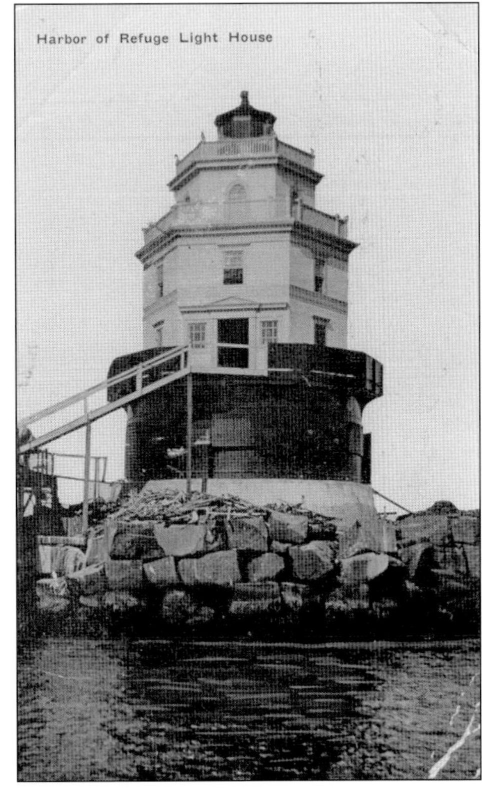

HARBOR OF REFUGE, LIGHTHOUSE, c. 1910. Completed about 1908, this lighthouse was built on the southern end of the National Harbor of Refuge Breakwater. It had a concrete block and iron substructure and its concrete block foundation was 40 feet in diameter. Even so, it toppled in a strong storm in 1920 and was replaced in 1926.

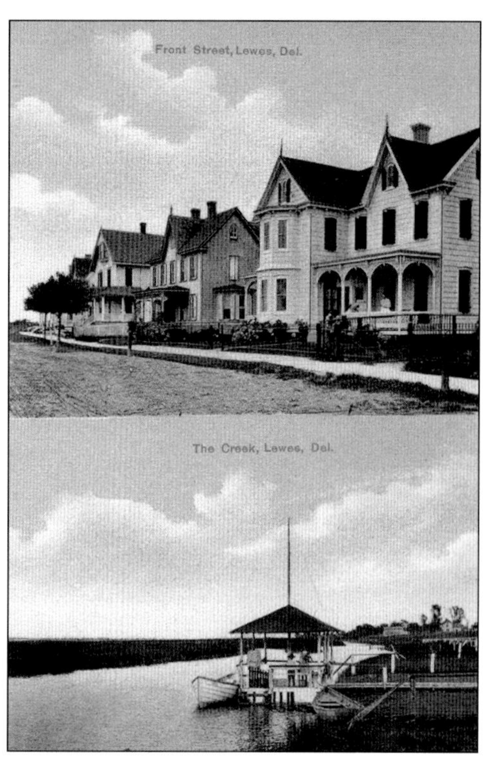

FRONT STREET AND THE CREEK, LEWES, c. 1900. The top view shows homes along the 100 block of Front Street, also known as Gills Neck Road. Many Delaware River and Bay pilots built their homes along Front Street to watch approaching ships from their "widow's walk." The bottom view shows private piers and a boathouse along Lewes Creek. Construction of the Lewes-Rehoboth Canal began in 1893.

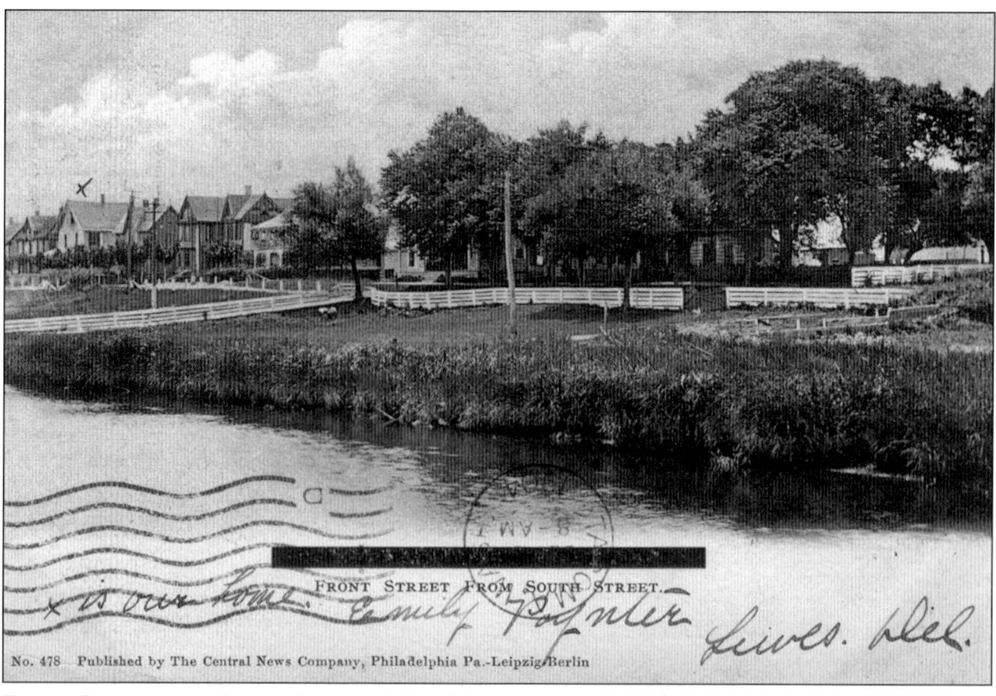

FRONT STREET FROM SOUTH STREET, 1904. This view looks across the Lewes Creek, now the Lewes and Rehoboth Canal, at the homes along Front Street in 1904. Emily Paynter marked an "X" above her family's home. At the time, William C. Paynter worked at the life-saving station.

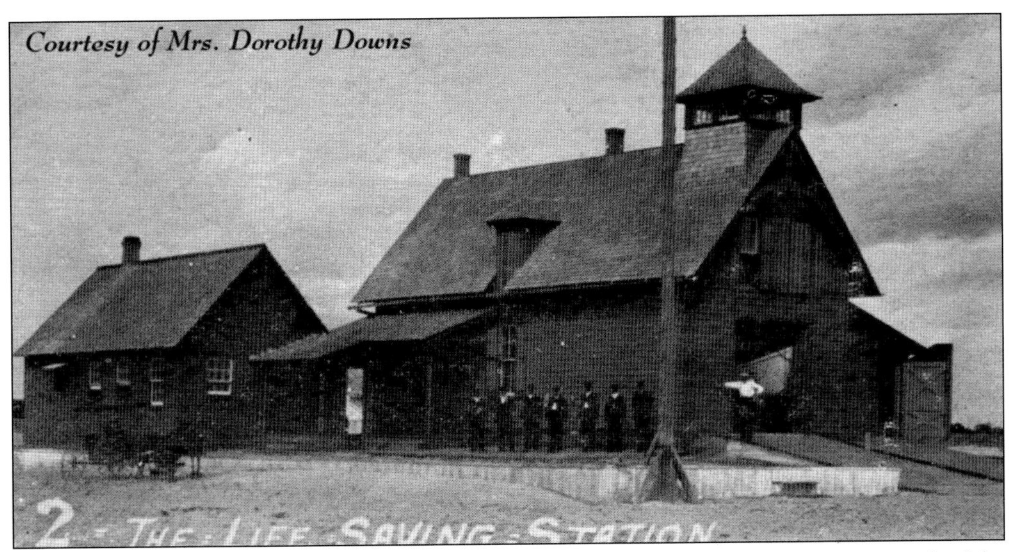

The Life Saving Station, Rehoboth, c. 1905. Because of treacherous storms and tricky sailing conditions, the United States Coast Guard established stations along the Atlantic coastline beginning in 1859. These stations, stocked with firewood, clothing, and food, had paid keepers. Stations at Indian River, Cape Henlopen, and Rehoboth were established in the 1870s. The stations had two purposes: to save the lives of seaman in trouble and to prevent the looting of stranded ships.

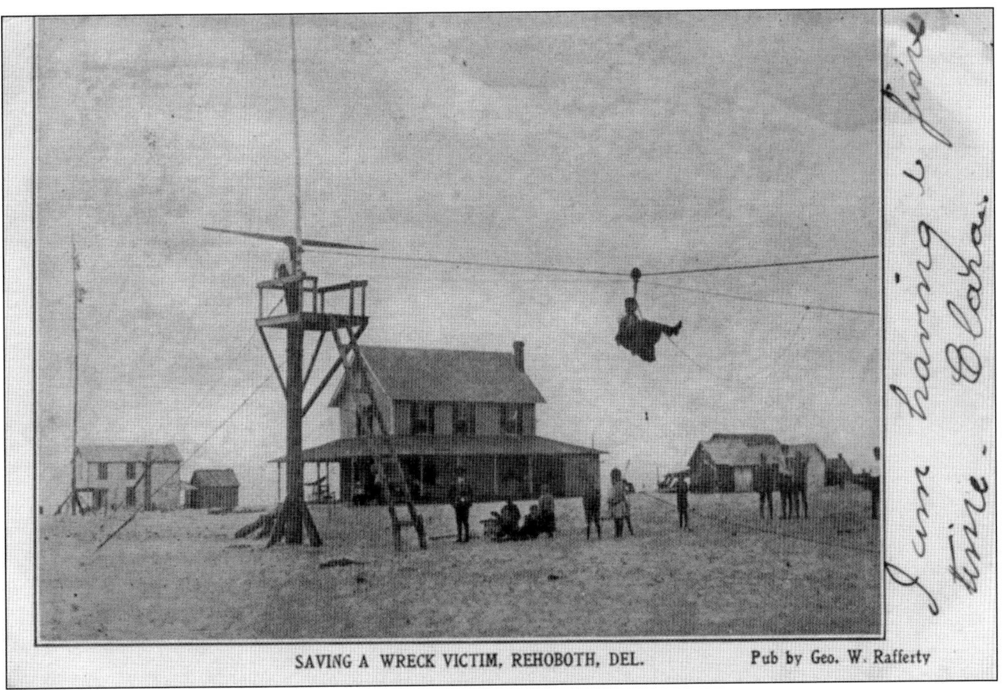

Saving A Wreck Victim, Rehoboth, 1907. This postcard shows one of the four life-saving stations in the area. The breeches buoy shown in use here aided in the rescue of people from beached ships.

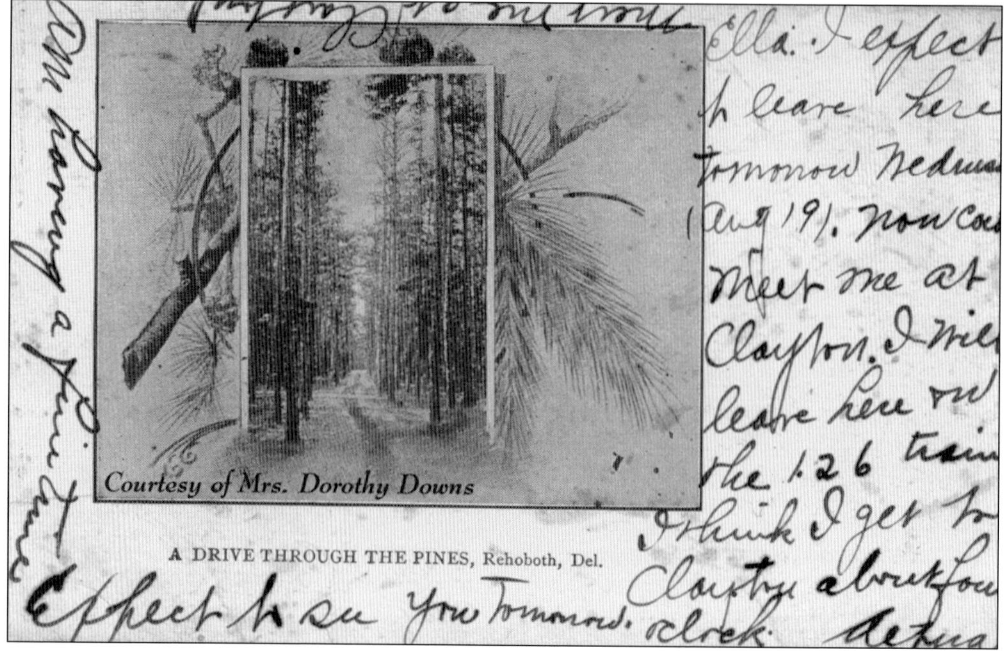

A Drive through the Pines, Rehoboth, 1908. One of the attractions of the Delaware beaches was their proximity to the dark, cool, fragrant pines that grew to within a few hundred feet of the ocean.

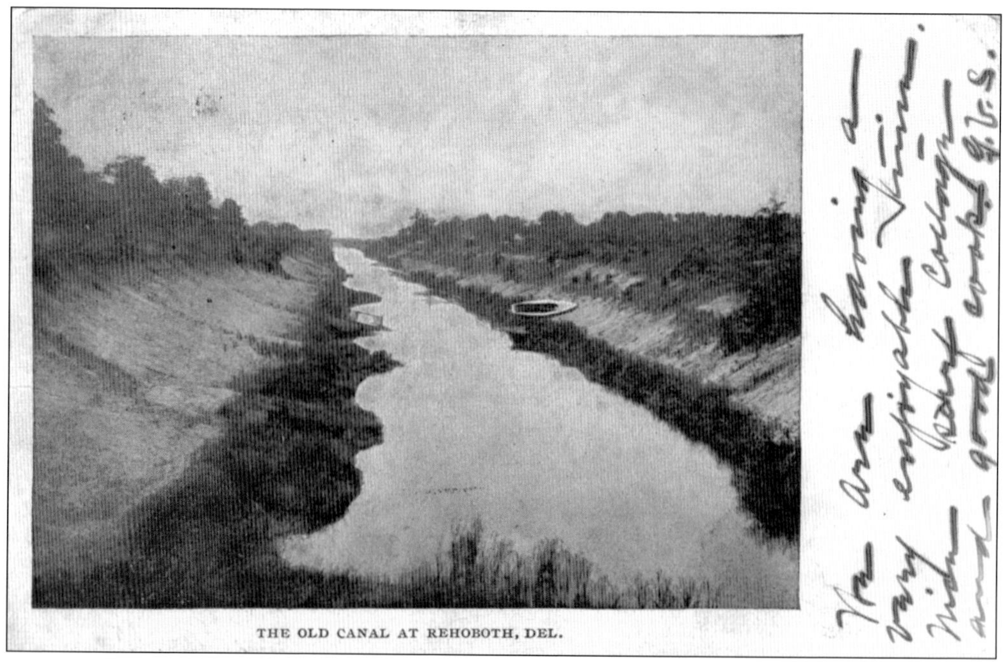

The Old Canal at Rehoboth, 1908. This view of the Old Canal was taken before the United States River and Harbor Act appropriated money to build the Lewes and Rehoboth Canal. The new canal linked the town and harbor with the Rehoboth and Indian Bays and, via the earlier Assawoman Canal, with the bays of the lower Delmarva Peninsula.

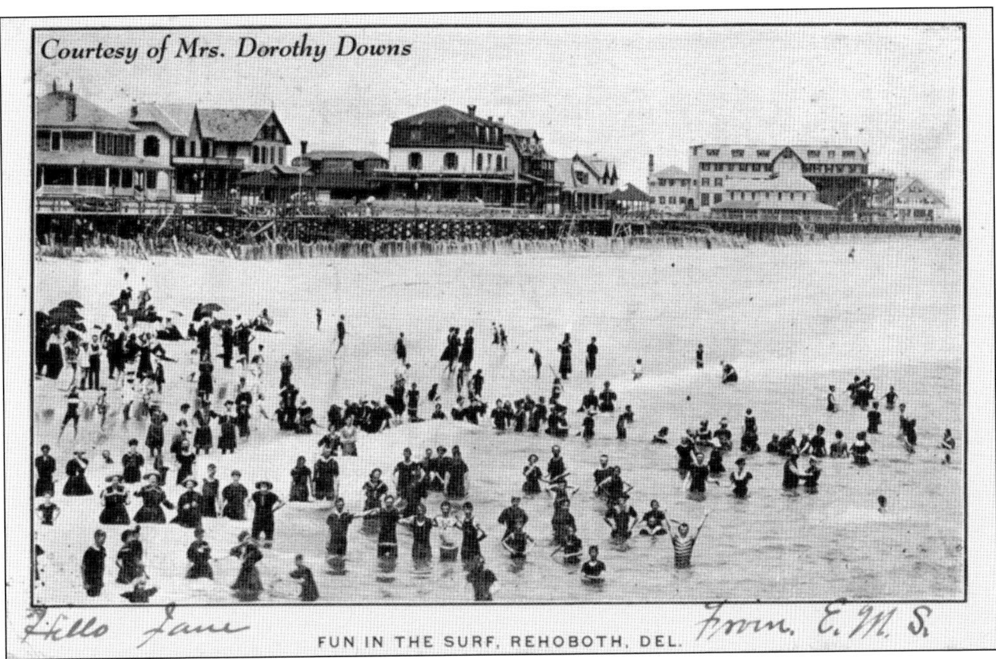

Fun in the Surf, Rehoboth, 1906. Looking toward the north end of the boardwalk, the large building at the far right is the Henlopen Hotel. In the early 1900s, the hotel sponsored "hops" or dances every Wednesday and Saturday night.

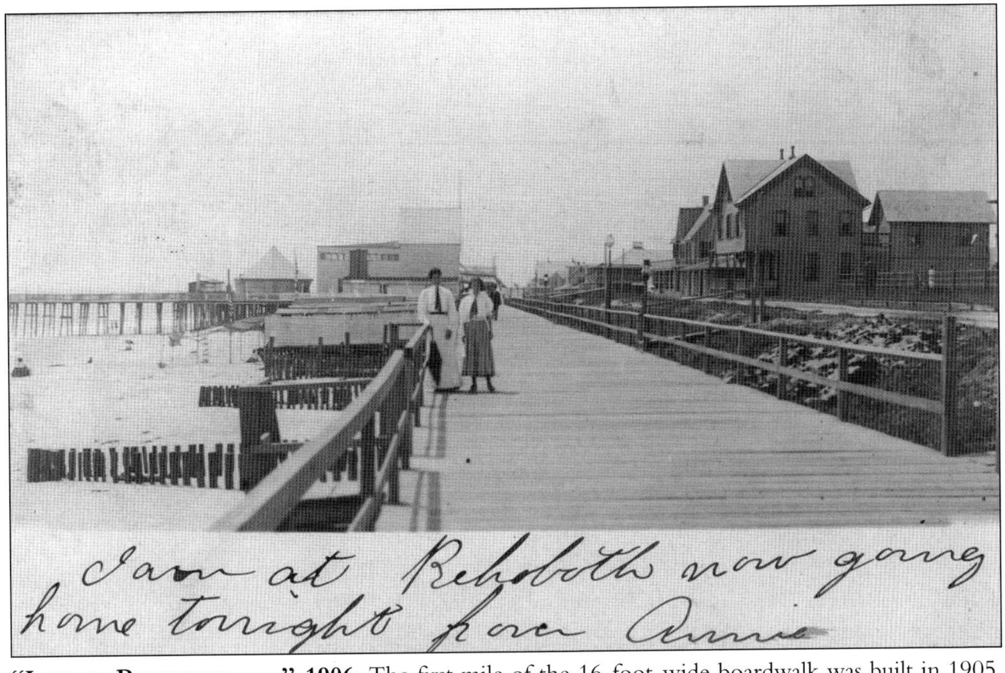

"I am at Rehoboth . . ." 1906. The first mile of the 16-foot-wide boardwalk was built in 1905, and gas lamps ran its length. In the center is Horn's Pavilion and pier. To the left of Horn's is the roundhouse—a pavilion used for gatherings. Horn's, the roundhouse, and the pier were destroyed in a 1914 storm. The store moved inland; the pier and roundhouse were never rebuilt.

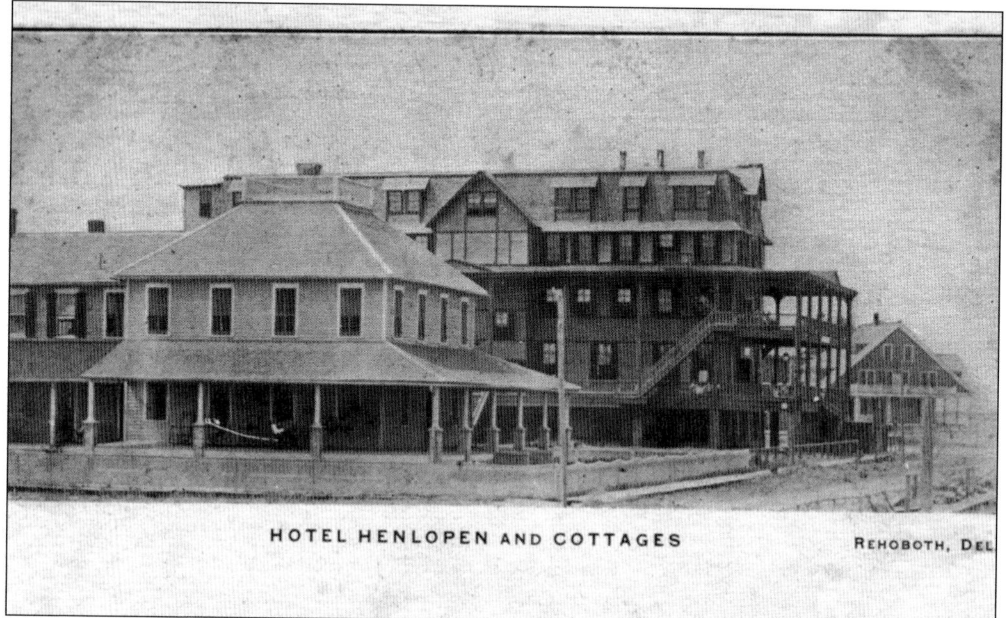

HOTEL HENLOPEN AND COTTAGES, REHOBOTH, BEFORE 1910. These two postcards span 30 years and show two of the faces of the Hotel Henlopen and Cottages, a landmark in Rehoboth. The earlier view is undated but was taken before 1910. The building then underwent an art deco renovation when it was stuccoed and given a brick beach facade. The next remodeling gave it an even more modern appearance as seen in the 1941 view.

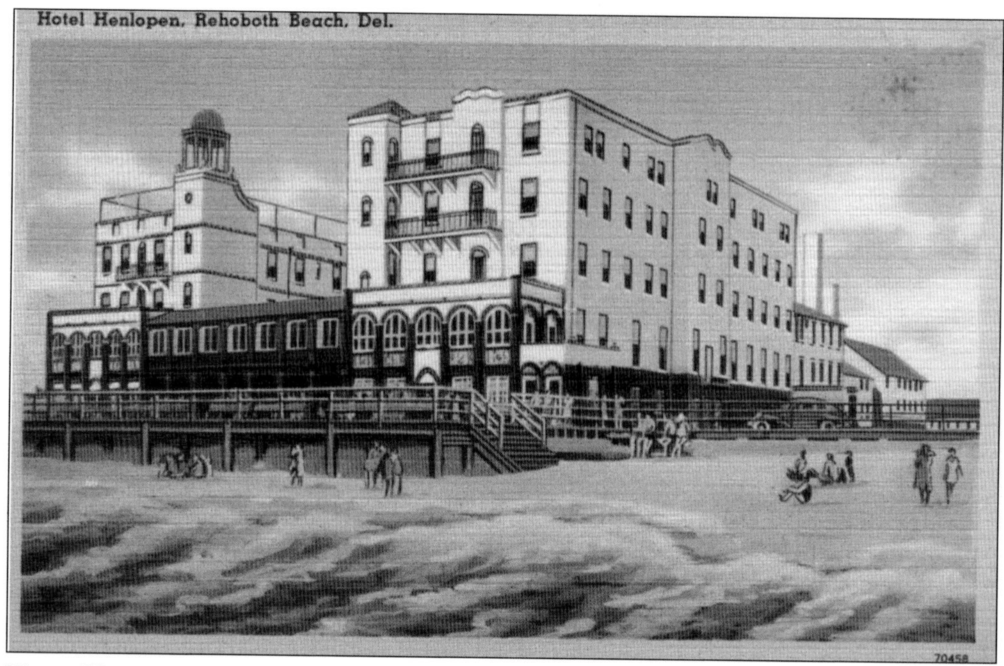

HOTEL HENLOPEN, REHOBOTH BEACH, 1941.

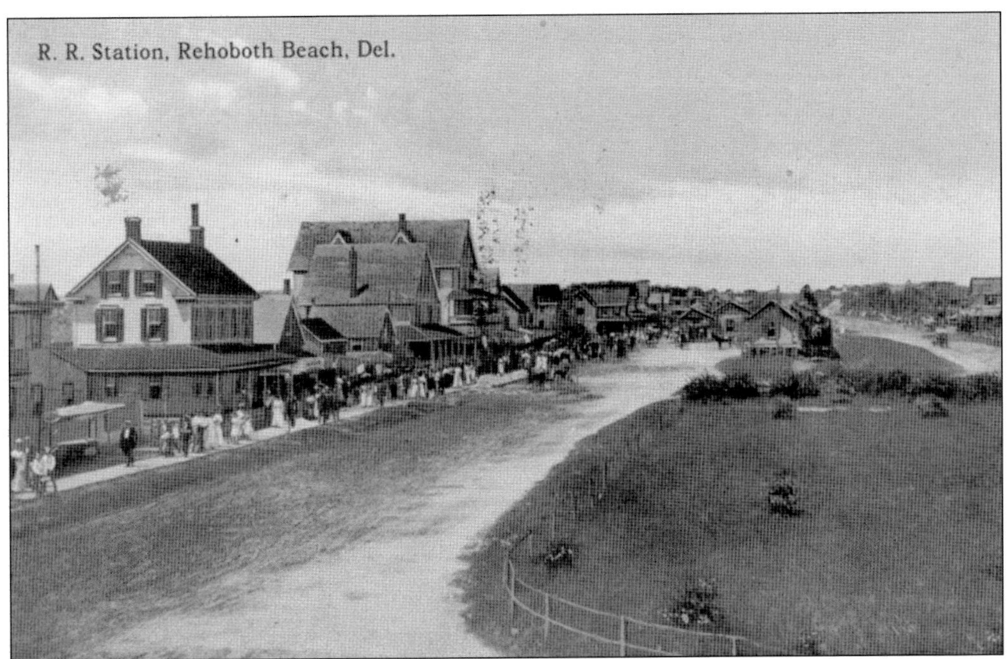

Railroad Station Rehoboth Beach, 1913. Rehoboth must have seemed like a perfect resort for one newly married couple. This postcard was sent to New Bedford, Massachusetts and reads, "We're here finishing our honeymoon. It is real nice down here. Had a good dip today and expect to take another tomorrow. All sun burnt to pieces. Herb & Ruthe."

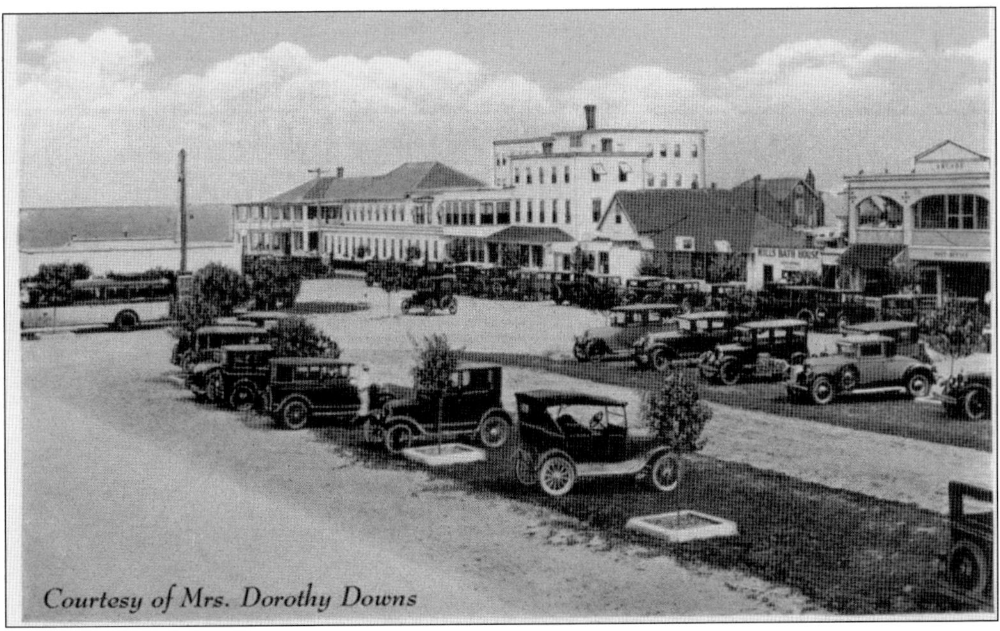

South Side of Rehoboth Avenue from Carlton Hotel, Rehoboth Beach, 1920s. A brochure described Rehoboth about 1920 as follows: "Here during the season may be found representations of the wealth, beauty, and fashions of our large cities, and while its walk may be crowded, it is always a well-behaved crowd."

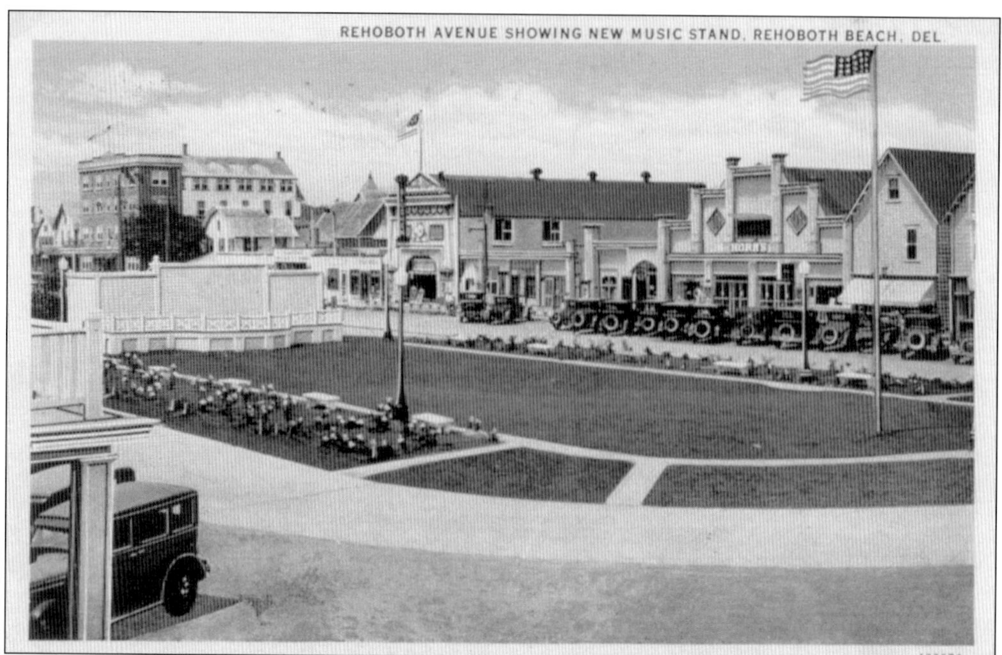

REHOBOTH AVENUE SHOWING NEW MUSIC STAND, REHOBOTH BEACH, 1929. Today, Rehoboth bustles with activity year-round, but it has not always been that way. This view, taken after a growth period during the late 1920s, shows the ocean end of Rehoboth Avenue. The large hotel on the far left is the Hotel Carlton; Horn's Souvenir Shop is the large, stair-stepped facade near the center of the view.

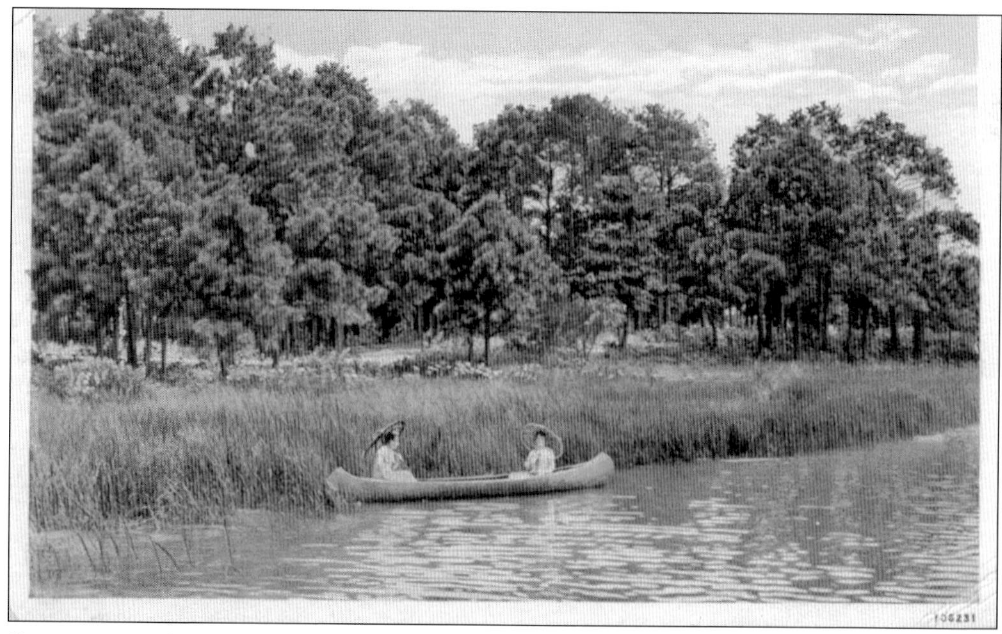

CANOEING ON SILVER LAKE, REHOBOTH BEACH, 1928. Some vacationers, like these two ladies, preferred the calm, serene waters of Silver Lake to the beach or bay. Silver Lake is in south Rehoboth Beach. Today it is a residential neighborhood.

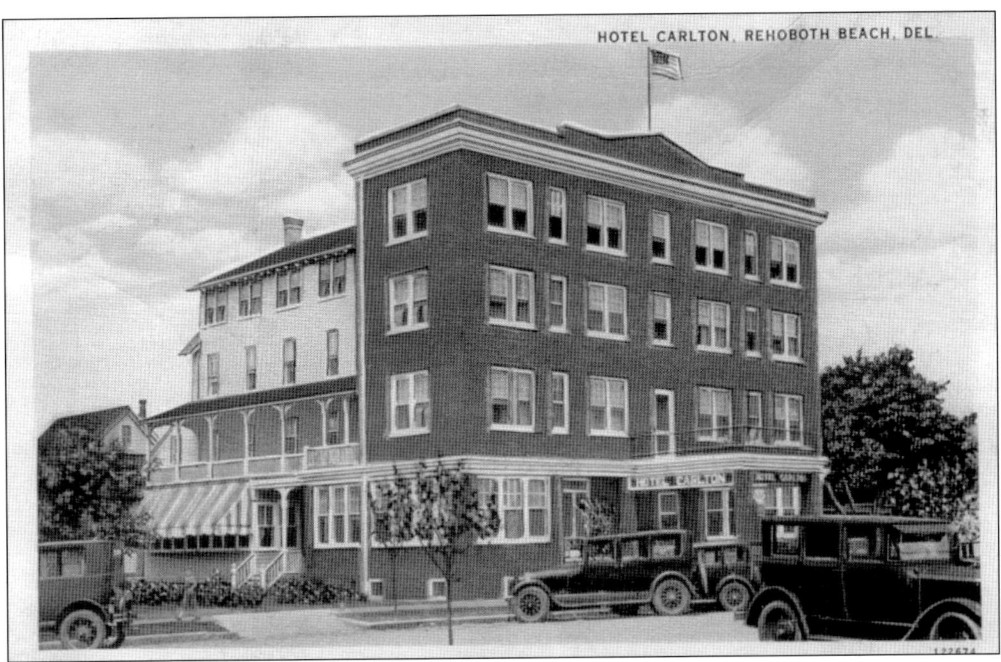

Hotel Carlton, Rehoboth Beach, 1929. Originally the Hotel Brayton, which opened in 1912, this hotel became known as the Hotel Carlton. During the 1920s expansion and modernization of Rehoboth, the hotel gave itself a facelift. The front of the hotel was transformed to the larger, brick facade seen in this view. The hotel went out of business in the 1970s.

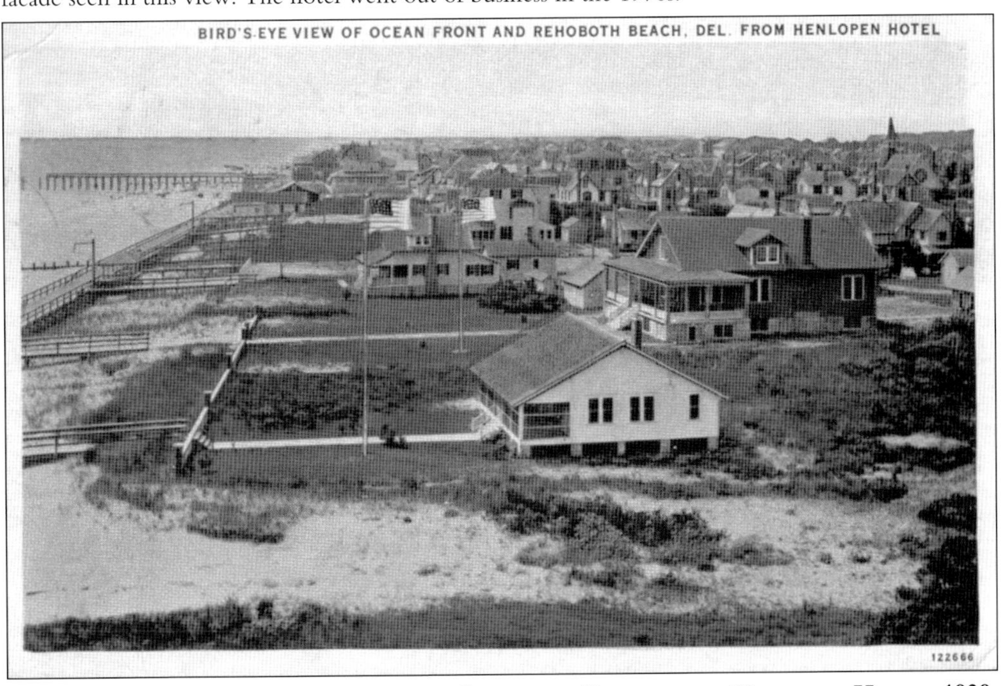

Bird's-eye View of Ocean Front and Rehoboth Beach from Henlopen Hotel, 1929. Featuring the northern end of town, this view taken from atop the Henlopen Hotel proudly displays the tremendous growth that Rehoboth underwent during the 1920s.

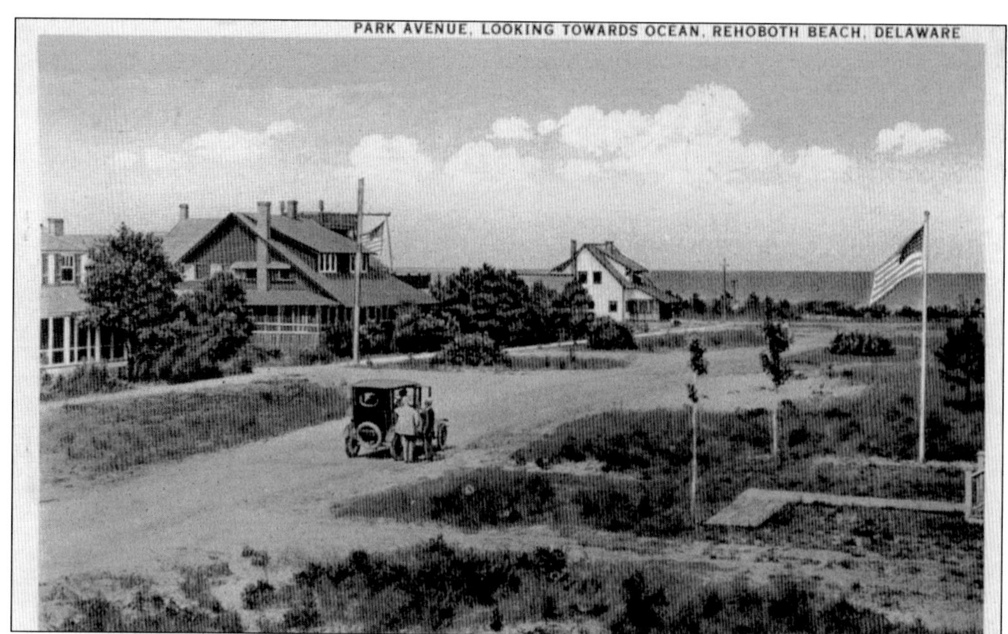

PARK AVENUE, LOOKING TOWARDS OCEAN, REHOBOTH BEACH, 1931. Both the completion of DuPont Highway in 1924 and the paving of the road from Georgetown to the beach, completed in 1925, led to a building and real estate boom in the late 1920s. Roads connecting the beach towns to the inland metropolitan areas of Baltimore and Washington brought growing numbers of tourists to Delaware. These two views show Rehoboth's development from the 1920s. While the new houses and cottages look meticulous, the yards have yet to be groomed and the roads remain unpaved.

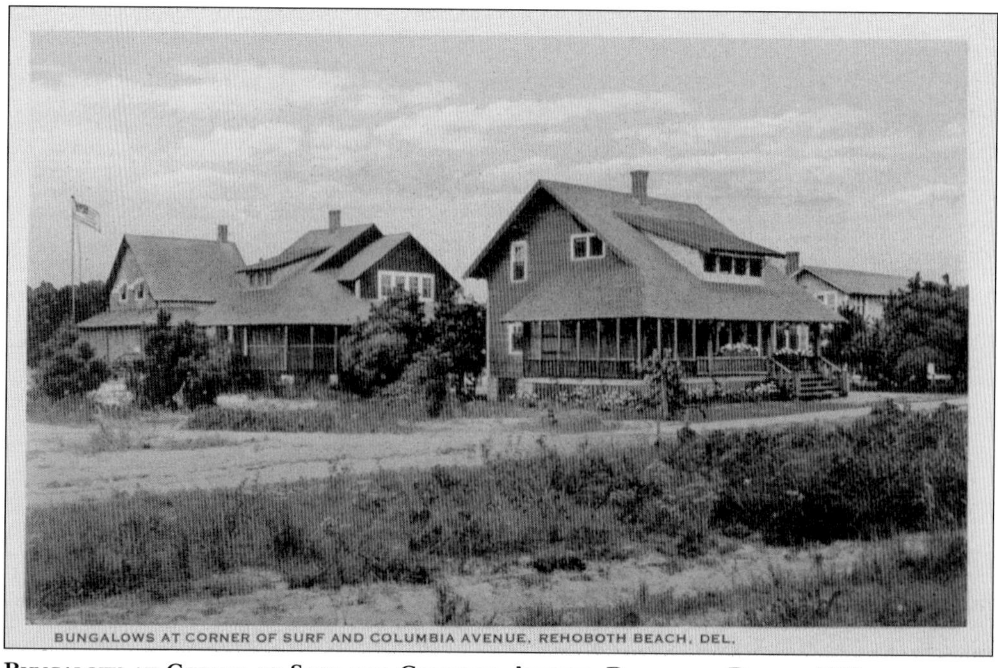

BUNGALOWS AT CORNER OF SURF AND COLUMBIA AVENUE, REHOBOTH BEACH, 1920S.

Two

Sussex County

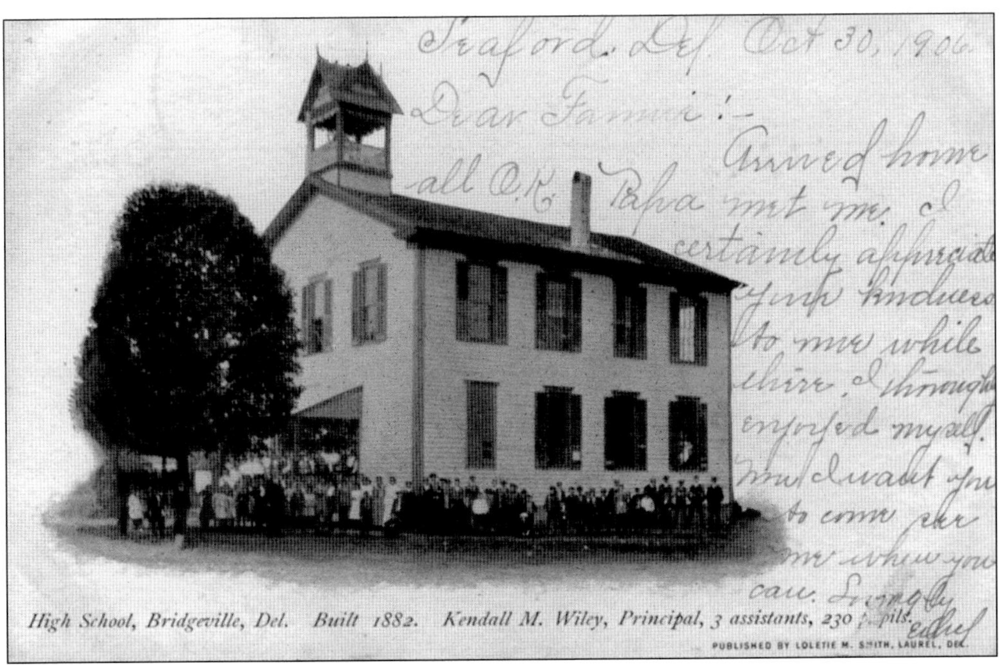

High School, Bridgeville, 1906. Students in all grades, not just in the high school, attended class in this frame school erected in 1883. The 1903 graduating class had only three members. In 1906, the principal was Kendall M. Wiley; he had 3 assistants and 230 pupils. A new brick building replaced this one by 1912.

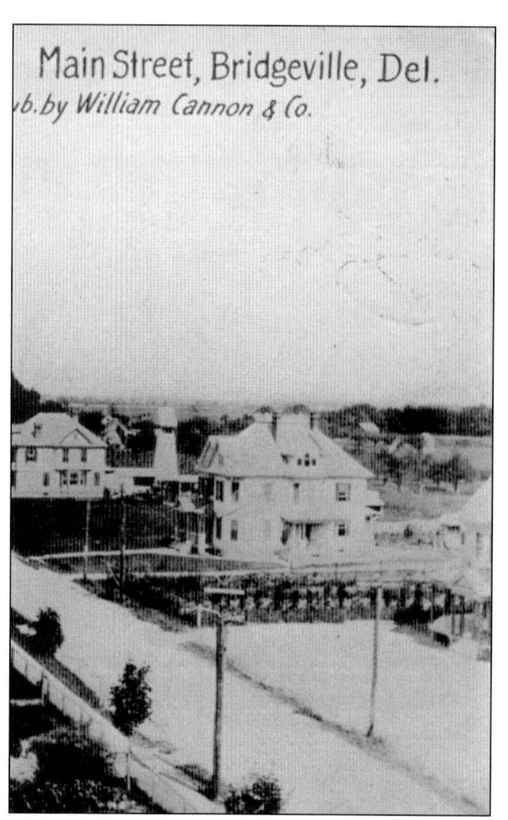

MAIN STREET, BRIDGEVILLE, *c.* 1908. Published by William Cannon & Co., this postcard view looks along Main Street from the eastern edge of town. Bridgeville, the oldest town in western Sussex County, traces its beginnings to the first bridge over Bridgeville Branch, erected in 1730. The village began to grow after the Delaware Railroad went through in 1858. H.P. Cannon and Son, a large local cannery, began in 1881.

BALTIMORE TRUST COMPANY, BRIDGEVILLE, 1907. Established in 1904 with capital in the amount of $73,090, the Bridgeville branch of the Baltimore Trust Company opened at 102 Market Street. By the end of the year it moved to this building at 302 Market Street. In 1907, the cashier was Charles N. Rawlins. The building was remodeled with a classical facade in 1925 and remained in service until 1973.

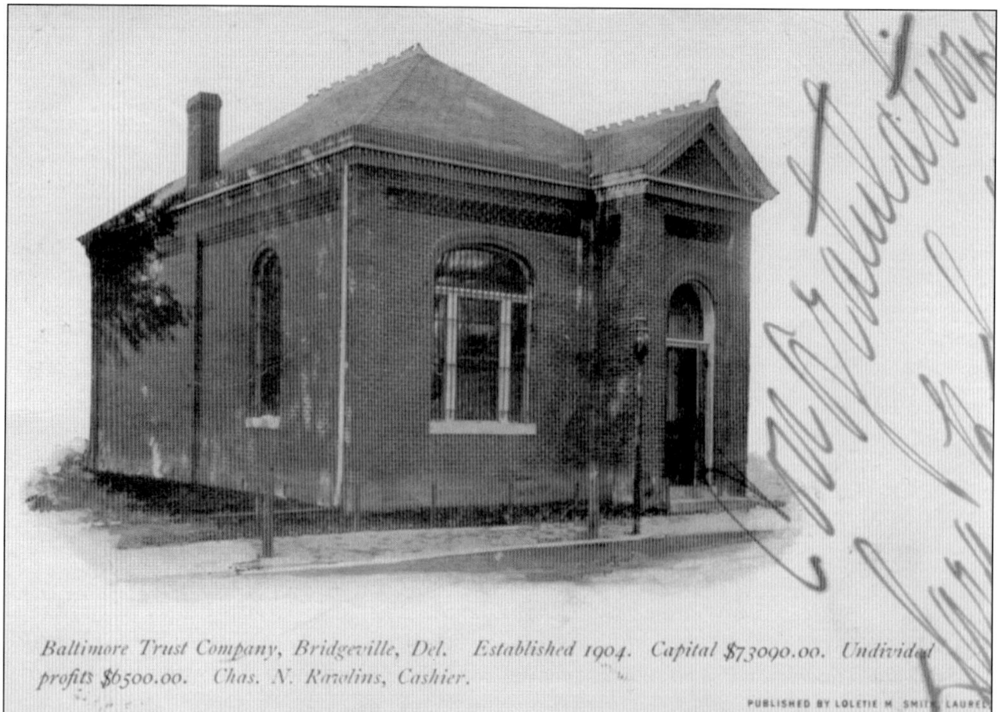

Baltimore Trust Company, Bridgeville, Del. Established 1904. Capital $73090.00. Undivided profits $6500.00. Chas. N. Rawlins, Cashier.

PUBLISHED BY LOLETIE M. SMITH, LAUREL

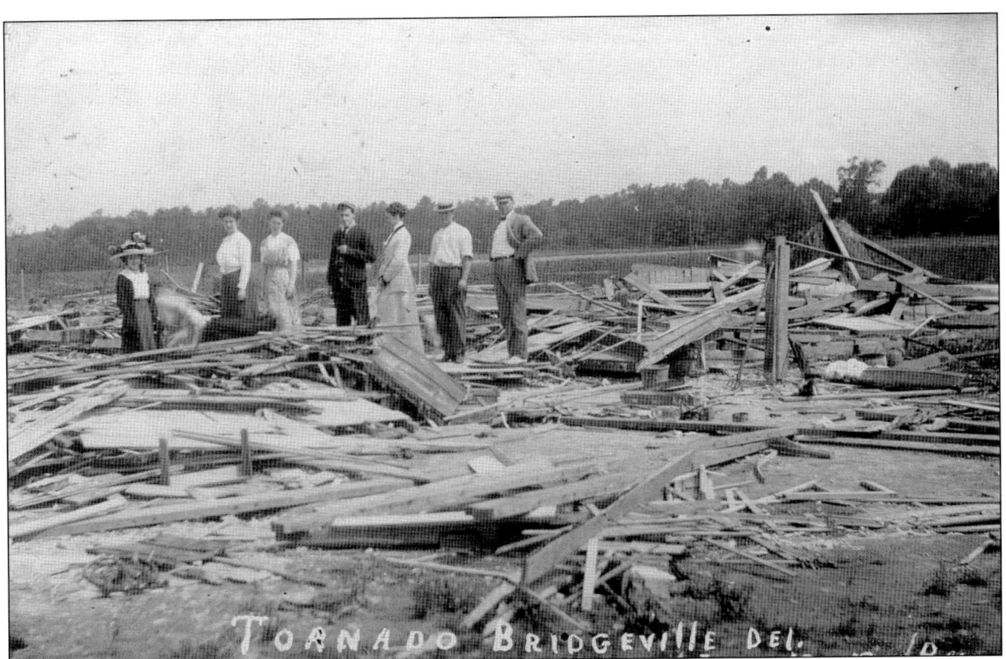

TORNADO BRIDGEVILLE, JUNE 18, 1911 (P.M.A.). During a period of tremendous storms, the tornado that caused this damage hit towns in Sussex County on June 14. It left a swath of destruction 60 feet wide and 10 miles long. One newspaper reporter wrote, "It was a sight of desolation to make the most hard-hearted person feel like weeping."

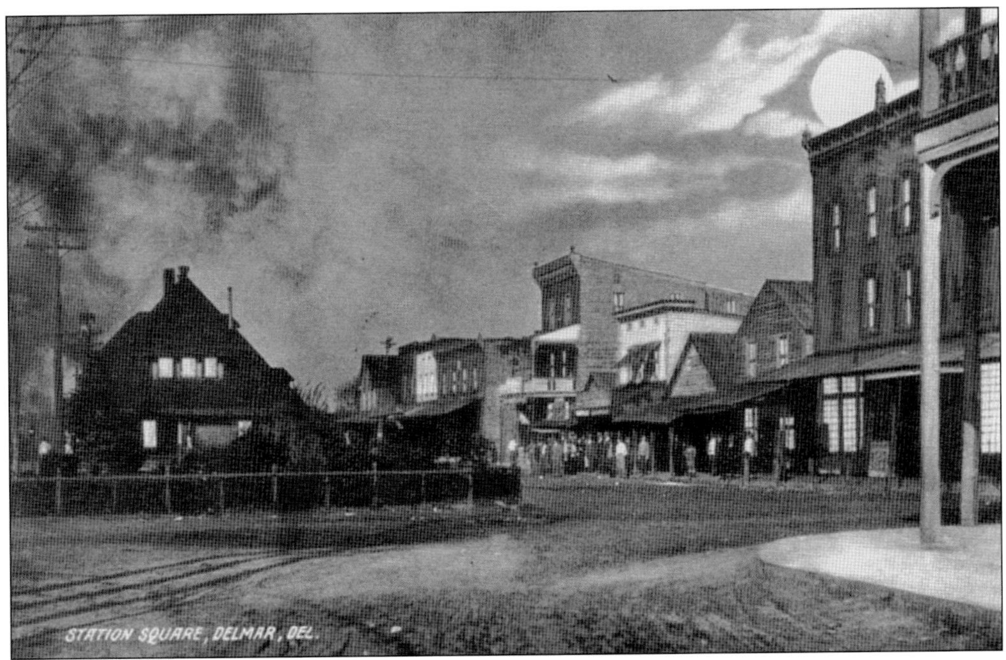

STATION SQUARE, DELMAR, 1911. Delmar straddles the boundary with Maryland at the southern end of Delaware. This view looks north along Delaware Street into Delaware. Devastating fires destroyed much of the town in 1892 and again in 1904.

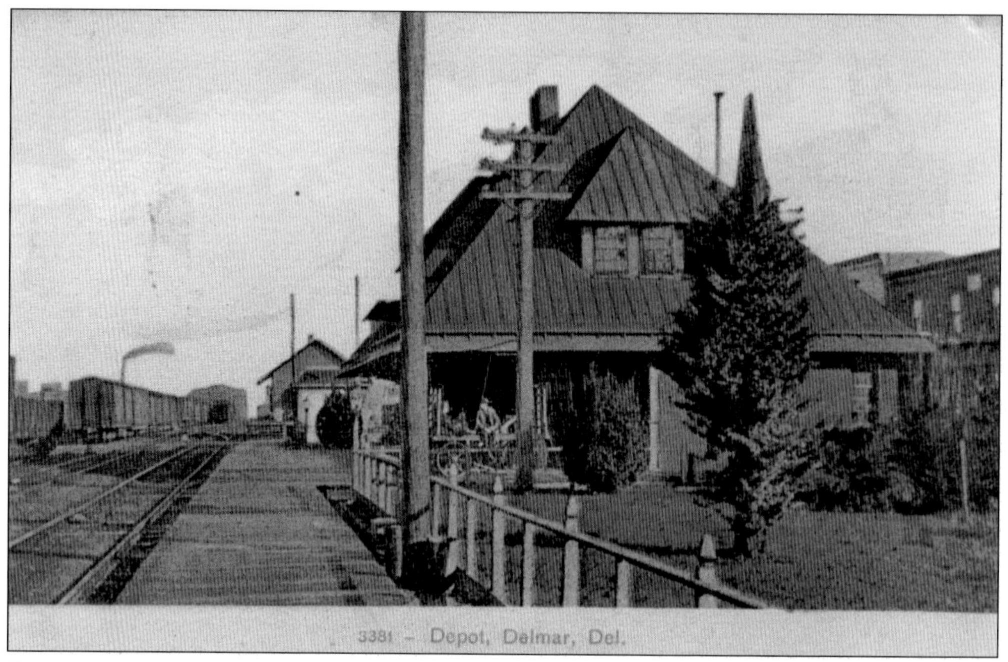

Depot, Delmar, after 1910. Before the Delaware Railroad crossed into Maryland in 1859, the area was a pine wilderness. That same year, Wilder Hastings and Elijah Freeny laid out Delmar. The railroad station is on the Delaware side of the boundary.

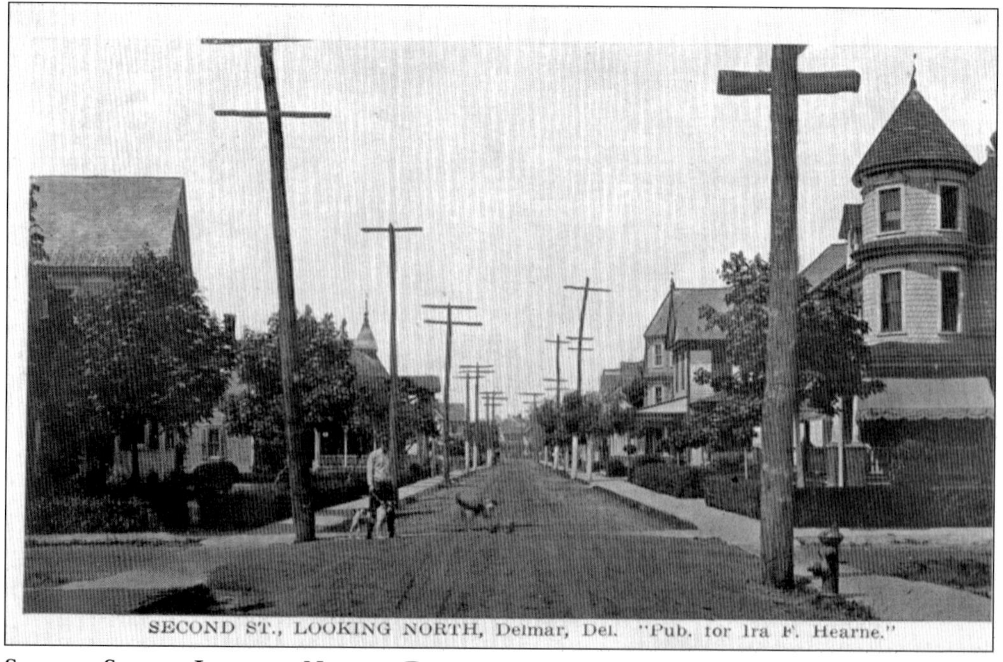

Second Street Looking North, Delmar, c. 1920. Pictured here is a quiet street of comfortable homes. As in many towns in western Sussex, almost all of the houses are of frame construction.

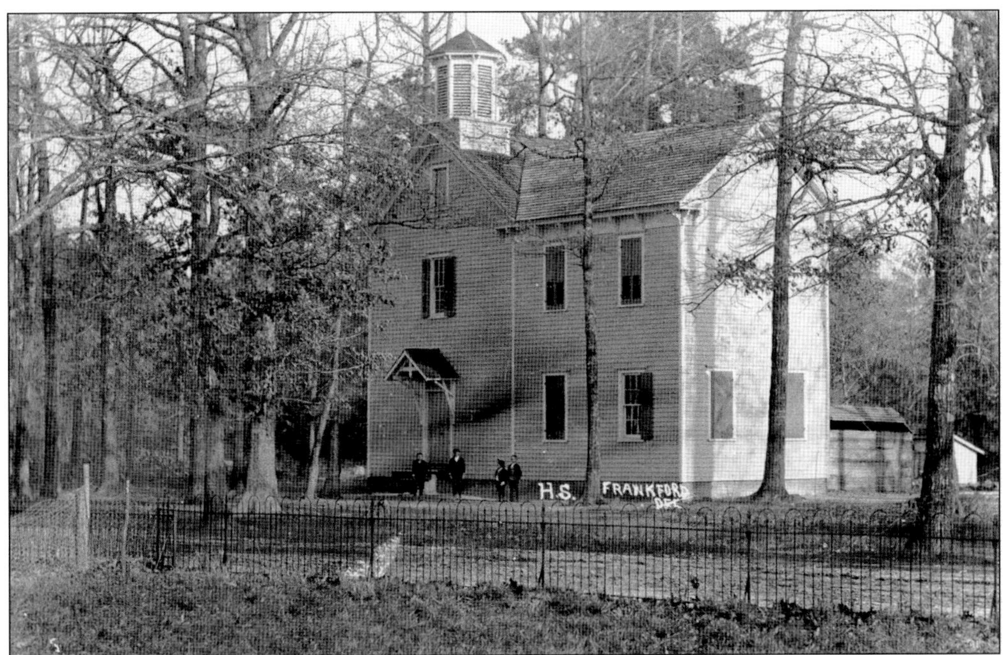

HIGH SCHOOL IN FRANKFORD, 1908. Students pose outside in this view of the public high school. The village of Frankford began in 1808 as Dagworthy's Conquest. When its post office opened in 1848 the town's name was changed to Frankford. Never growing very large, Frankford's population was less than 500 by the 1930s.

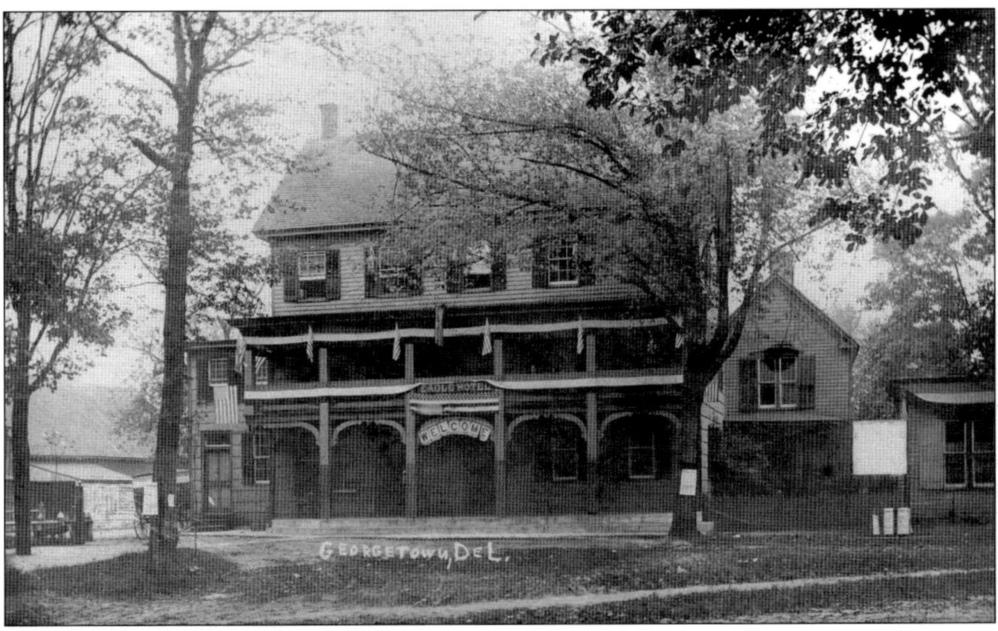

EAGLE HOTEL, AFTER 1910. Located on the Circle, this is one of three early hotels in Georgetown. Shortly after the county seat was moved to Georgetown, the Eagle Hotel, Rising Sun Tavern, and Brick Hotel were built to accommodate visitors. The Eagle Hotel was razed in 1930 to make room for the post office.

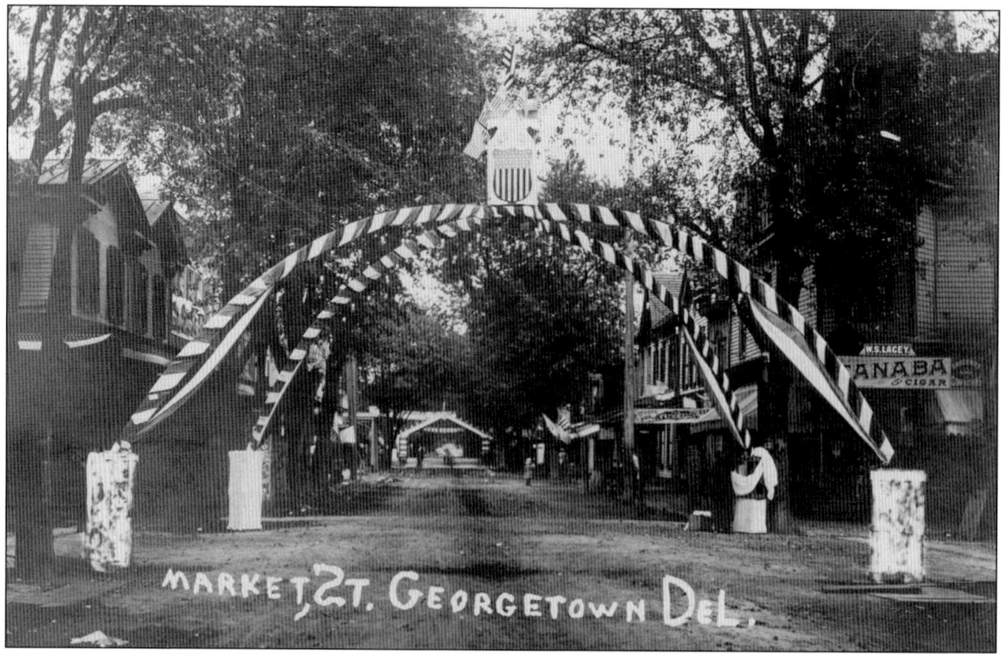

MARKET STREET, GEORGETOWN, 1907–1910. At the turn of the century, the people of Georgetown enjoyed traveling carnivals brought to town to benefit local organizations. In 1909 citizens petitioned their government for a town carnival. The council agreed and appointed a committee, funding the project with $25.

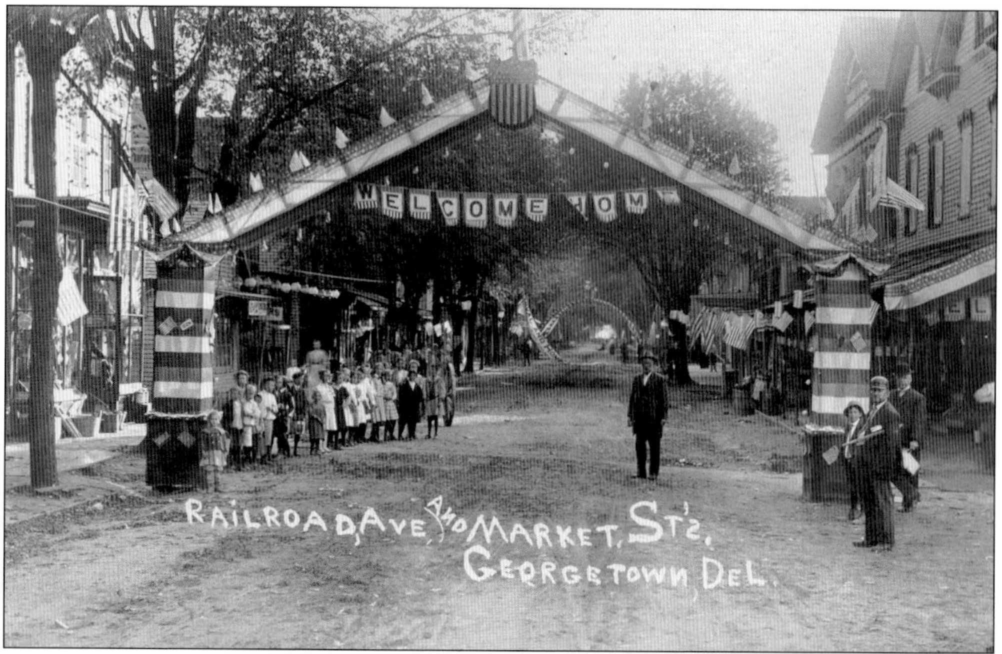

RAILROAD AVENUE AND MARKET STREET, 1907–1910.

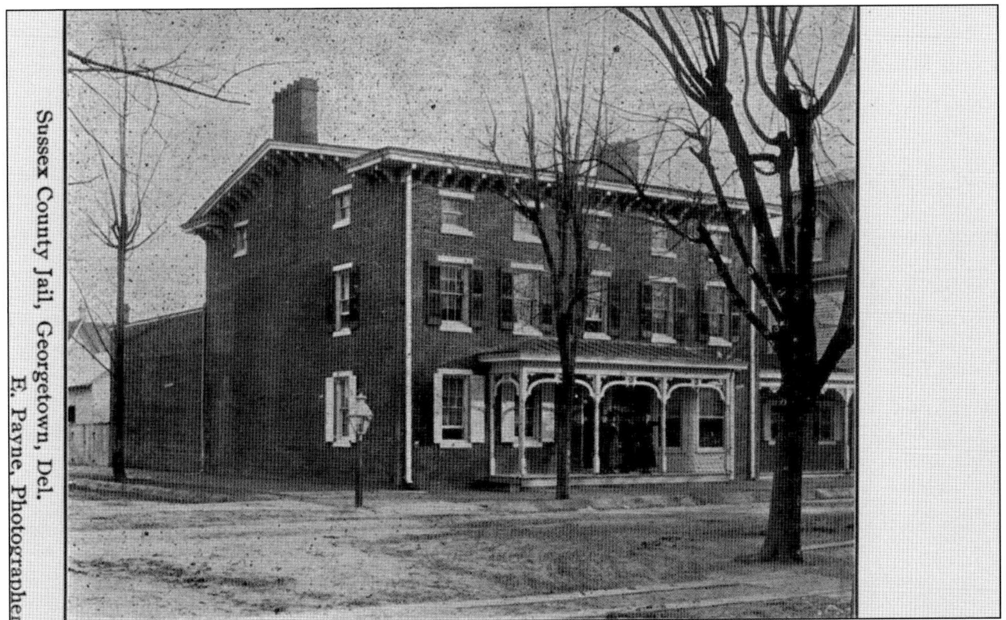

SUSSEX COUNTY JAIL, GEORGETOWN, 1900–1905. In 1791 the state legislature passed the Act for Removing the Seat of Justice from Lewes. Georgetown was laid out and then governed by the state for years. The jail seen here at the southwest corner of Market and Race Streets was the county's third. A larger jail was necessary in 1931 and this building became the Court House Annex.

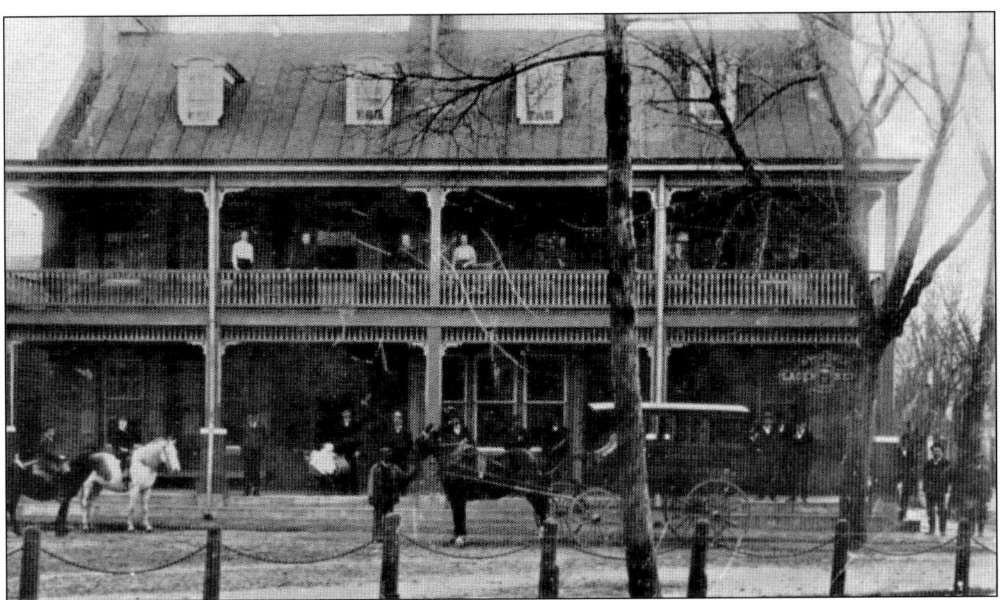

THE BRICK HOTEL, GEORGETOWN, 1910S. The Brick Hotel at Green and West Market Streets was built in 1836 by Joshua S. Layton and Caleb B. Sipple, who also erected the courthouse and jail. During the construction of the courthouse, the seat of justice moved into this hotel. In 1954 the hotel closed its doors. Until 1999 the building housed Wilmington Trust. It now belongs to the State of Delaware.

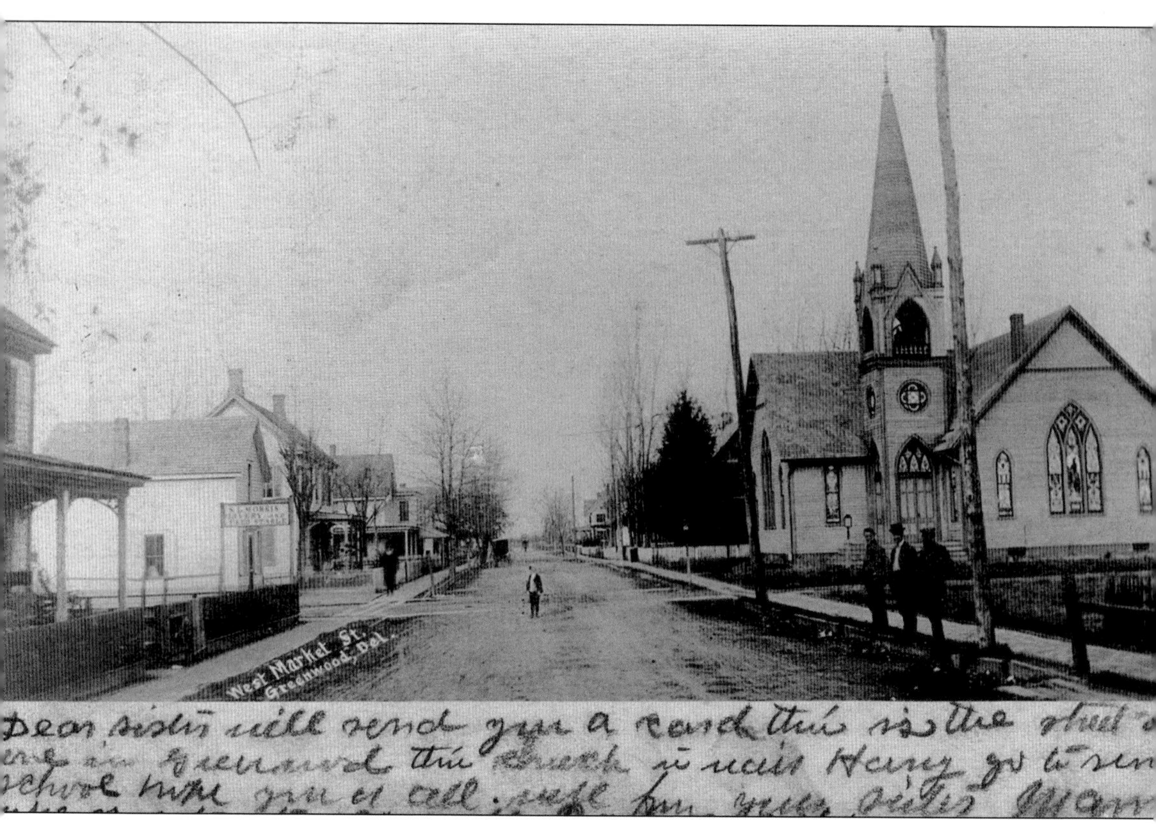

West Market Street, Greenwood, 1907. Greenwood owes its existence to the Delaware Railroad. When the railroad was routed slightly west of Saint Johnstown, its people founded a new town by the railroad in 1858. They called their new town Greenwood for the abundance of holly and other evergreens in the area. The Greenwood M.E. Church, founded in 1880, is on the right. The building shown was built in 1901.

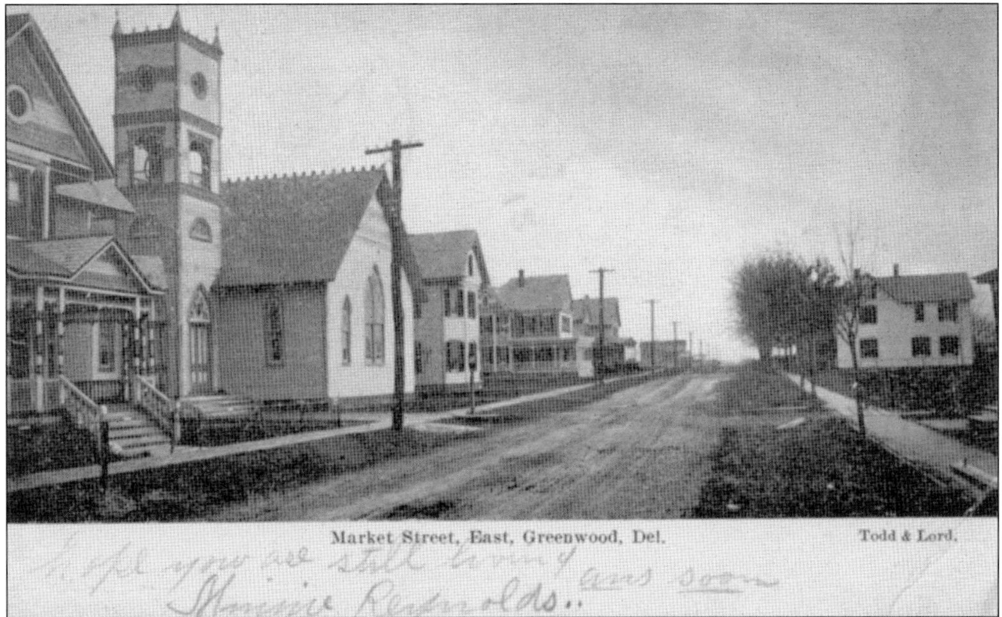

EAST MARKET STREET, GREENWOOD, 1907. Greenwood Methodist Protestant Church, on the left, was founded in 1880 and erected a new building in 1903. Just a few months later, on December 2, 1903, a rear-end collision between two freight trains ignited a fire and explosion. Many houses in town were damaged, as was this church. This postcard shows the church after it was rebuilt.

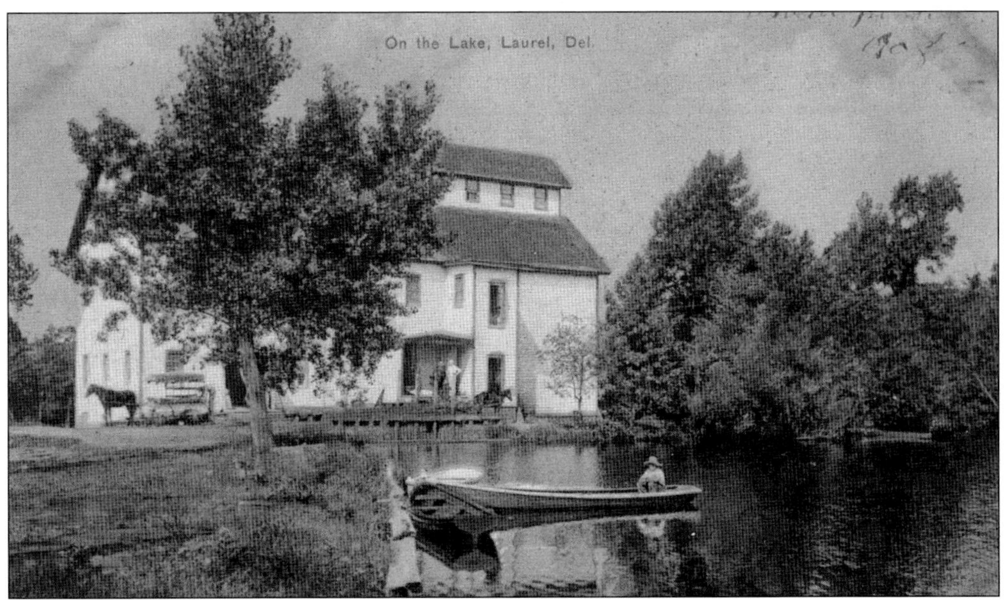

ON THE LAKE, LAUREL, 1909. John Mitchell erected a dam and mills on Broad Creek before 1800. But over the years, the mill buildings and their owners changed regularly. The structure shown here was built in 1878. W.T. Records and Son operated the grist mill from 1902 and 1934, and in the early 1950s, the mill was still in operation as the Laurel Flour and Feed Mills, Inc. The pond is called Records Pond.

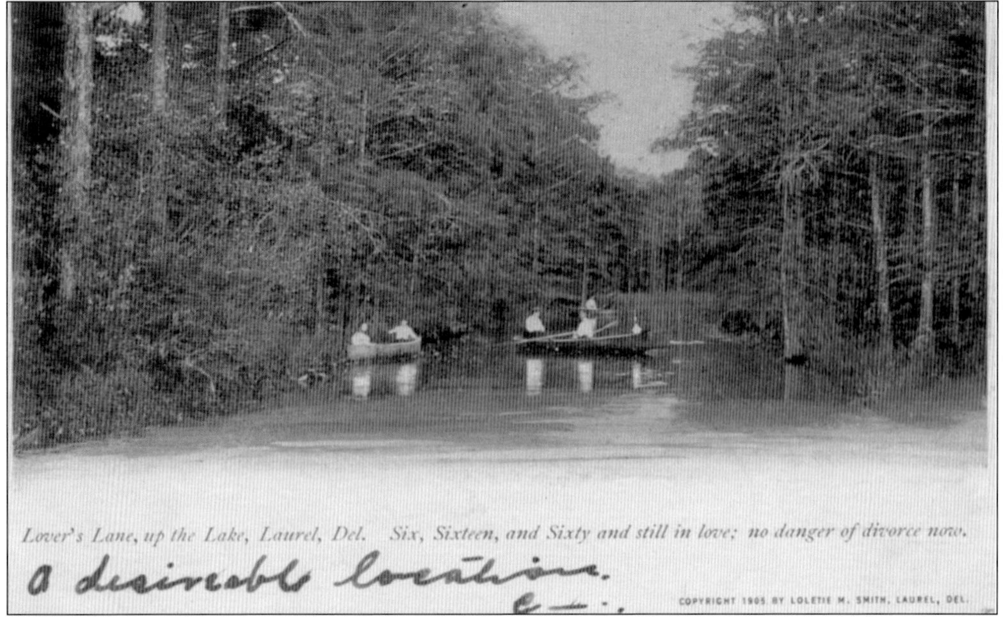

LOVER'S LANE, LAUREL, 1905. In season, lilies bloom in Lover's Lane, a beautiful stretch of water one-eighth mile long extending from Records Lake. This dreamy postcard view was taken by Mrs. Loletie M. Smith, the assistant postmaster of Laurel.

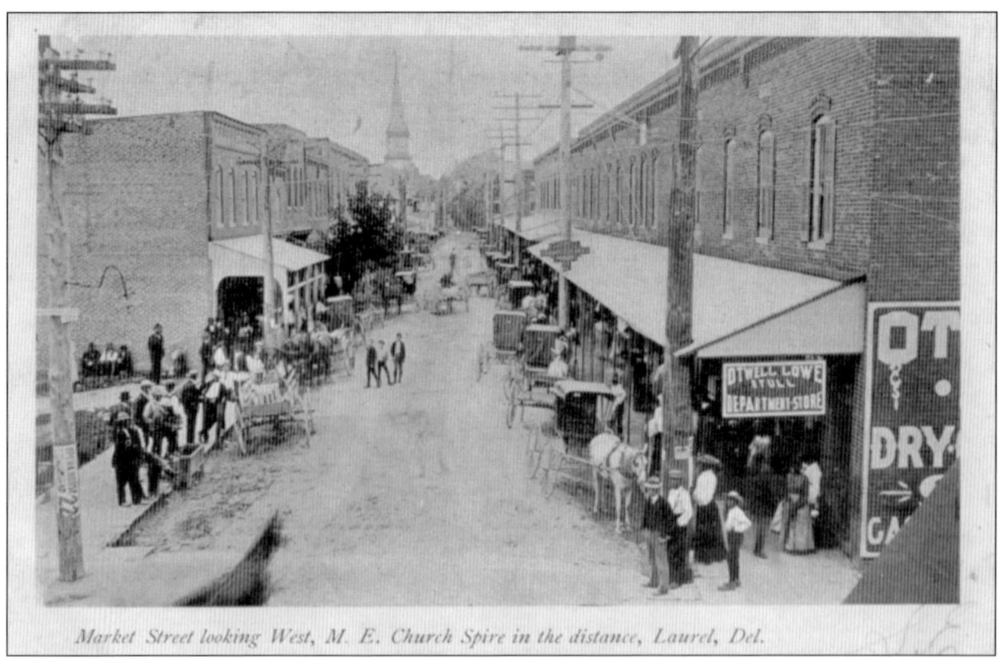

MARKET STREET LOOKING WEST, LAUREL, 1906. In 1799 Barkley Townsend, a large landowner and shipbuilder, laid out a town and named it for the laurel bushes growing along the banks of Broad Creek. In 1899 Laurel's entire business district burned. Laurel had no volunteer fire company, so firefighters from Salisbury, Maryland, and Wilmington were called in. The town's new brick buildings are seen here, with the Methodist Episcopal church's spire in the distance.

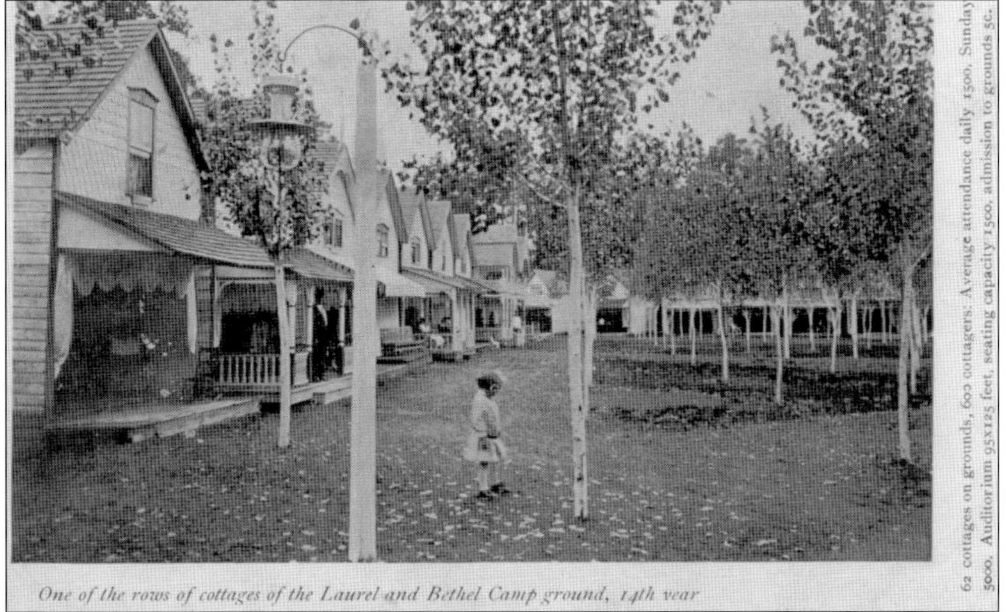

COTTAGES ON THE LAUREL AND BETHEL CAMPGROUND, 1905. Summer camp meetings, popular throughout Delaware, offered a wonderful opportunity for people to renew their faith in a relaxed, congenial atmosphere. According to the legend on the postcard, this camp meeting, seen in its 14th year of operation, had 62 cottages and 600 cottagers. The average daily attendance was 1,500, with 5,000 attendees on Sundays. Loletie M. Smith of Laurel produced this postcard in 1905.

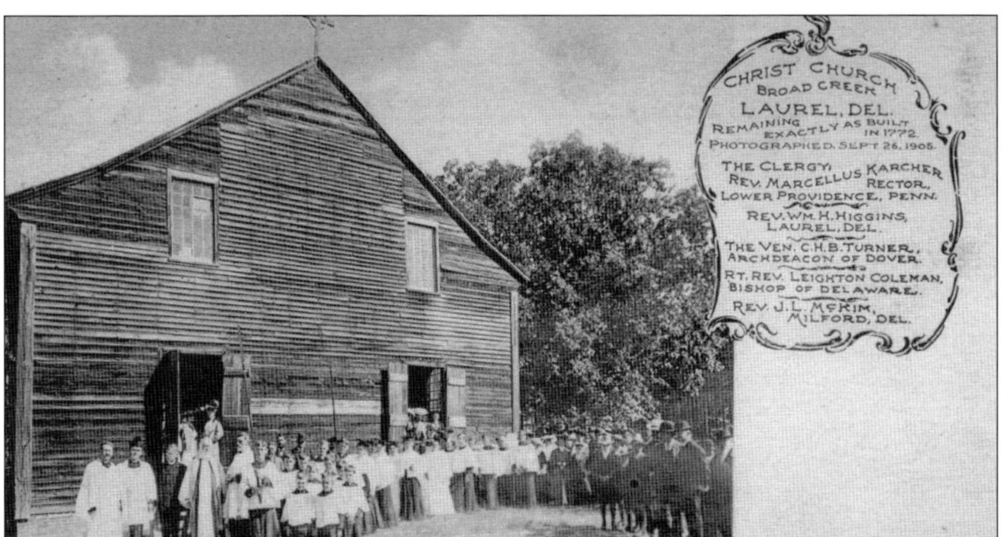

CHRIST CHURCH, LAUREL, SEPTEMBER 26, 1905. Located east of Laurel on Chipman's Pond, Christ Church was built in 1772 as a chapel of ease for Stepney Parish in Maryland. This building, which may have replaced an earlier structure, was used for regular services until St. Philip's Church, more conveniently located in town, was built in the mid-1800s. Built entirely of wood, inside and out, the interior of Christ Church has never been painted or altered in any way and is a wonderful example of a colonial country church in this region. Christ Church is cared for by St. Philip's Church. This is another postcard by Loletie M. Smith.

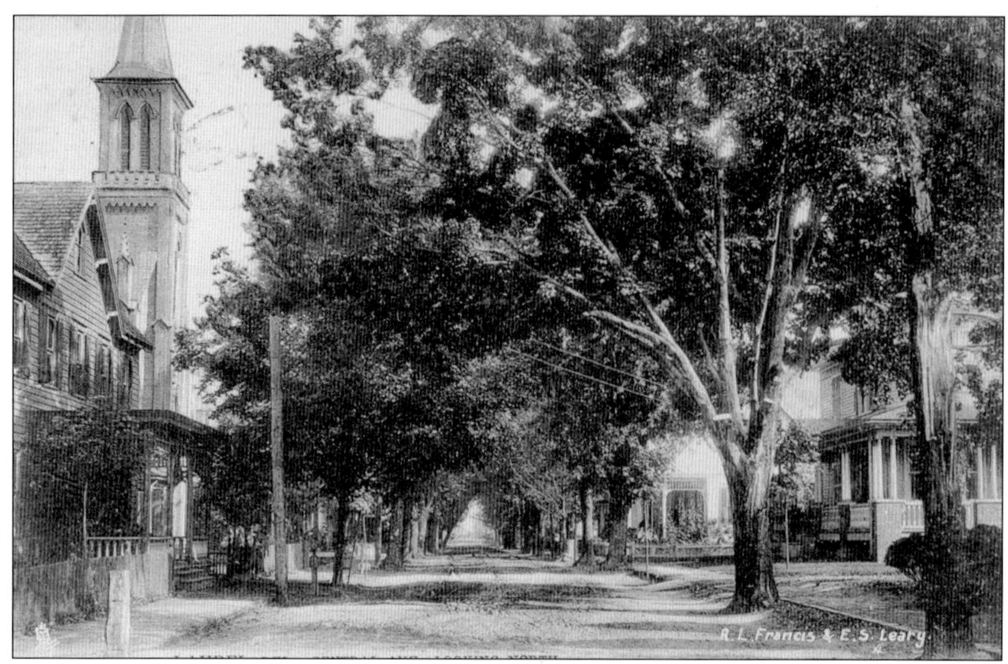

Central Avenue Looking South, Laurel, 1908. Substantial, comfortable homes line Laurel's streets. On the left in the above view is Christ Methodist Protestant Church, which was organized in 1831. The building pictured served the congregation from 1867 until 1912.

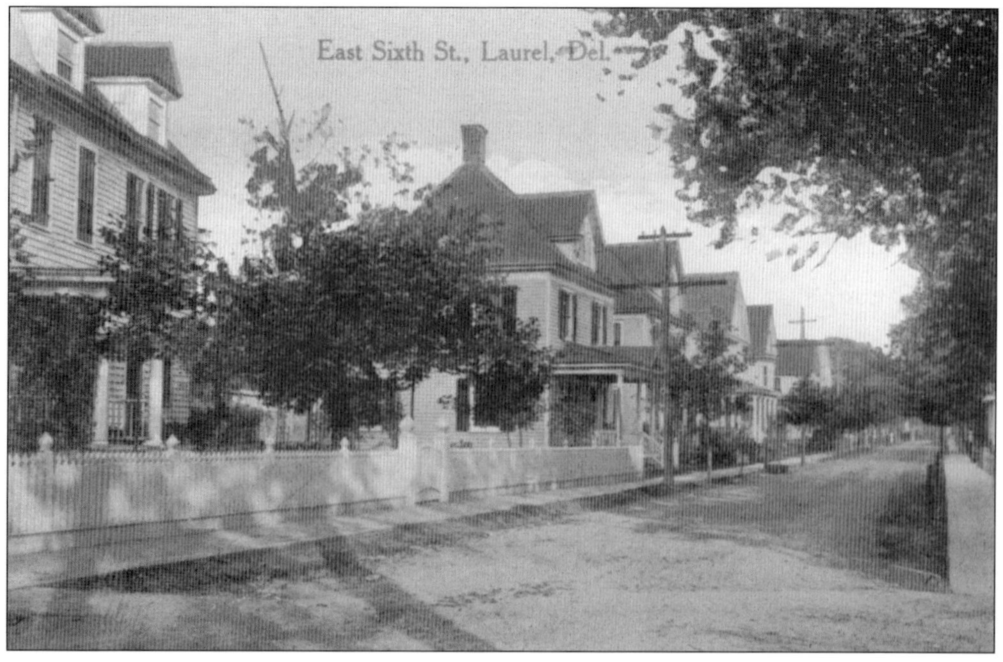

East Sixth Street, Laurel, 1911.

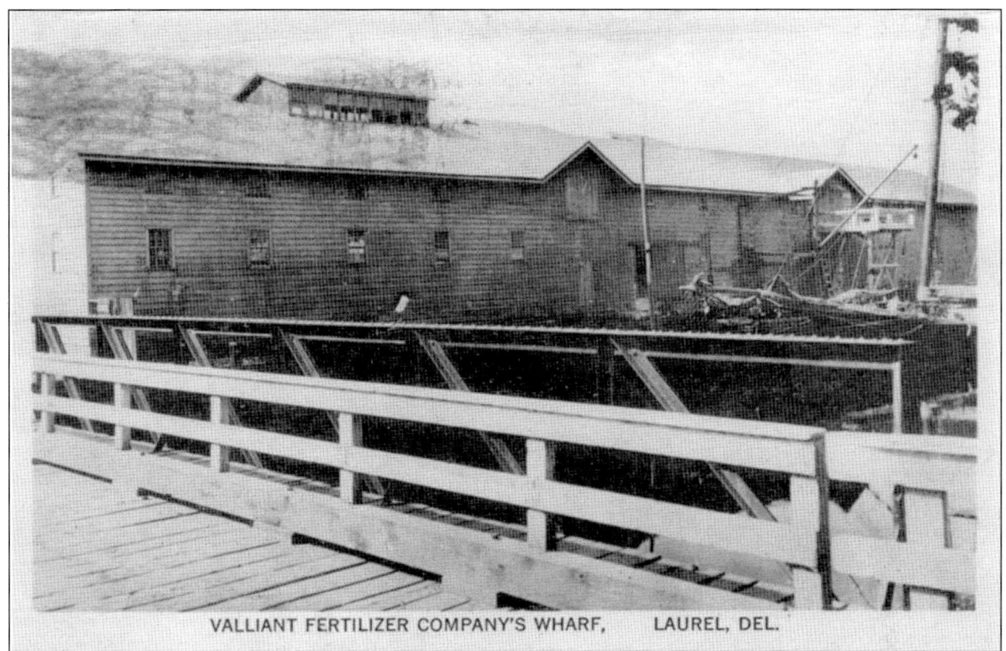

VALLIANT FERTILIZER COMPANY'S WHARF, LAUREL, 1924. Edwin Stearns Valliant and Edwin Stephens Valliant began the Valliant Fertilizer Company around 1912. The company was based at the wharf and warehouse, shown here, just east of the Central Avenue bridge over the Laurel River. Gov. Elbert N. Carvel came to Laurel as general manager and treasurer of the company in 1936. The firm is now known as the Milford Fertilizer Company.

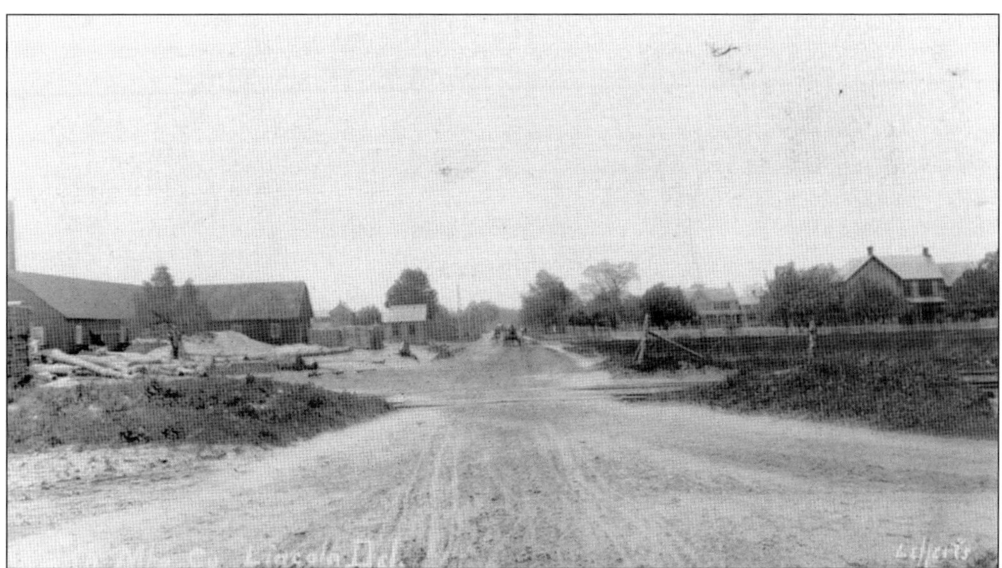

LINCOLN, *c.* 1910. Speculator Col. Abel S. Small hoped to develop Lincoln, founded just after the Civil War and named after the recently assassinated president, into a "metropolis of Southern Delaware." He sought to attract residents with exaggerated claims of a tropical climate. His plans even included a racetrack. But the dream ended with his death in 1889, and the Junction and Breakwater Railroad crossing provided the town's only lasting economic asset.

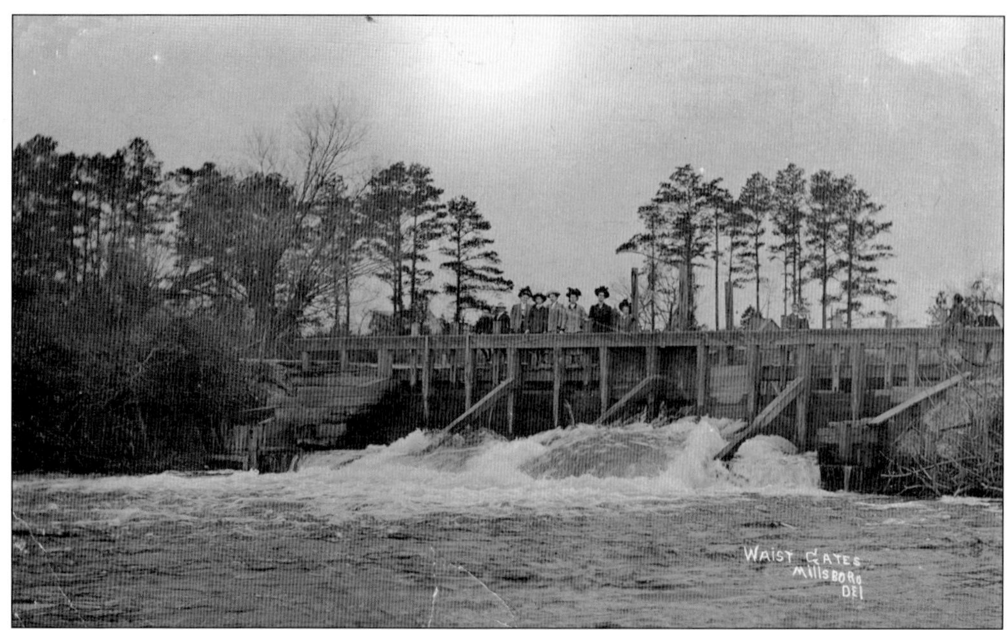

WAIST [SIC] GATES, MILLSBORO, C. 1910. This dam is located just north of the center of town at Zoar Road (Route 30). A waste gate is a dam built across a river or canal to raise or divert the water. According to local tradition, boys were tossed overboard at the milldam when they reached a certain age.

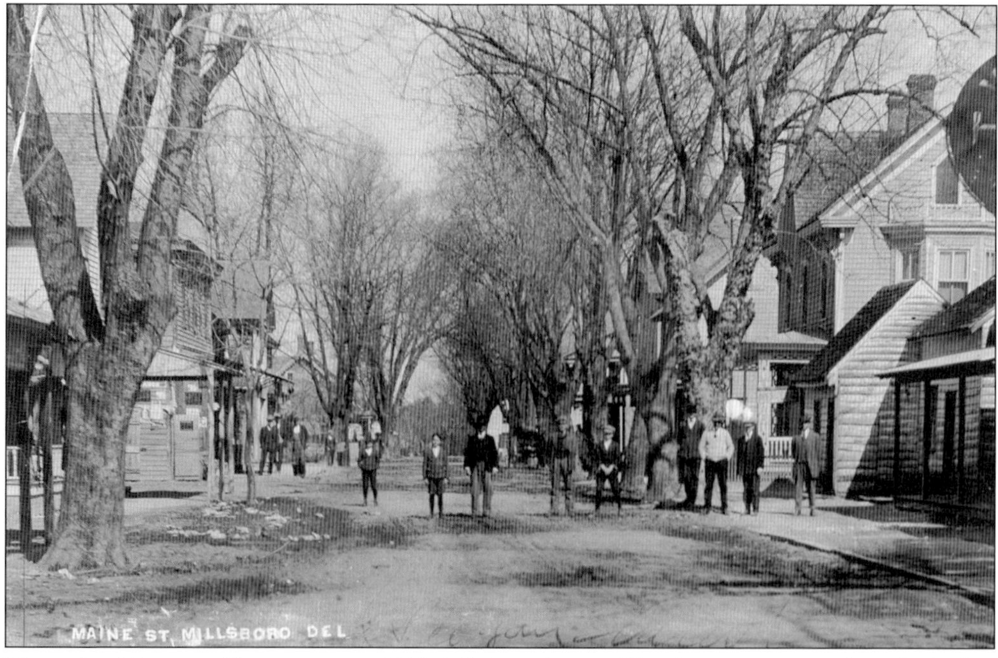

MAINE [SIC] STREET, MILLSBORO, C. 1910. Millsboro is a small but important town along the Indian River. In the early 1800s it was the center of the holly and strawberry seasons for the area. To the far right in this view is the Millsboro Hotel, with a small part of its distinctive sign showing. The hotel was moved in the 1930s to clear the site for the Ball Theater.

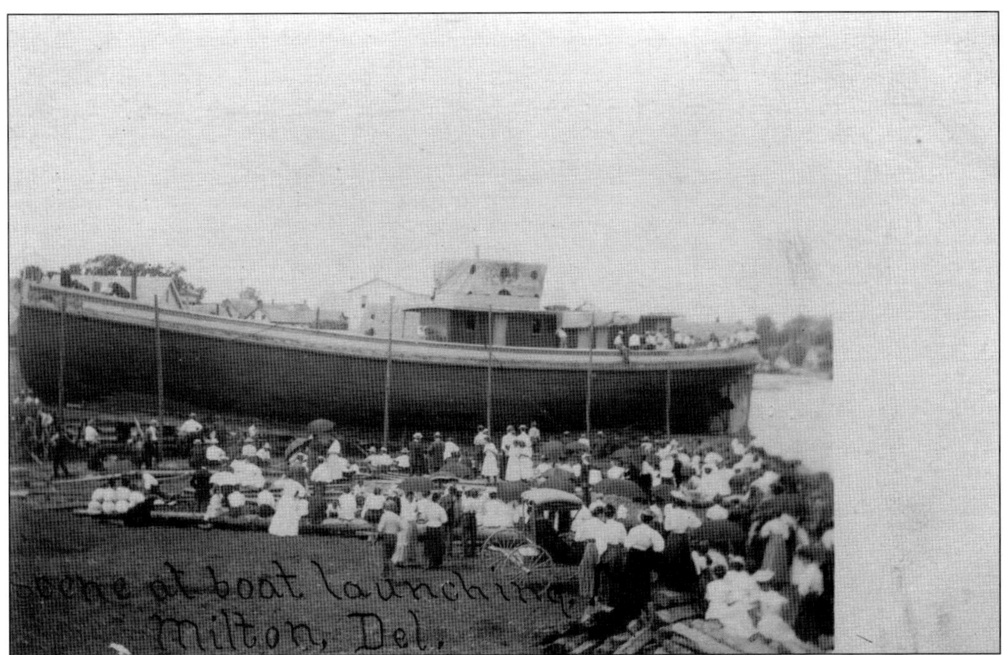

Boat Launching in Milton, c. 1905. Shipbuilding formed the early economic base of Milton, which is located at the head of the Broadkiln River. Festive ship launchings attracted as many as 1,000 people. By the early 1900s, however, Milton's shipbuilding industry had nearly collapsed because most of the local timber had been cut and new wooden ships became too large for the Broadkiln to accommodate.

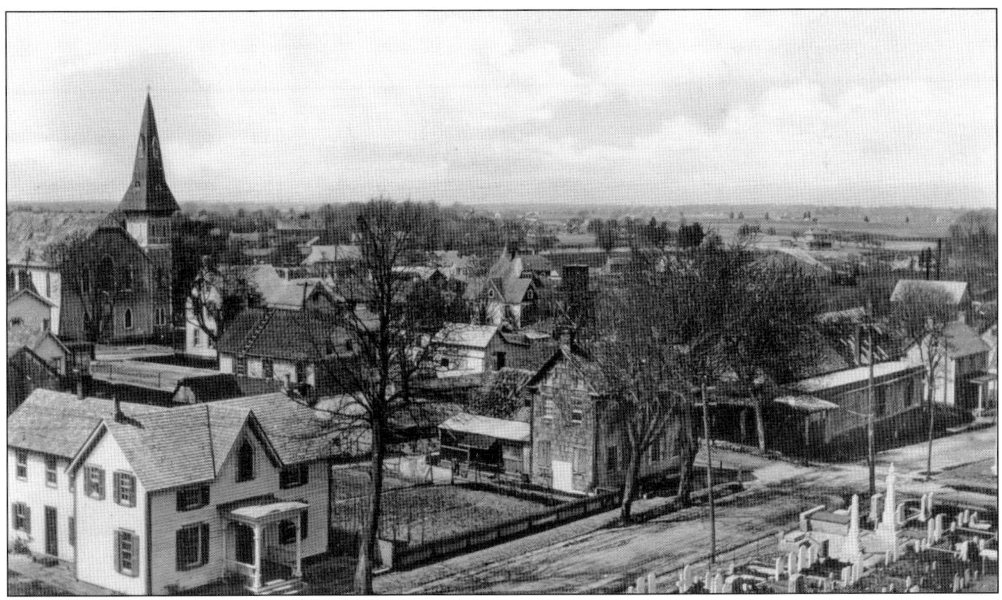

Bird's-eye View of Milton, c. 1910. A 19th-century writer once described Milton as "laid out with great regularity and taste." From the 1740s through the late 1800s, Milton served as the main shipping center for Eastern Sussex County. On Federal Street, to the left in this view, is the steeple of Goshen Methodist Church, which was torn down in 1967.

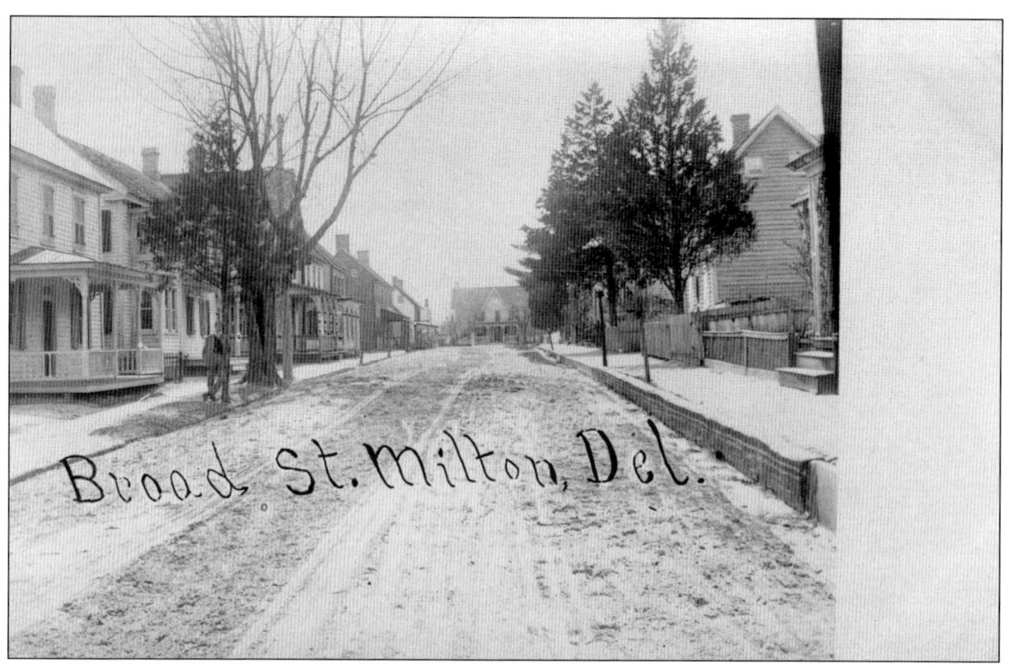

Broad Street, Milton, c. 1910. This postcard scene was taken looking toward Mulberry Street. A dapper man leans against a tree on the left.

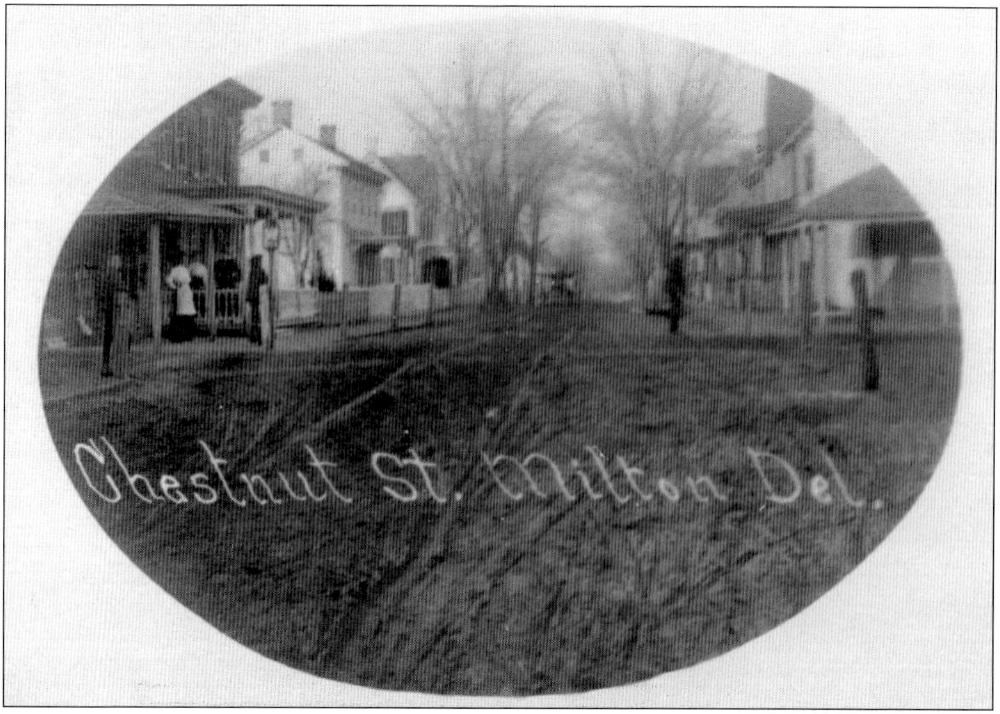

Chestnut Street, Milton, c. 1910. Looking down muddy Chestnut Street in south Milton, this picture shows one of the oldest sections of homes in the city. Chestnut Street was once known as Apple Tree Street because of the apple trees lining it.

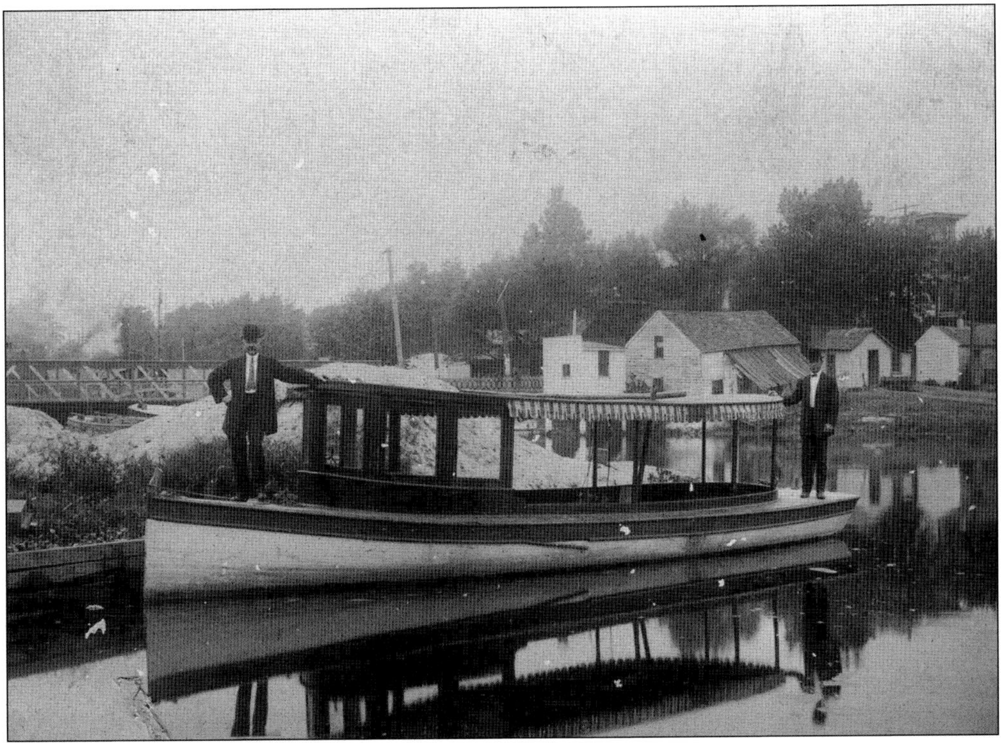

Shuttle Boat, 1910s. Rodgers shuttle boat used to take people across the Indian River at Oak Orchard.

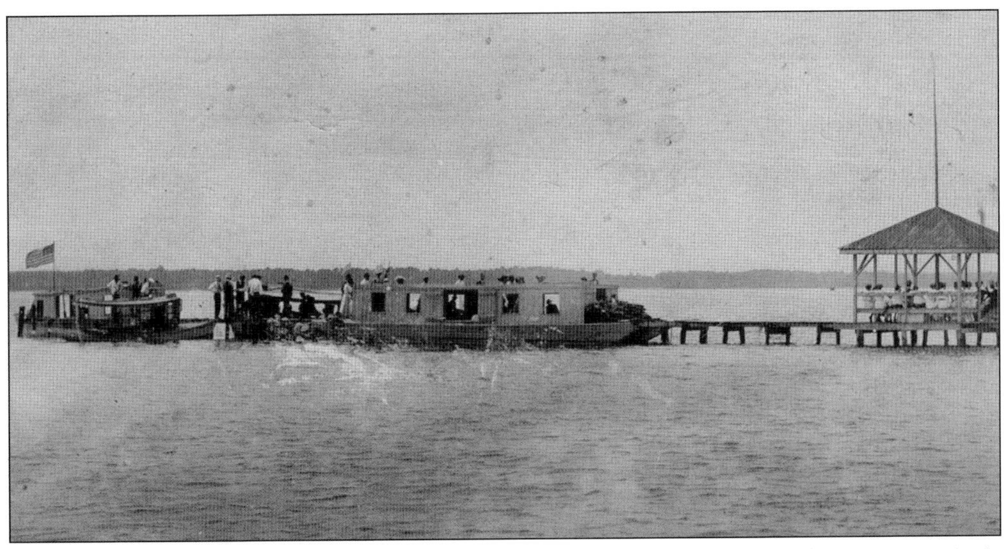

Docking at the Pier, 1910s. Visitors can drive to Oak Orchard, primarily used as a summer picnic grounds, along the "Jersey Road," Route 24, which runs between Oak Orchard and Millsboro. Oak Orchard and nearby Riverdale were popular bathing spots for locals. This pier was operated by the River House, also known as the River Hotel, a local landmark. Destroyed by Hurricane Hazel in 1954, the hotel was torn down in the 1980s. Today the Whitecaps Café occupies the site.

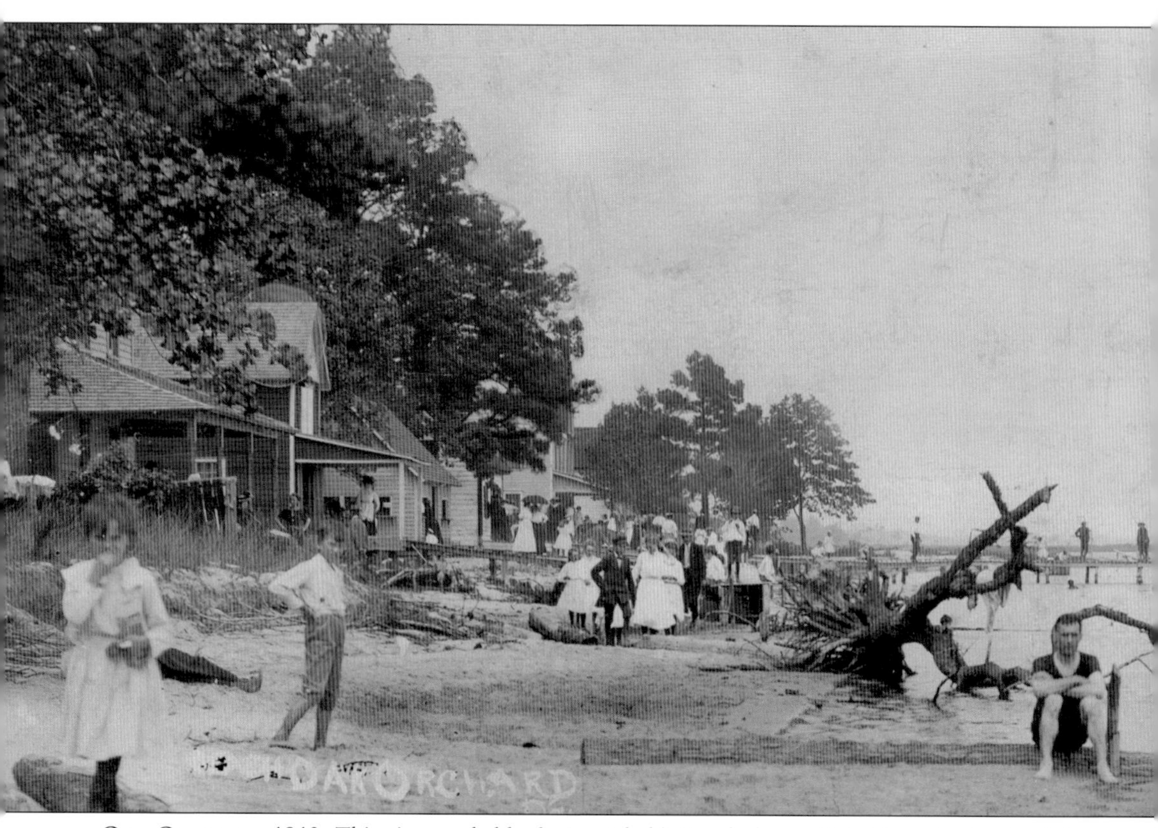

OAK ORCHARD, 1913. This view probably depicts Clark's Beach during "Big Thursday," a local day of gathering at the Delaware beaches. Not well known to out-of-state visitors, Oak Orchard is a small summer resort of cottages and boarding houses on the shores of Indian River. By the 1950s, it had food stands, a pavilion, a dance hall, a small boardwalk, and hotels.

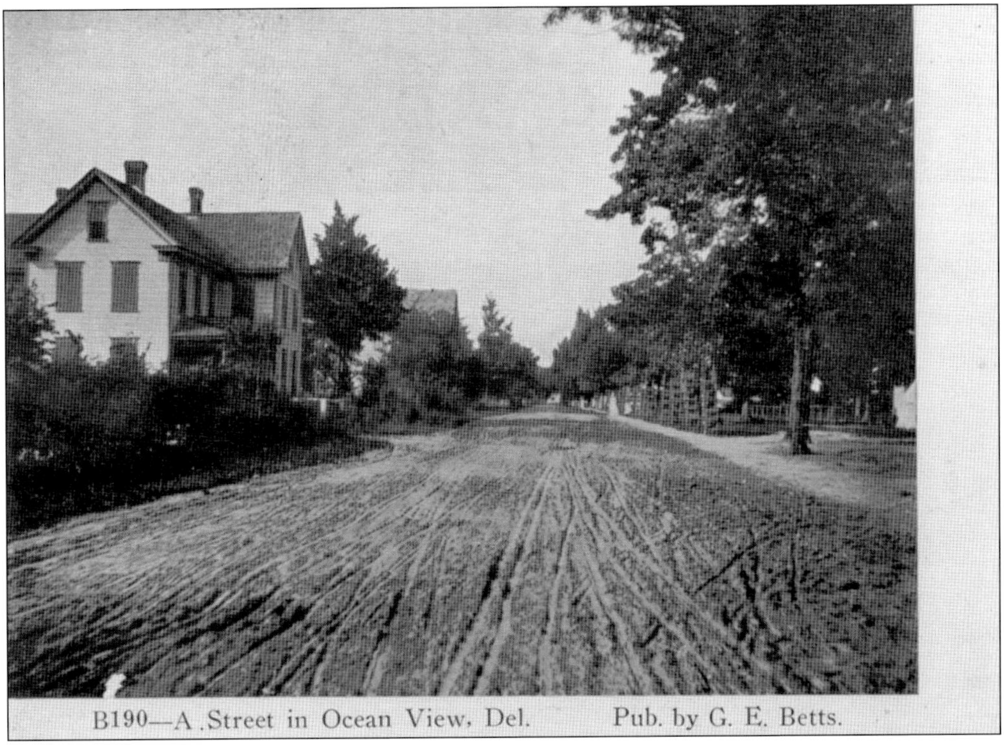

B190—A .Street in Ocean View, Del. Pub. by G. E. Betts.

A Street in Ocean View, 1910s. Surprisingly, Ocean View doesn't have an ocean view! The town, described in *Delaware: A Guide to the First State* as a small rambling village, was once known as Hall's Store. Legend has it that a boy climbed up a tree and, looking eastward, exclaimed that he could see the ocean. Both of these views were taken looking east toward Cedar Neck. The house at the far left was built by Capt. James Bennett. In the postcard by G.E. Betts, the trees lining the right side of the street have fruit ladders leaning up against their trunks.

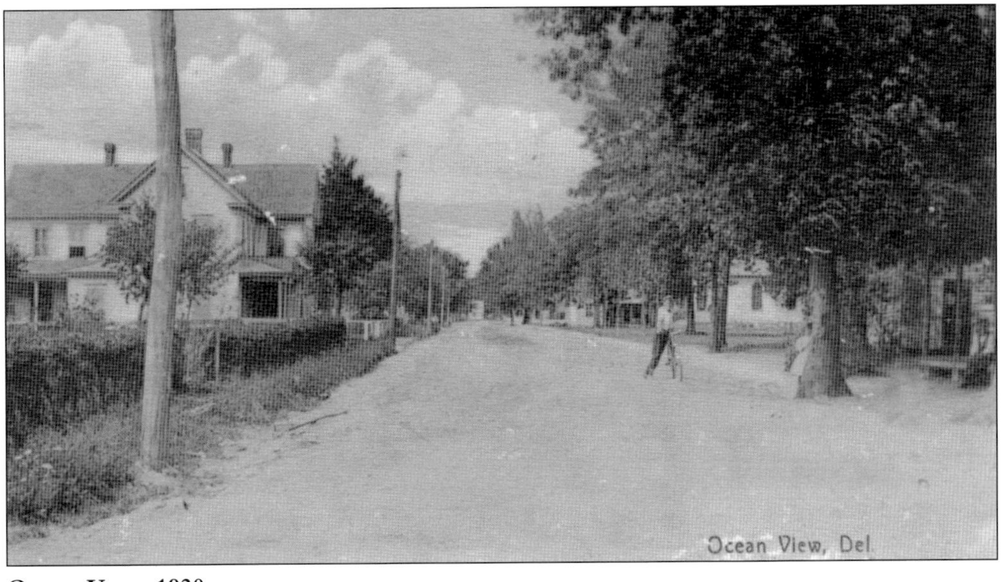

Ocean View, 1920.

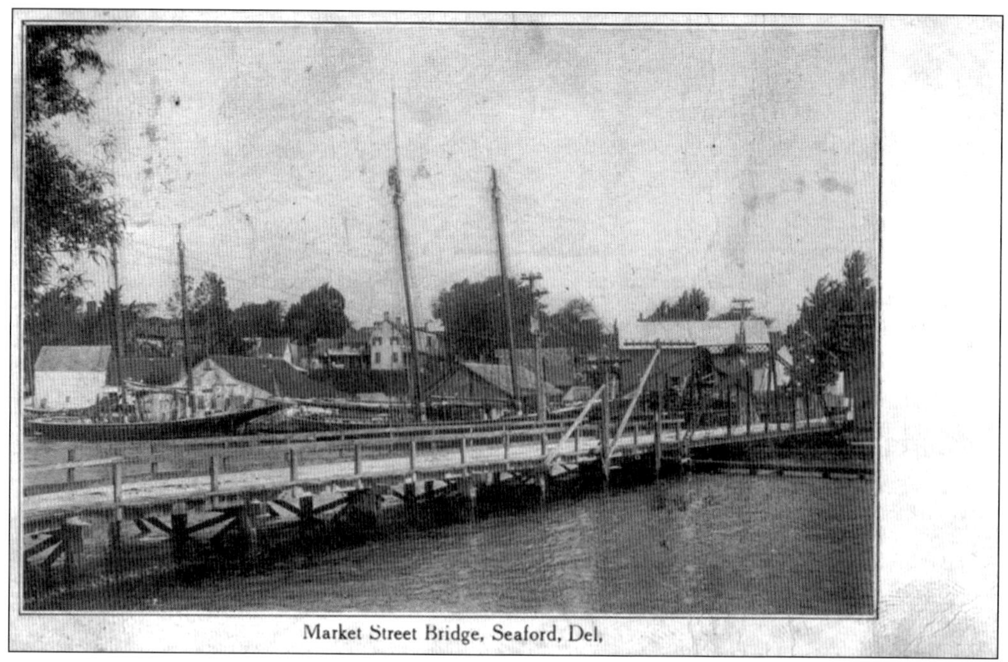
Market Street Bridge, Seaford, Del.

MARKET STREET BRIDGE, SEAFORD, 1908. Seaford was laid out in 1799 at the head of navigation on the Nanticoke River. The river was the community's lifeline—harvesting and processing Chesapeake oysters were an important part of the economy. The river made it easy to ship crops to market, and shipbuilding was also an important industry. The coming of the railroad in 1856 gave the town another means of transportation.

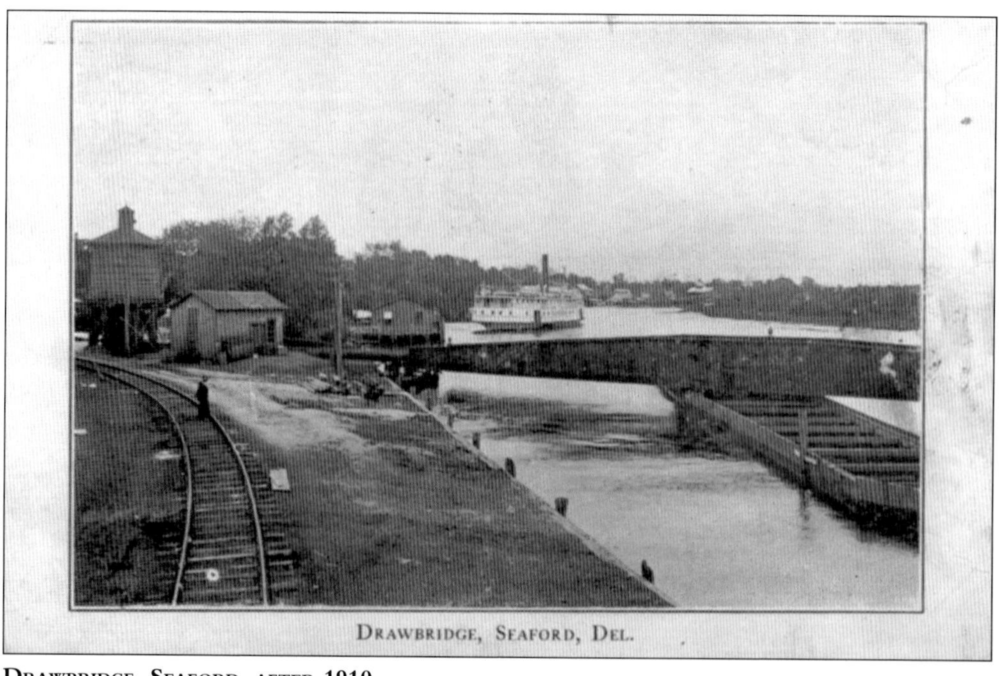
DRAWBRIDGE, SEAFORD, DEL.

DRAWBRIDGE, SEAFORD, AFTER 1910.

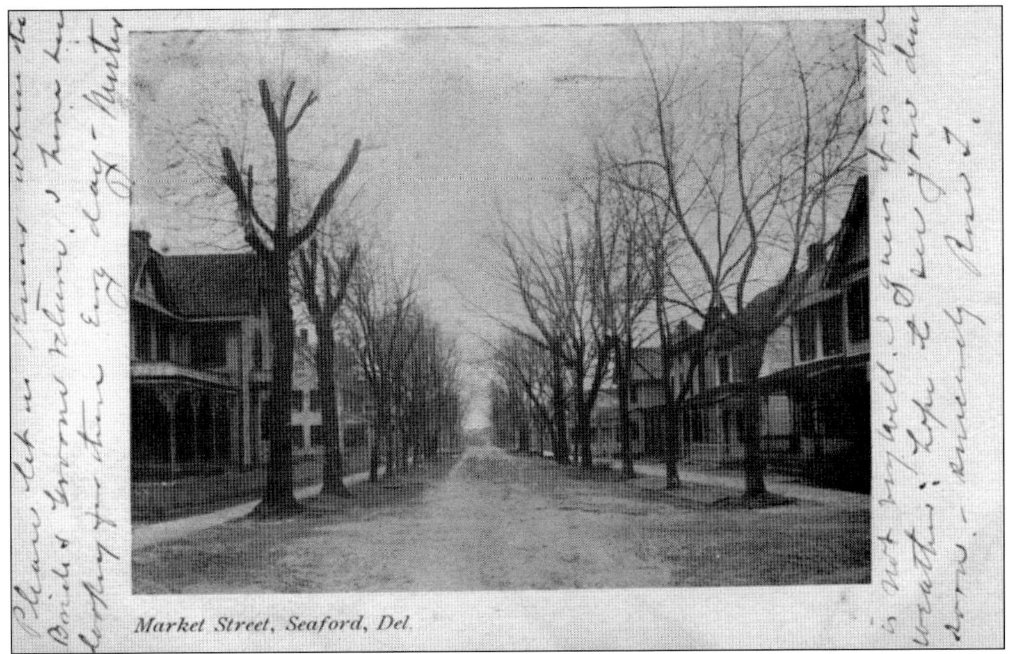

Market Street, Seaford, 1911. These postcards show two neighborhoods in Seaford. The houses are all from the same era, but those on Market Street are more modest.

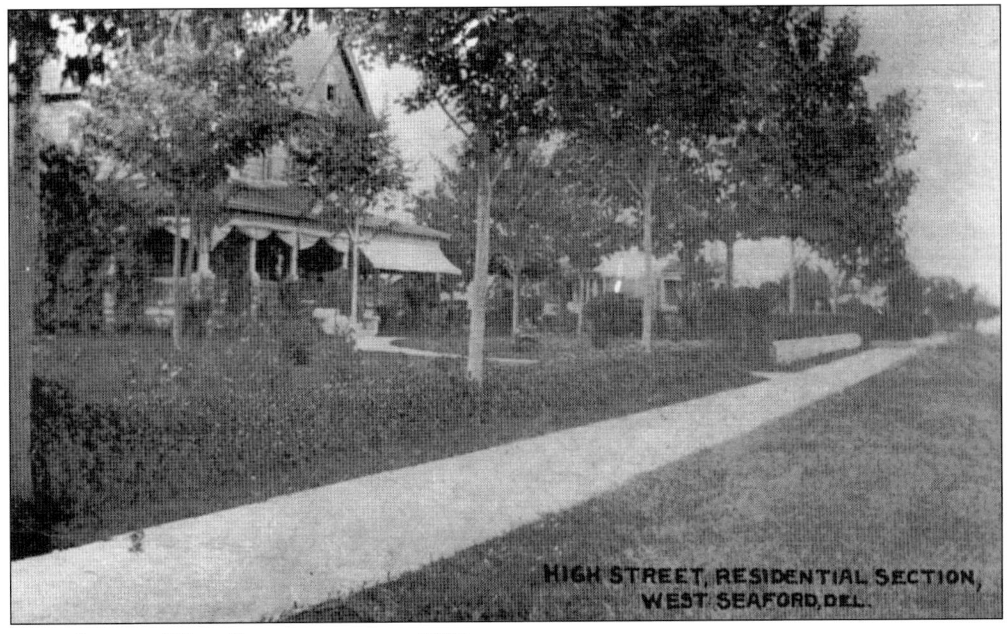

High Street, West Seaford, before 1909.

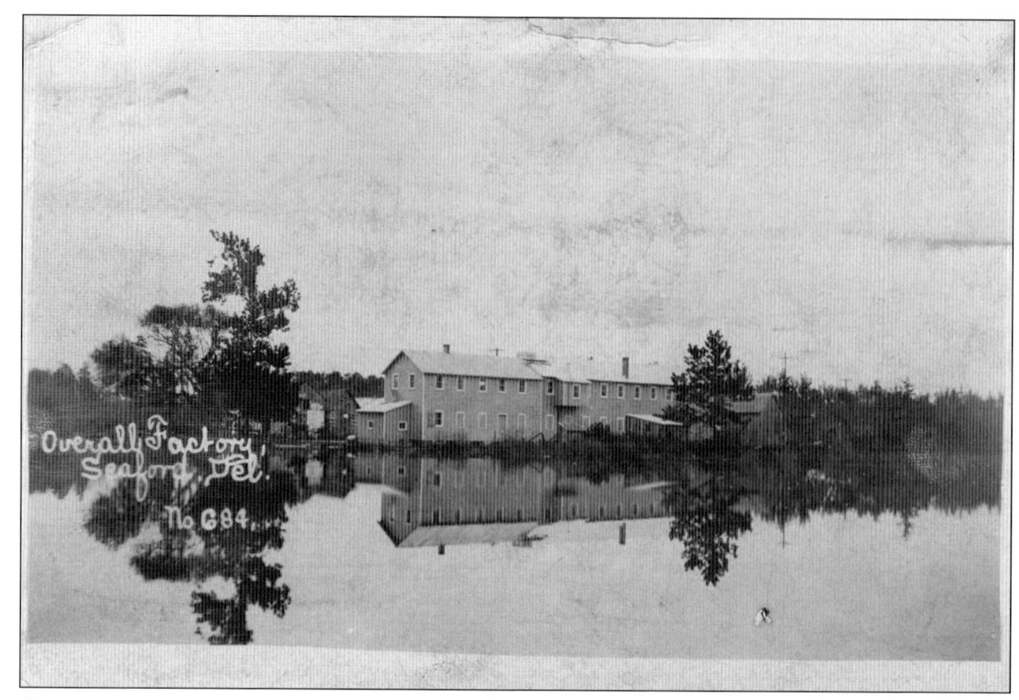

Overall Factory, Seaford, 1909. The "Overall Factory," owned by Carter, Webster, and Company of Baltimore, made work shirts, pants, and overalls. Fire destroyed the building in 1914.

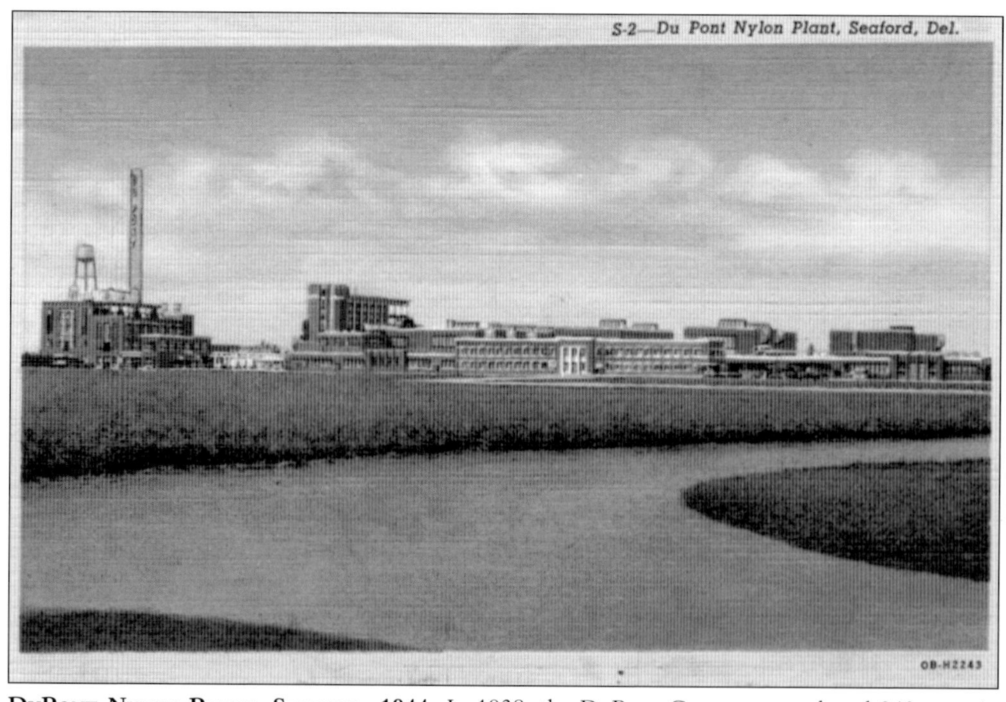

DuPont Nylon Plant, Seaford, 1944. In 1938, the DuPont Company purchased 340 acres in Seaford and erected a large, modern plant to manufacture nylon, its new synthetic fiber. The nylon plant opened late in 1939, bringing growth and change to Seaford.

MT. OLIVET METHODIST PROTESTANT CHURCH, SEAFORD, AFTER 1910. The site of Mt. Olivet, which was established in 1831, was originally part of the Hooper family burial ground. Thomas Hooper was the first recorded owner, in the early 1700s, of the land that became Seaford. This building, the congregation's third, was constructed in 1897.

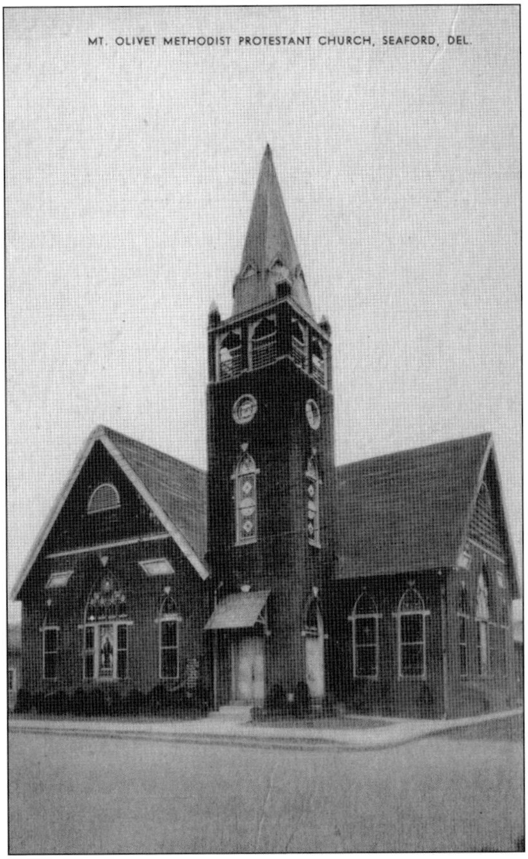

MT. OLIVET METHODIST PROTESTANT CHURCH, SEAFORD, DEL.

SCENE AROUND SLAUGHTER BEACH, 1920S. The origin of the name of this summer community of about 75 cottages is unclear. Settlers may have brought the family name from Gloucestershire, England. Another possibility revolves around a man named Brabant, who, despite escalating tension between Native Americans and colonists, was trusted by both groups. Fearing a deadly attack on the colonists, Brabant tricked the Indians, killing or maiming the troublemakers, but preserving peace.

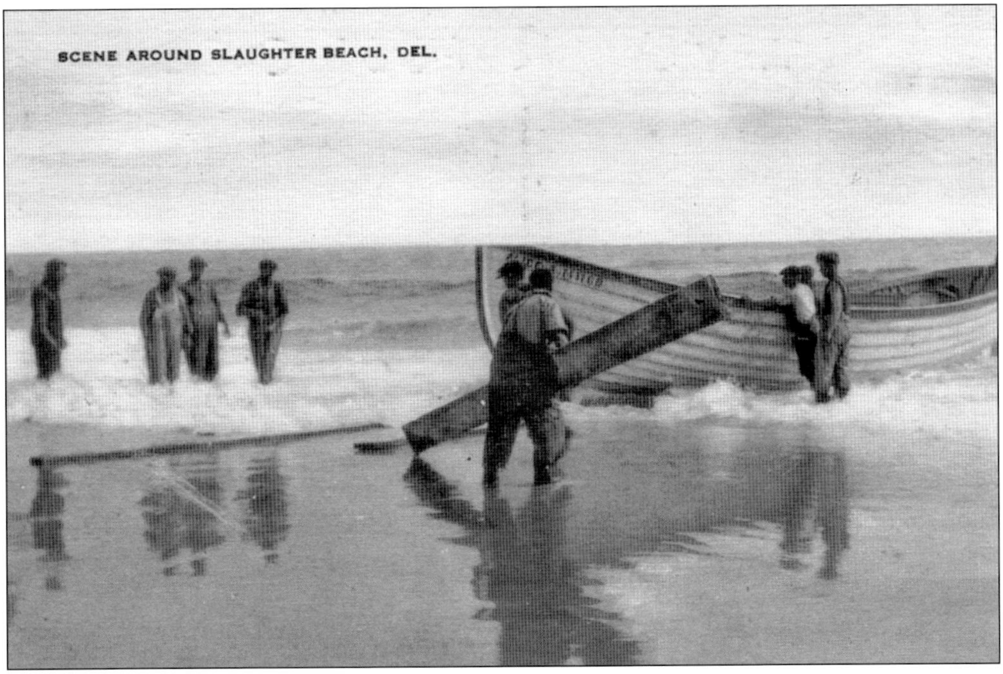

SCENE AROUND SLAUGHTER BEACH, DEL.

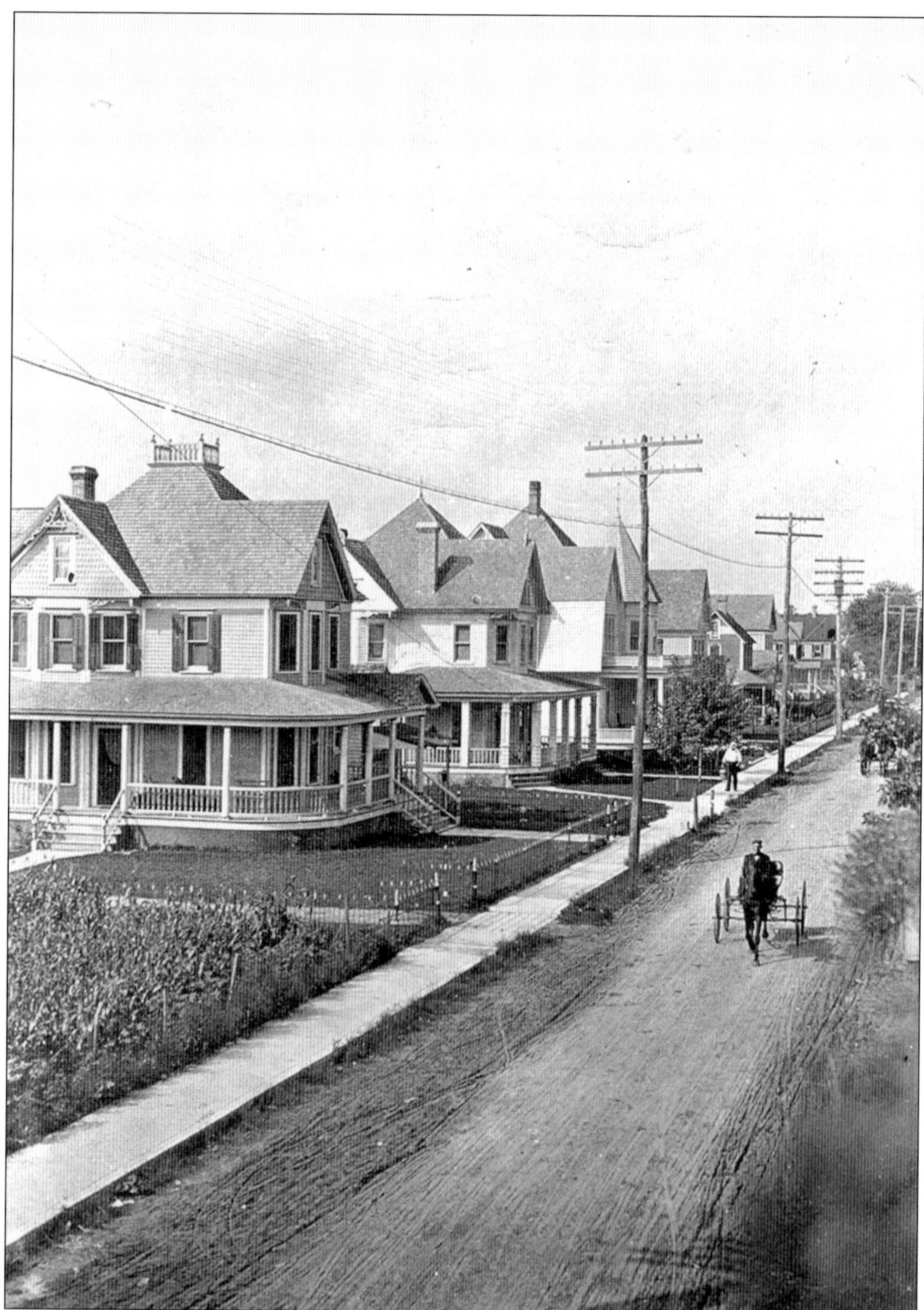

Church Street, Selbyville, c. 1910. Looking from Main Street toward the railroad tracks, this view shows just a portion of Church Street. The first house on the left is no longer standing. The house with the pointed cupola near the closest telephone pole is the Victorian Rose Bed and Breakfast, situated across from Salem United Methodist Church.

Three

Kent County

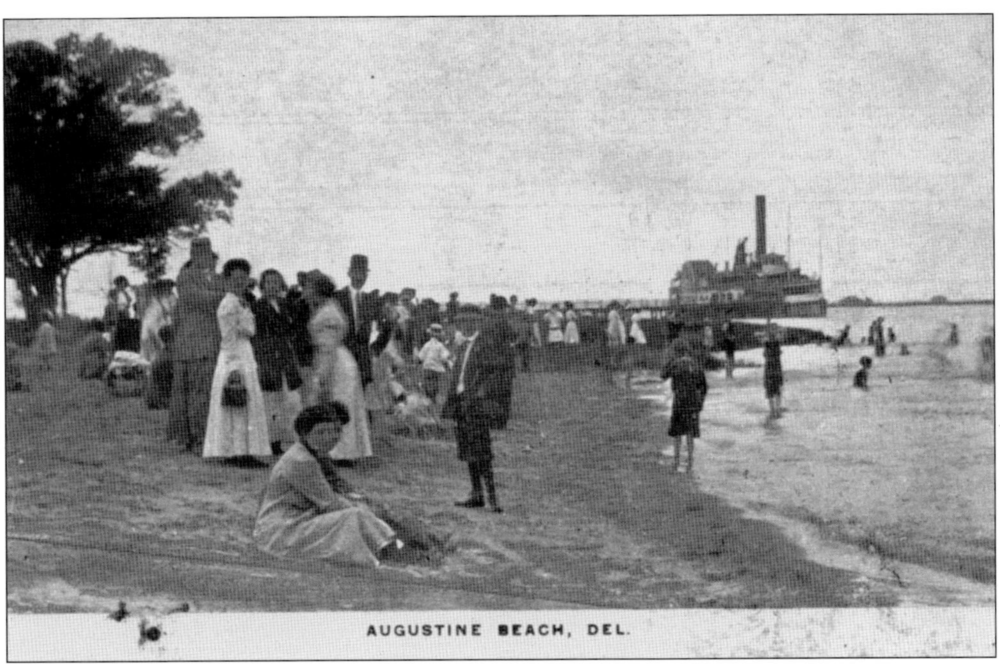

Augustine Beach, 1910s. Named after 17th-century mapmaker Augustine Hermann, the beach enjoyed great popularity from 1870 to 1920. The Wilmington Steamboat Company charged 30¢ in 1900 for a trip from Wilmington to Augustine Beach, which boasted a fine hotel, swimming, and picnic tables. Three steamers made daily stops at "The Piers" on regular trips south to Woodland Beach and Bombay Hook.

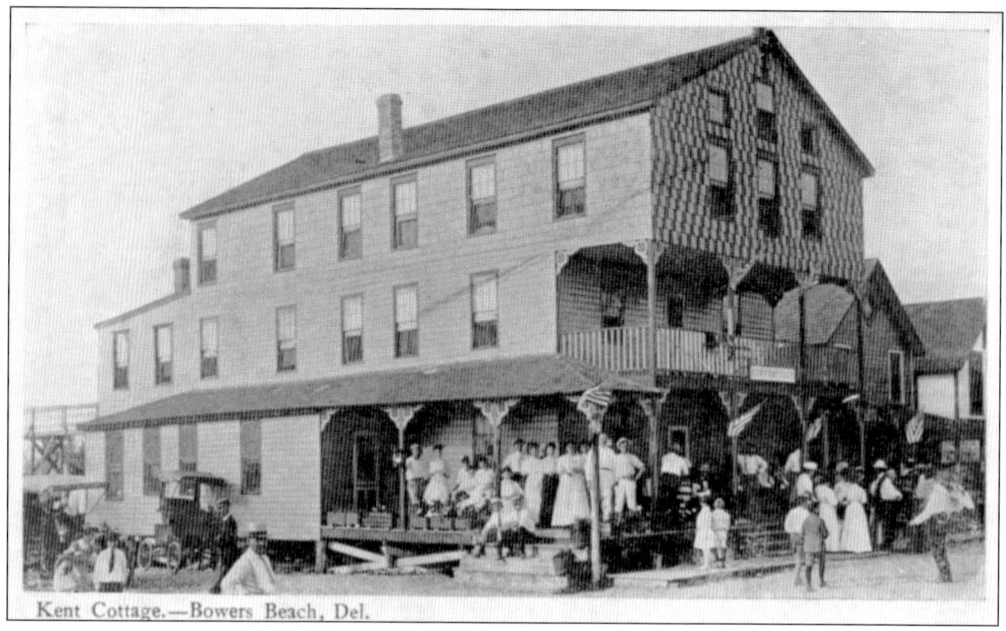

KENT COTTAGE 1916. Both of the buildings pictured here were fashionable hotels at Bowers Beach. During the summer months, Bowers was known for its good bathing and bathhouses, extensive strolling, and excellent hotels.

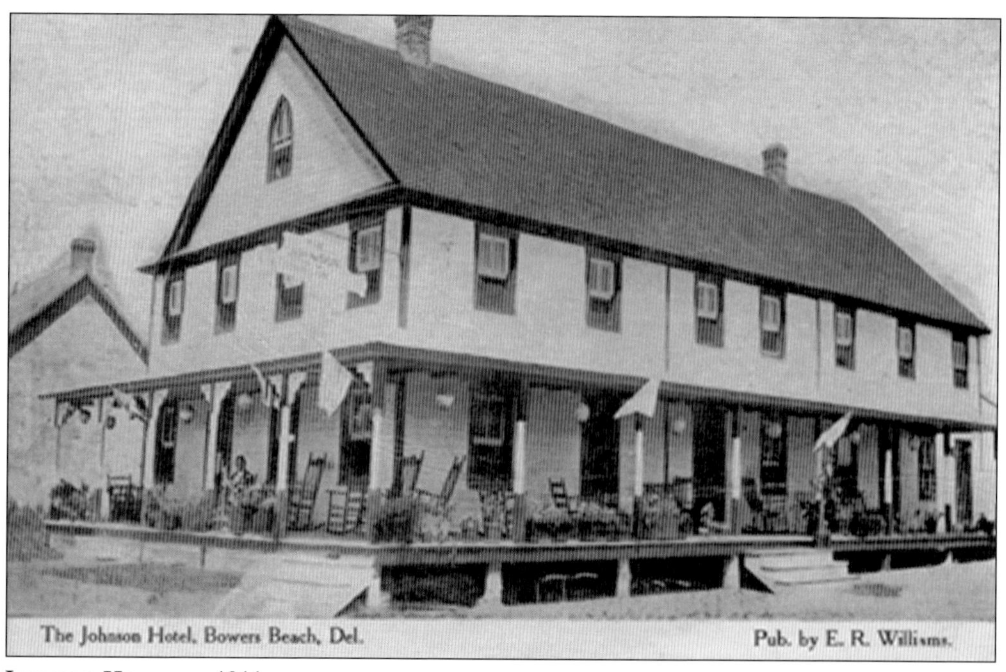

JOHNSON HOTEL, c. 1911.

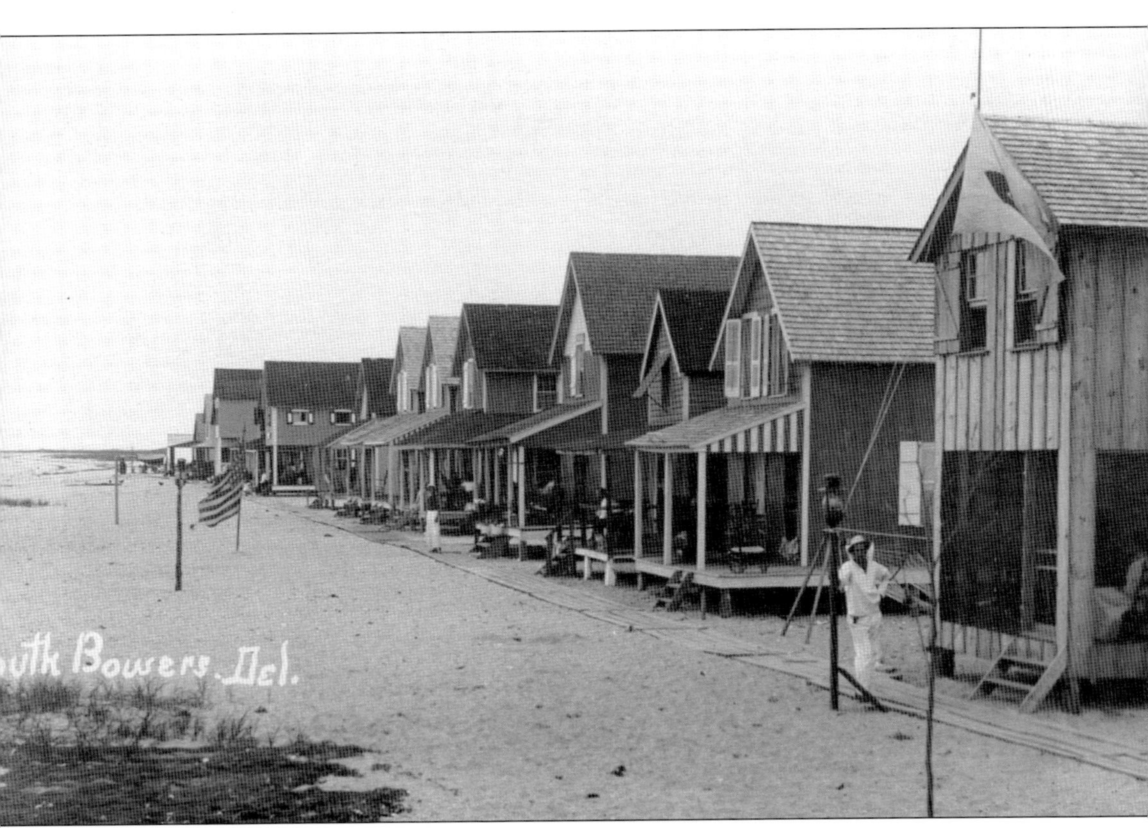

COTTAGES IN SOUTH BOWERS, C. 1910. Bowers was a popular summer spot for thousands of visitors each summer from towns along the St. Jones and Murderkill Rivers and for the steamers that plied between Bowers and cities to the north along the Delaware Bay. Fire almost destroyed Bowers Beach in 1920.

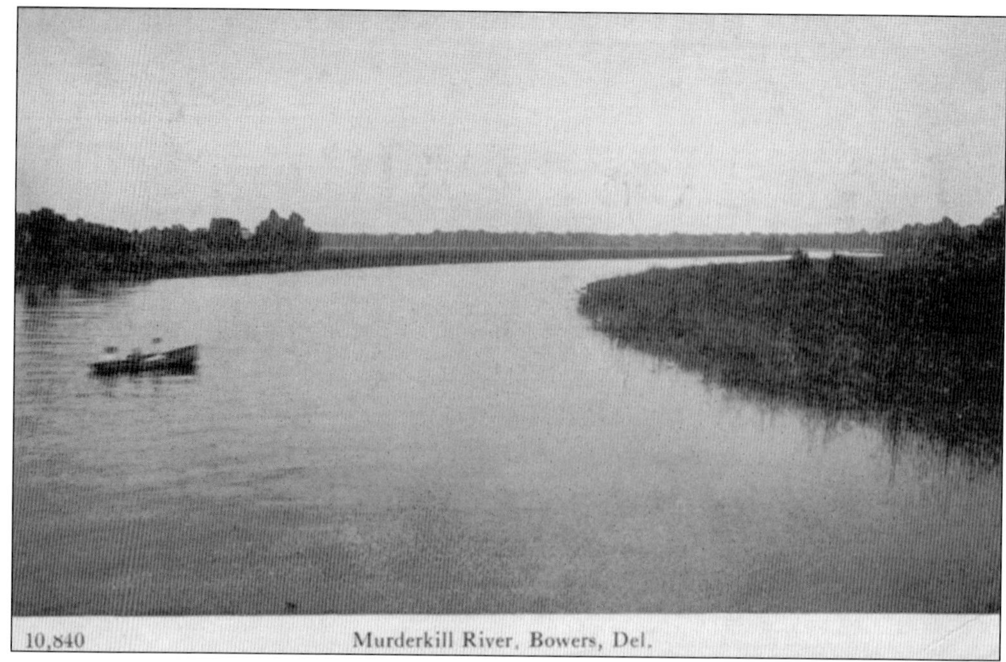

10,840 Murderkill River, Bowers, Del.

MURDERKILL RIVER, BOWERS, 1907–1909. The origin of the name Murderkill is not known, though the earliest form appeared on Peter Lindestrom's map in the 1650s as Modare Kijhlen, which can be translated as "The Murder Creek." In addition to year-round steamer traffic, during the winter Murderkill was known for good oystering and muskrat trapping. In the summer, Bowers became a salt-water fishing resort for croaker, sea trout, flounder, blue fish, and shark.

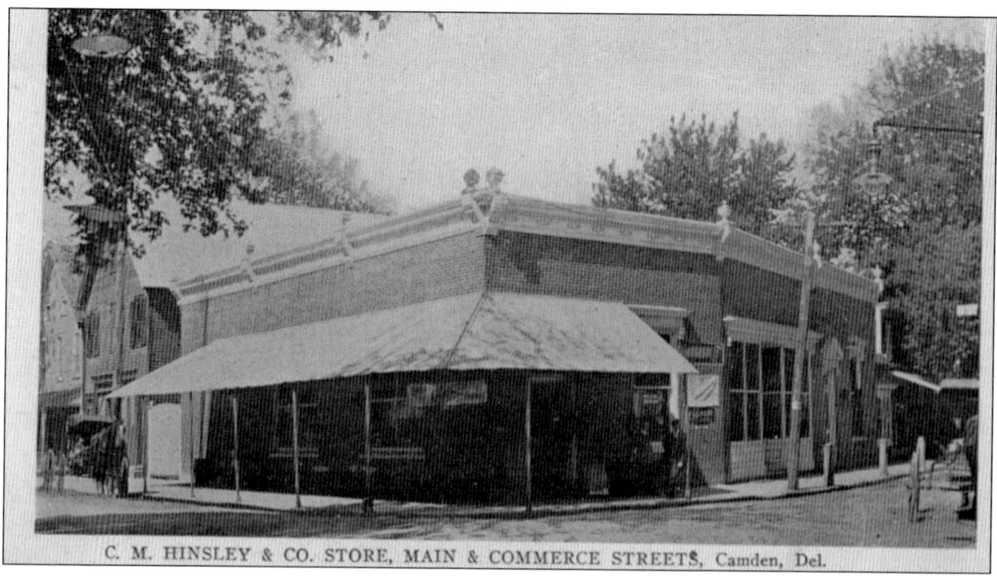

C. M. HINSLEY & CO. STORE, MAIN & COMMERCE STREETS, Camden, Del.

C.M. HINSLEY & CO. STORE, CAMDEN, AFTER 1905. This new brick store on Main and Commerce Streets contrasts with the frame dwellings on the left. One of the few early Delaware towns not located on navigable water, Camden, founded in 1783, shipped its produce through nearby Lebanon and Forest Landing on the St. Jones Creek. Similarly, the Delaware Railroad built its station at nearby Wyoming rather than in Camden.

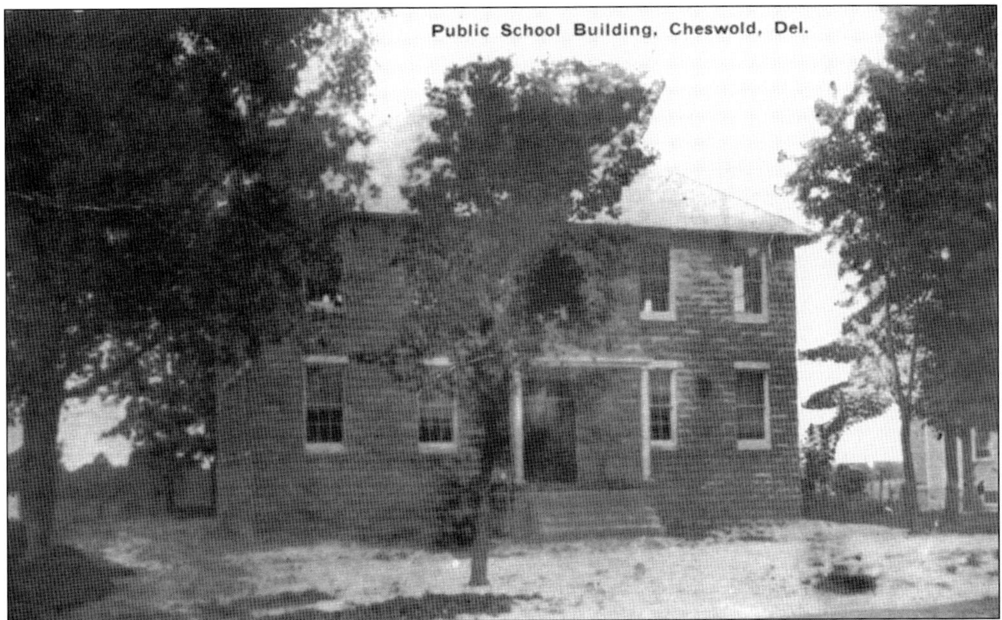

Public School Building, Cheswold, 1916. Cheswold, once a stop on the Delaware Railroad, is the birthplace of former governor and U.S. senator J. Caleb Boggs. It is probably best known for the community of Moors, a unique racial group, who live there.

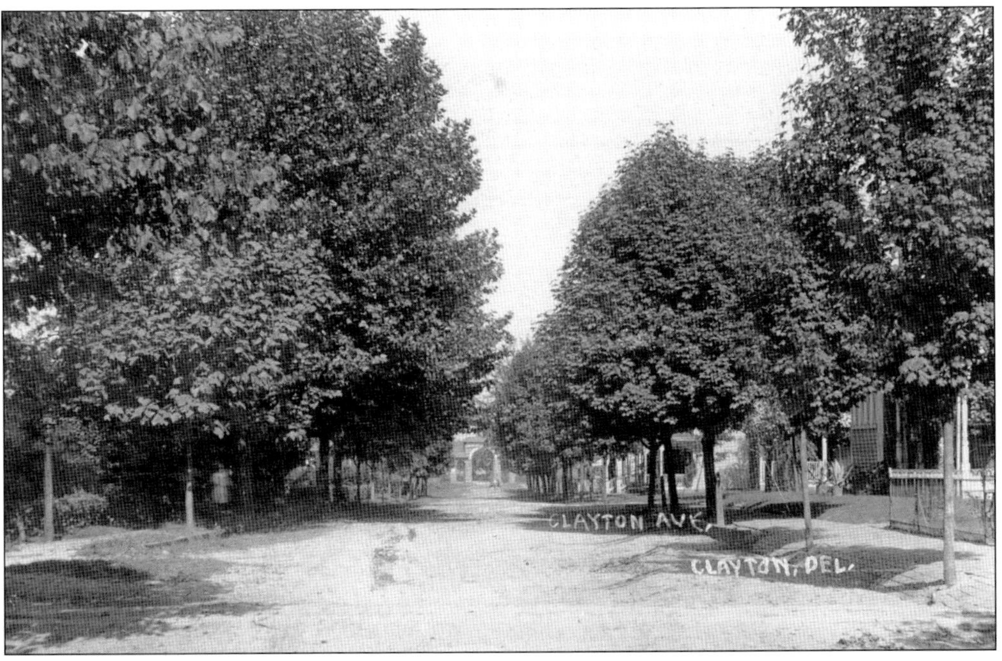

Clayton Avenue, Clayton, 1907. At the far end of the street is the entrance to St. Joseph's Industrial School. Founded in 1896 by St. Joseph's Society of the Sacred Heart of the Roman Catholic Church, the school admitted African-American boys between 10 and 14 years of age and "of good character." Boys could stay at St. Joseph's for five years, receiving their first two years of high school.

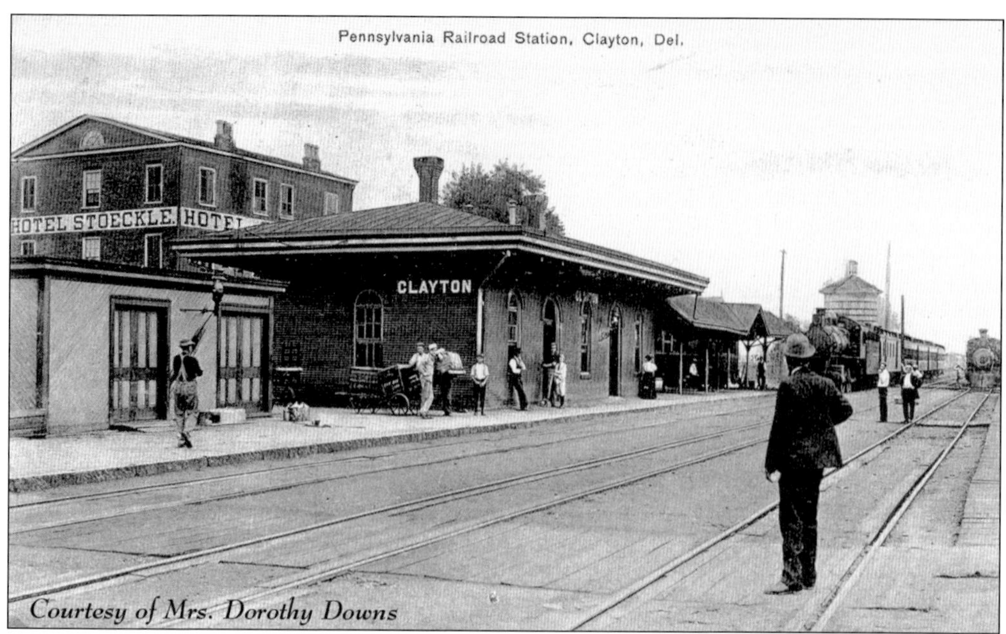

PENNSYLVANIA RAILROAD STATION, CLAYTON, 1910. In 1855 the crossroads station of the Oxford, Maryland branch of the Pennsylvania Railroad was named Smyrna Station. The name was changed in 1877 to honor John M. Clayton, the Delaware statesman responsible for bringing the railroad to Clayton. In 1920 the railroad's offices and repair shops closed, leaving the town with only a few industries, a cannery, and a cold storage plant.

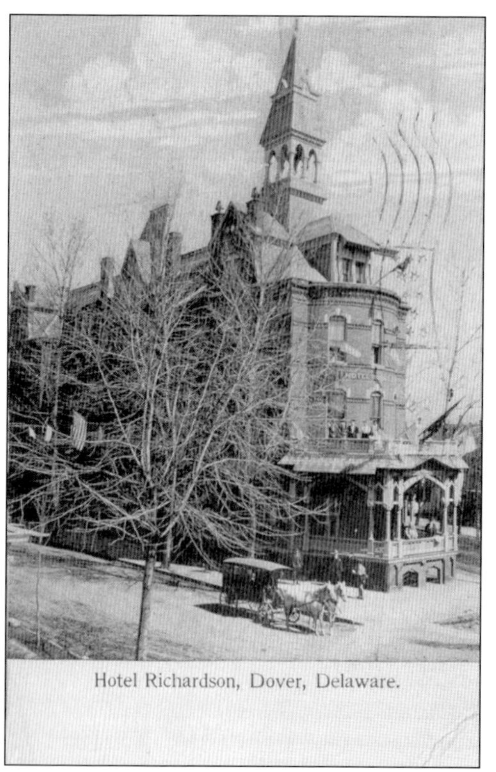

HOTEL RICHARDSON, DOVER, 1912. Built by Alden Richardson of the Richardson and Robbins Company, the hotel opened in 1882 at State and King Streets. With elegant architecture and furnishings, steam heat, gas light, electric call bells, and bathrooms on every floor, the 68-room hotel represented the height of elegance. The hotel's dining room became the town's social center. The building was torn down in 1954.

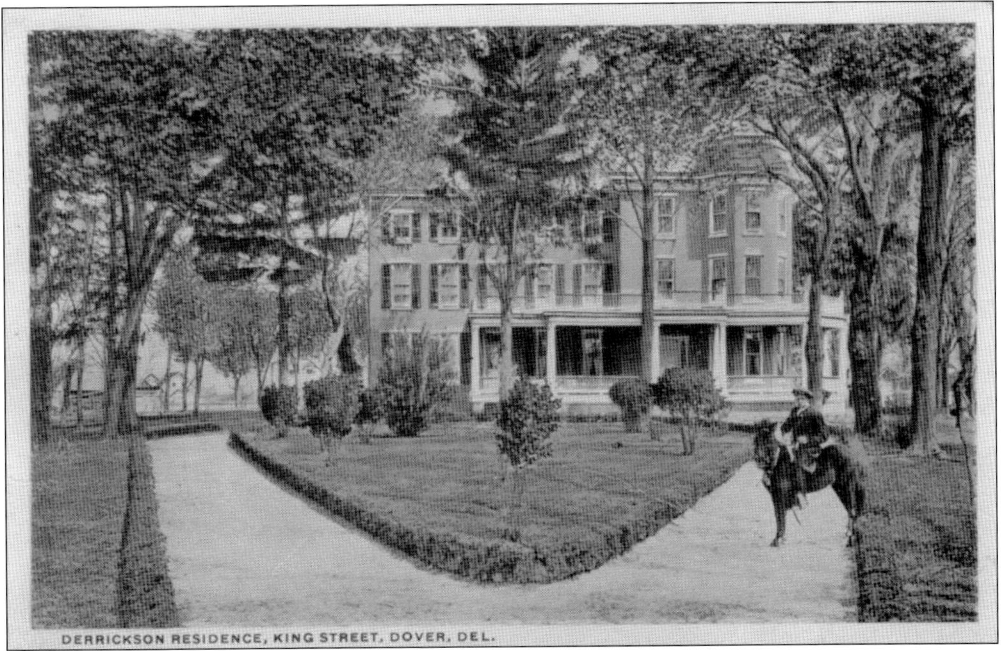

Derrickson Residence on King Street, Dover, after 1910. Large, gracious homes built in a variety of styles in the late 1800s and early 1900s sit on the quiet, tree-lined streets of the older sections of Dover.

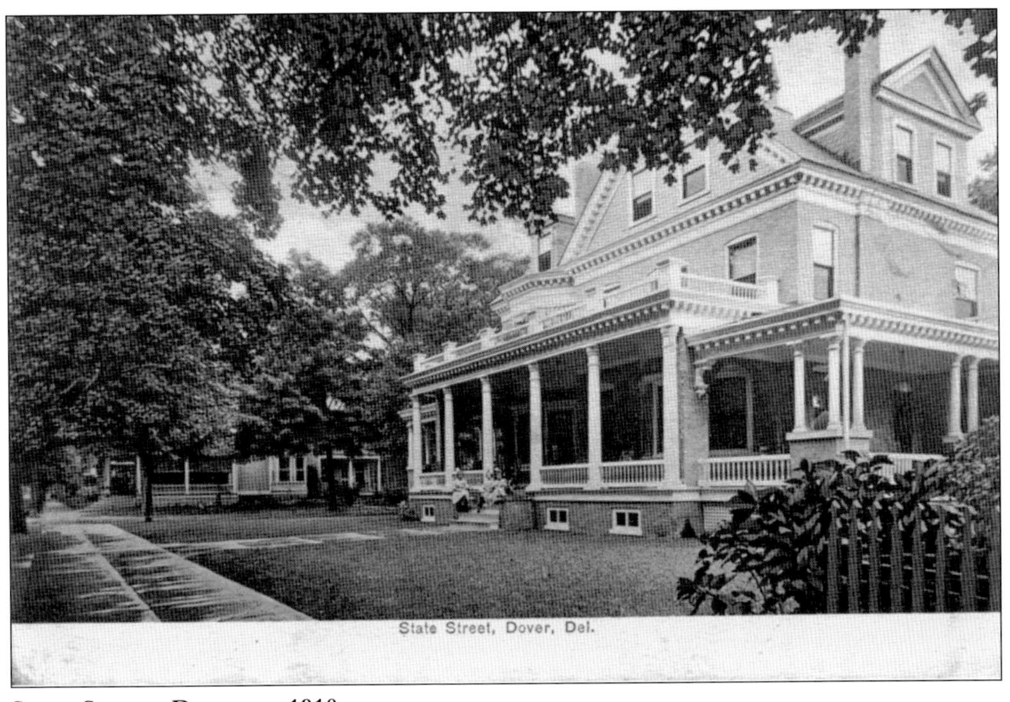

State Street, Dover, c. 1910.

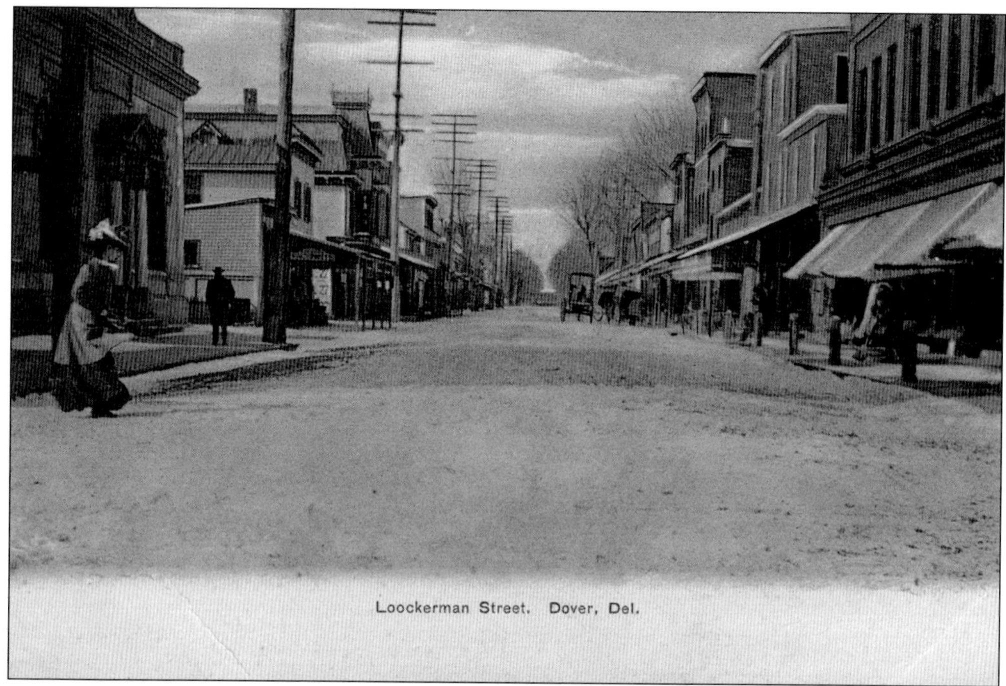

LOOCKERMAN STREET, DOVER, BEFORE 1905. These postcards show different views of Dover's main commercial street. The 1905 card above looks up the street from the post office at State Street, while the 1926 view below looks towards the post office. Many of the buildings were erected in the late 1800s and early 1900s. Even though only 20 years separate the two views, change is evident.

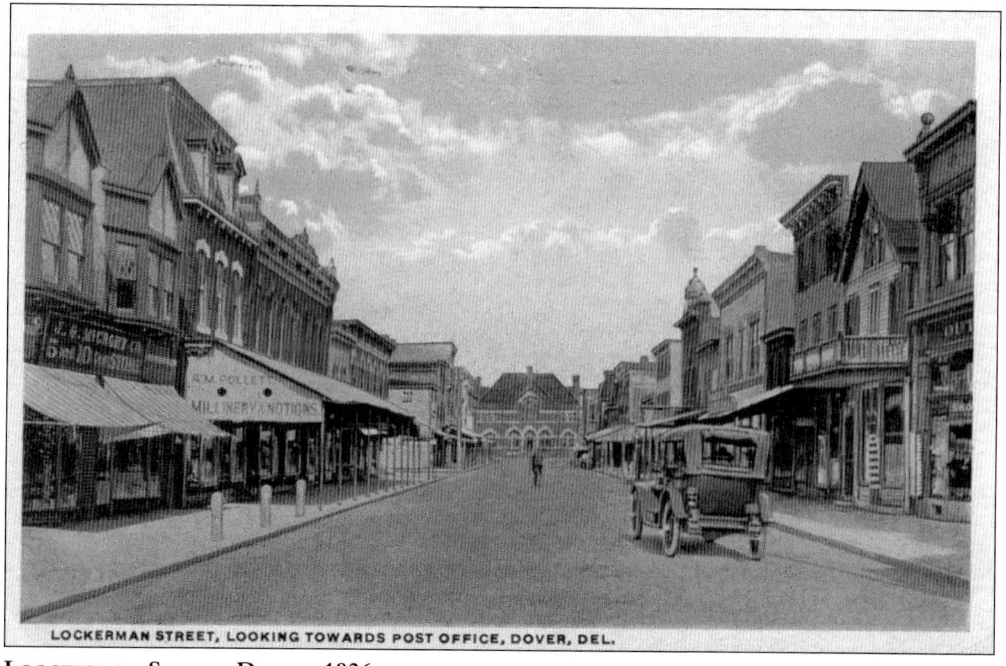

LOOCKERMAN STREET, DOVER, 1926.

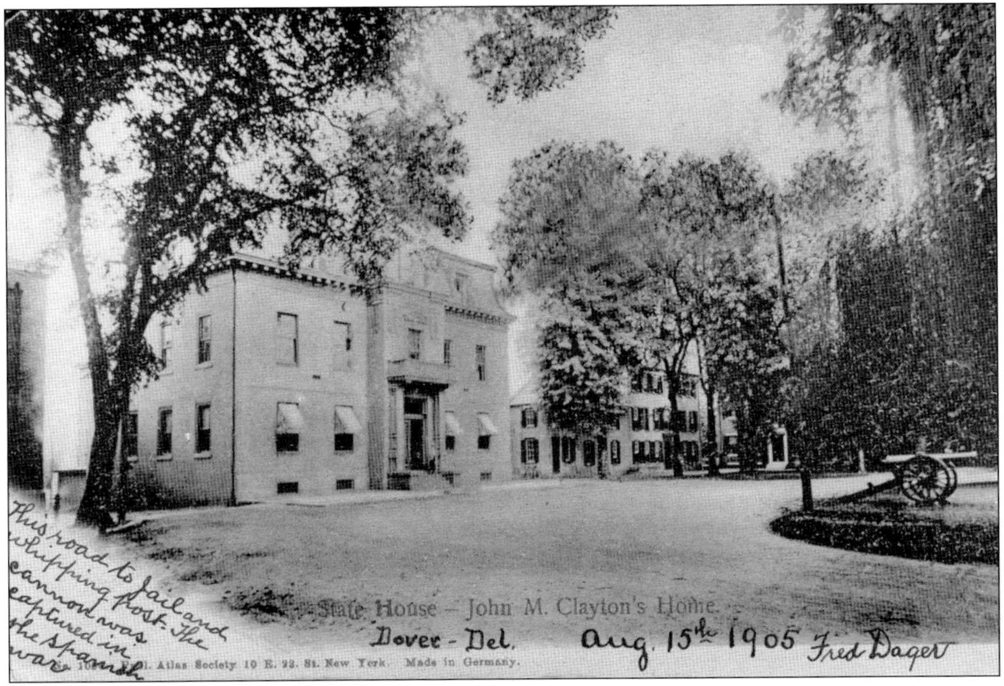

State House and John M. Clayton's Home, August 15, 1905. These postcards show two versions of the same building just nine years apart. Erected between 1787 and 1792, the Old State House, as it is now known, served both as the state capital and the Kent County Courthouse until 1874. The building received a Victorian facelift in 1873–1875, and in 1909–1910 the building was restored to a Georgian style. Additions required the demolition of John M. Clayton's home, also known as the Chew Mansion, next door.

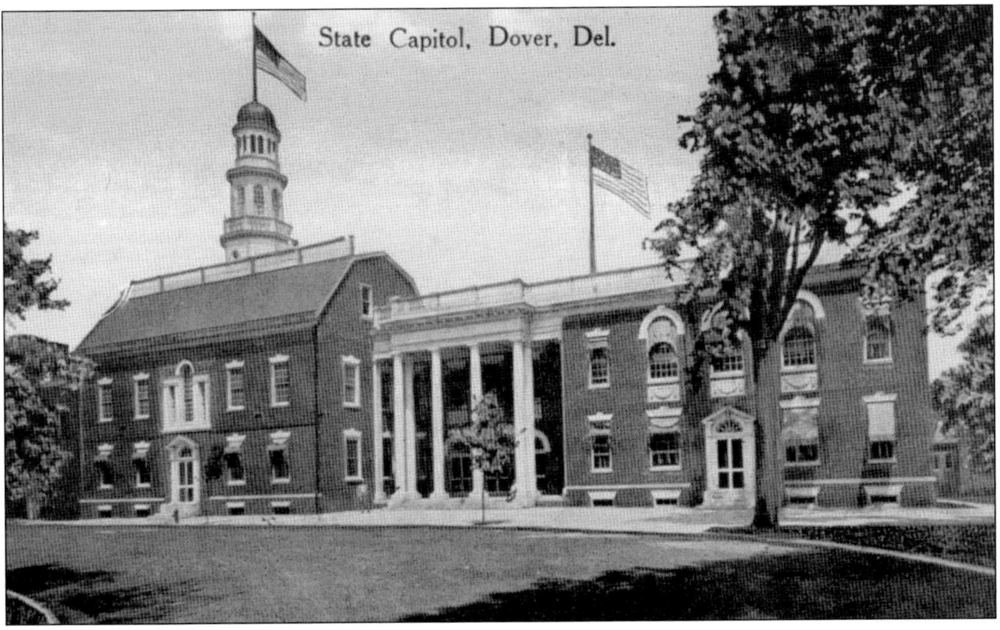

State Capitol, Dover, 1914.

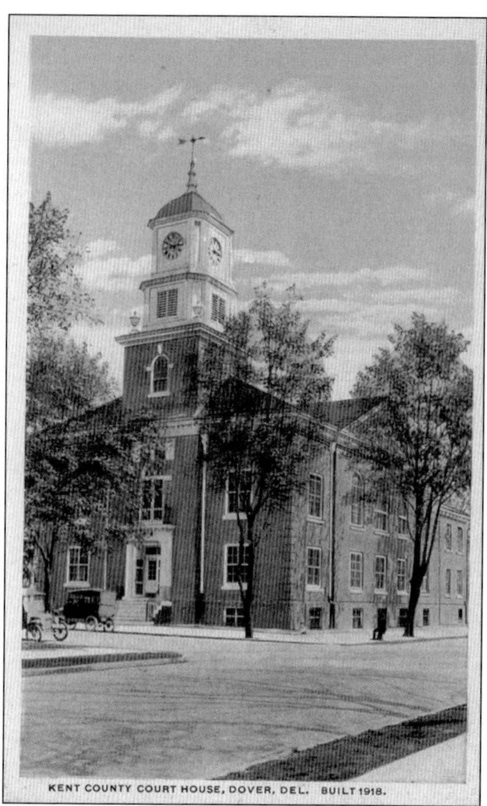

KENT COUNTY COURTHOUSE, DOVER, AFTER 1918. This building was actually erected in 1874 as a four-story, Victorian-style structure. In 1918, a complete renovation removed the top story and gave the courthouse a Georgian appearance. The building still serves Kent County.

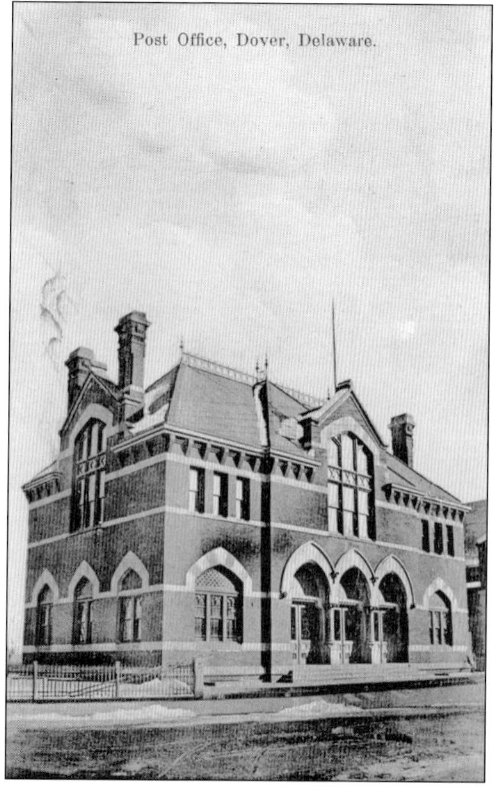

POST OFFICE, DOVER, 1911. This Romanesque-style post office on Loockerman Street was built in 1873. The location, however, prevented the extension of the street as the city grew. In 1933, the building was moved to a new site northeast of its original location. It then became Dover's city hall and part of the new City Plaza that was created. The building is no longer standing.

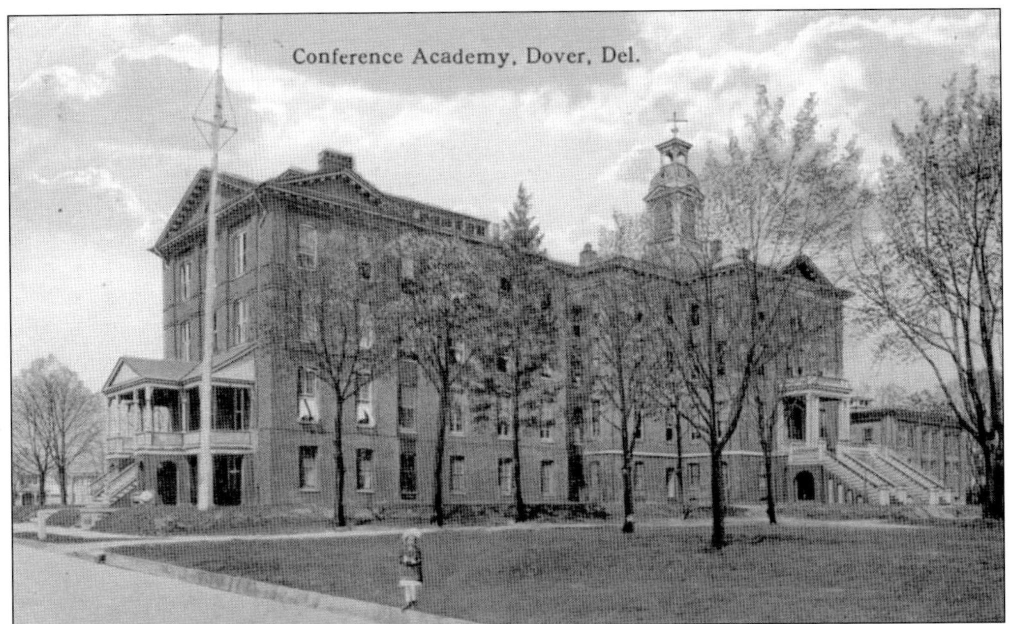

CONFERENCE ACADEMY, DOVER, 1910. The Methodist Church established the Wilmington Conference Academy in 1873 as a high school for young men and women. The school became Wesley Collegiate Institute in 1918. After closing during the Great Depression, it reopened as Wesley Junior College in 1942, and then became Wesley College. "Old Main," the school's original building, is still part of the campus.

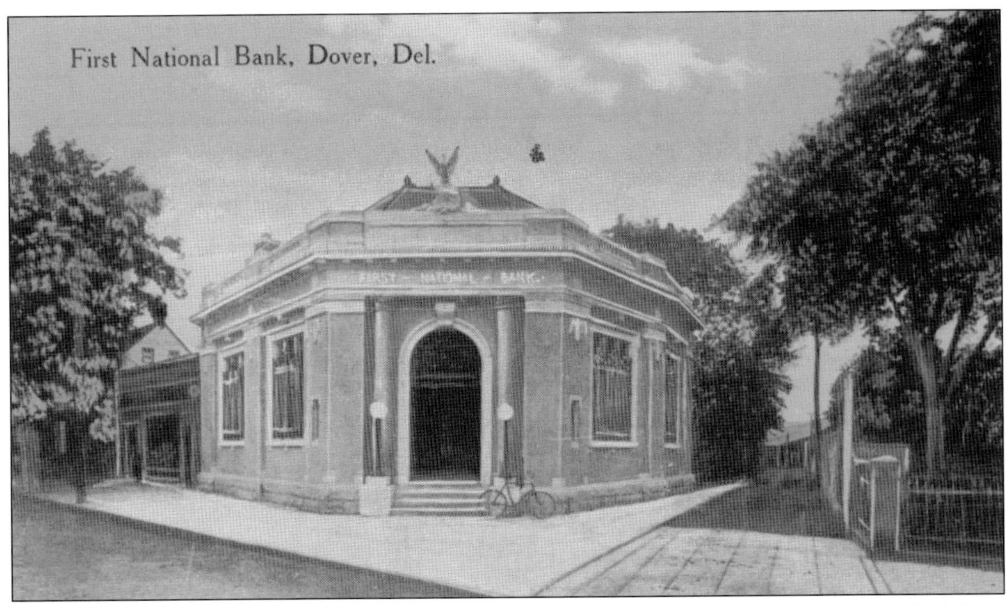

FIRST NATIONAL BANK, DOVER, C. 1912. Dover's First National Bank, founded in 1865, had three homes before this small but imposing edifice at King and Loockerman Streets was built in 1912. In 1954, the bank merged with Equitable Security Trust Company of Wilmington, which became the Bank of Delaware in 1958. This building was demolished and replaced with a new Bank of Delaware facility in 1965.

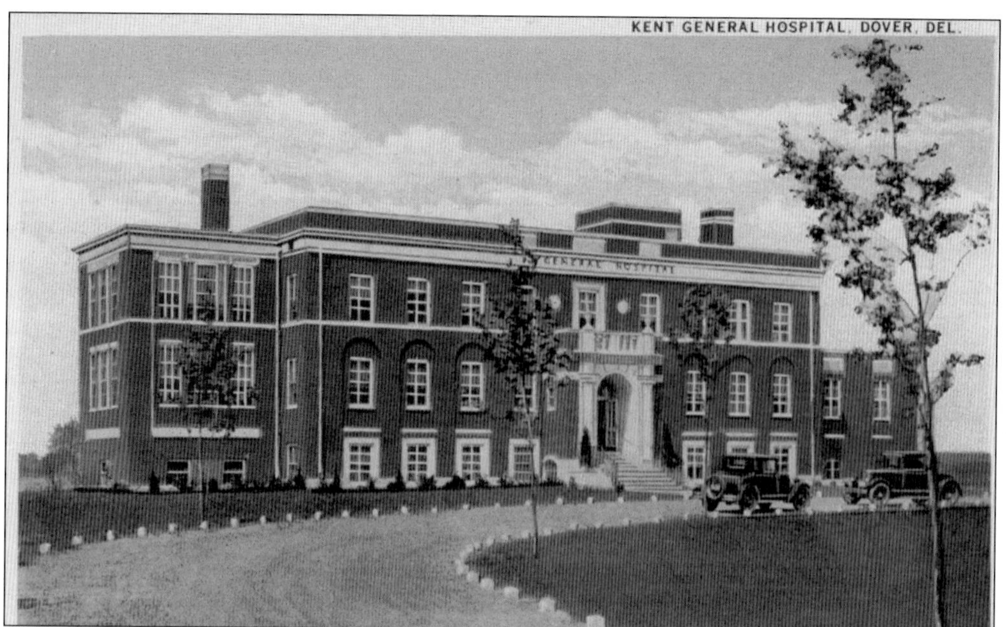

KENT GENERAL HOSPITAL, DOVER, 1920s. In 1924, the Rotary Club of Dover began a fund-raising campaign to build a hospital to serve central Kent County. The campaign succeeded and the new hospital, at the south end of State Street, opened in 1927. Greatly expanded, Kent General Hospital continues to serve the area today.

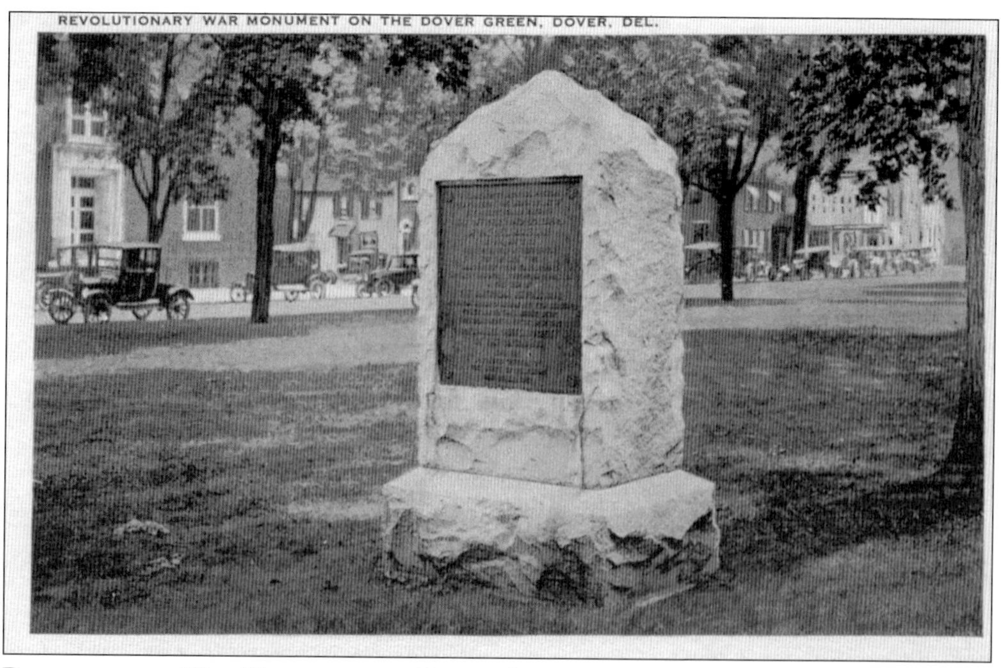

REVOLUTIONARY WAR MONUMENT ON DOVER GREEN, DOVER, AFTER 1912. This monument, erected by the Delaware State Society of the Cincinnati in 1912, honors Delaware's soldiers in the Continental Army.

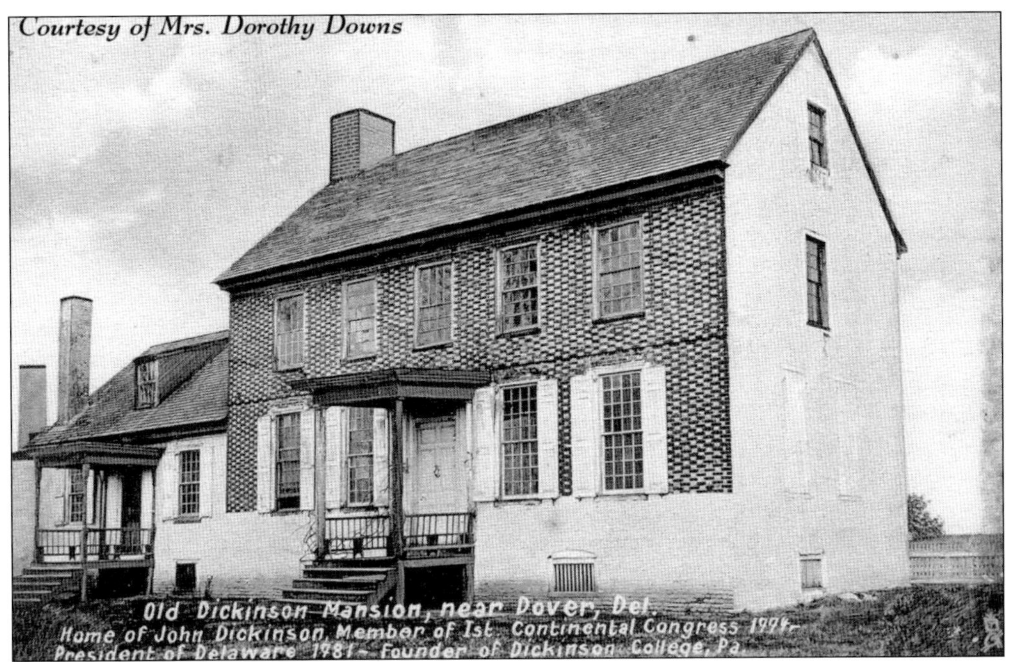

OLD DICKINSON MANSION NEAR DOVER, *c.* 1910. Samuel Dickinson built this house in 1740. His son John, one of Delaware's signers of the U.S. Constitution, grew up here and returned to the house and farm throughout his life. The State of Delaware acquired the house, by then run down, in 1952. After restoration, it opened as a museum in 1956.

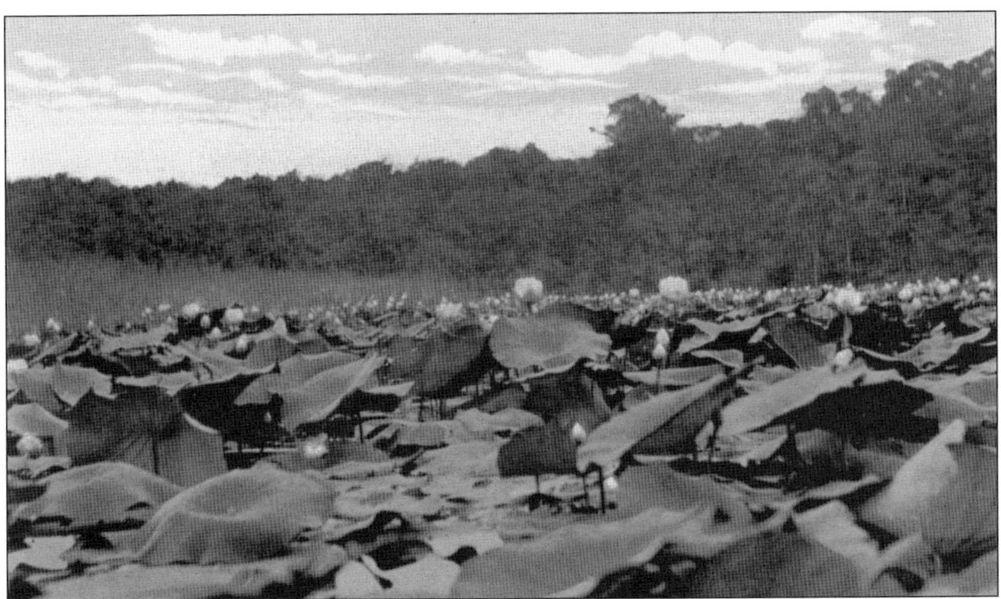

LOTUS BLOSSOMS ON ST. JONES RIVER, DOVER, 1906. During the Victorian era, lotus lilies—not native to the area—began to grow in the Saint Jones River. People made excursions by boat to see the blossoms each August, and they praised the rare flowers in prose and poetry. The federal government straightened the river channel after World War I, causing the lotus plants to die out in the changed environment.

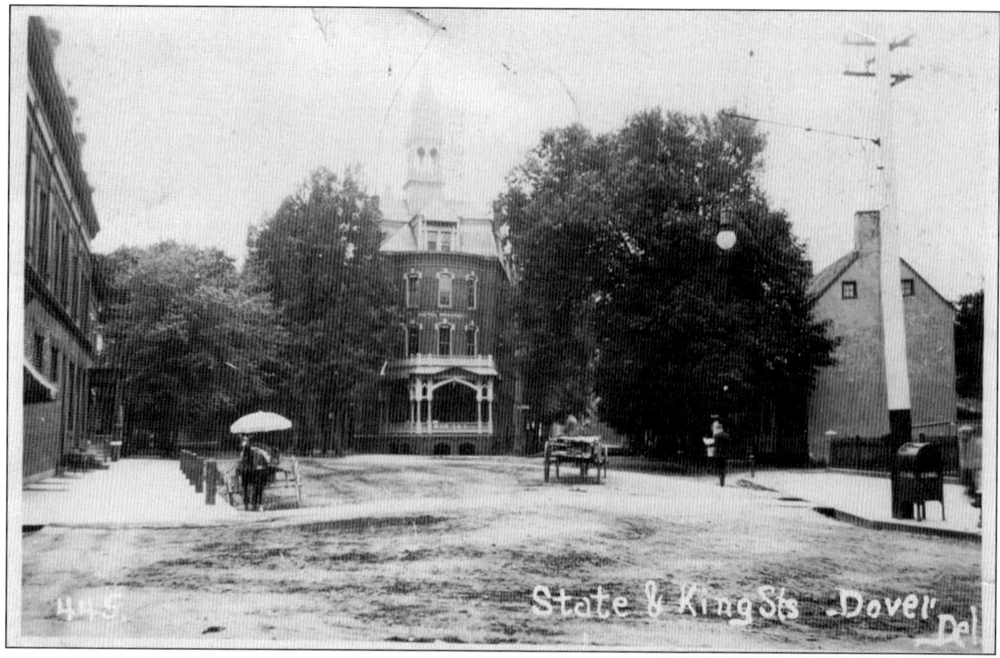

STATE AND KING STREETS, DOVER, C. 1910. The Hotel Richardson stands in the center while the new building for the First National Bank would soon stand to the right.

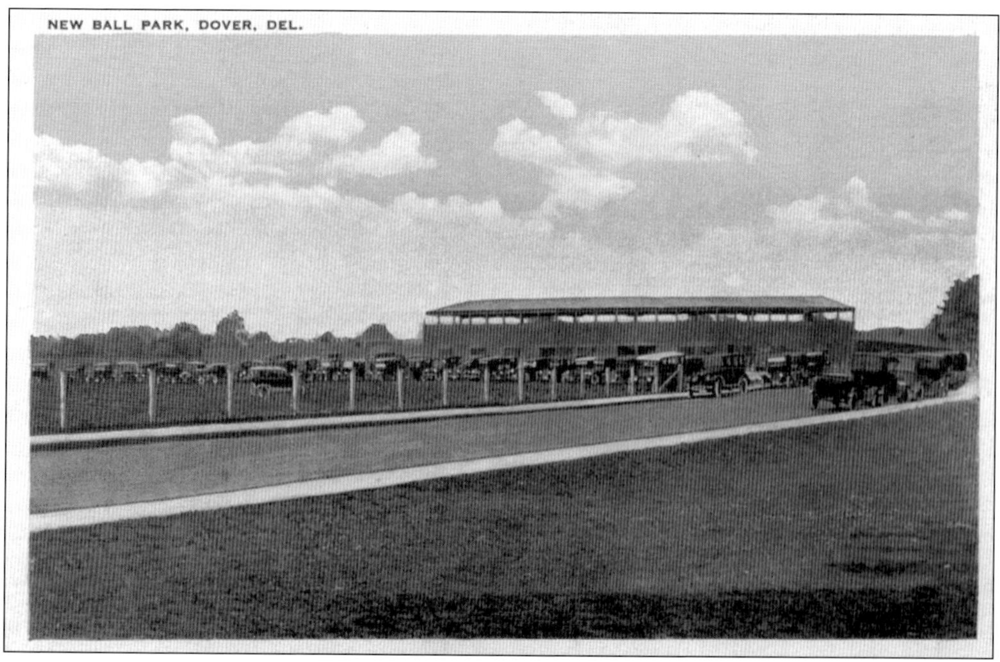

NEW BALL PARK, DOVER, C. 1923. The 1,800-seat Dover Baseball Stadium opened in 1923. Located on the site of the current Legislative Hall, it was the home field for the Dover team in the Eastern Shore Baseball League.

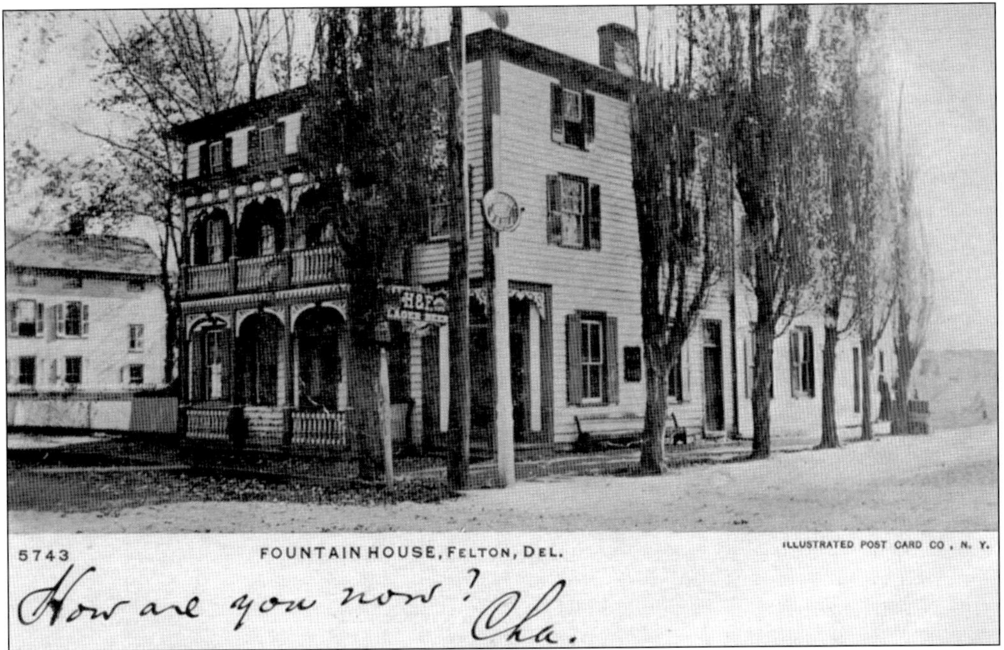

FOUNTAIN HOUSE, FELTON, c. 1900. Felton was founded in 1856 when the Delaware Railroad and Adams' Express opened offices there. The town was named for Samuel Felton, president of the railroad. The Fountain House, a 21-room hotel, opened the same year. The sign for "H&F Lager Beer" in this scene advertises Hartmann and Fehrenbach, which was brewed in Wilmington. Since 1910, the building has served as a residence and grocery store.

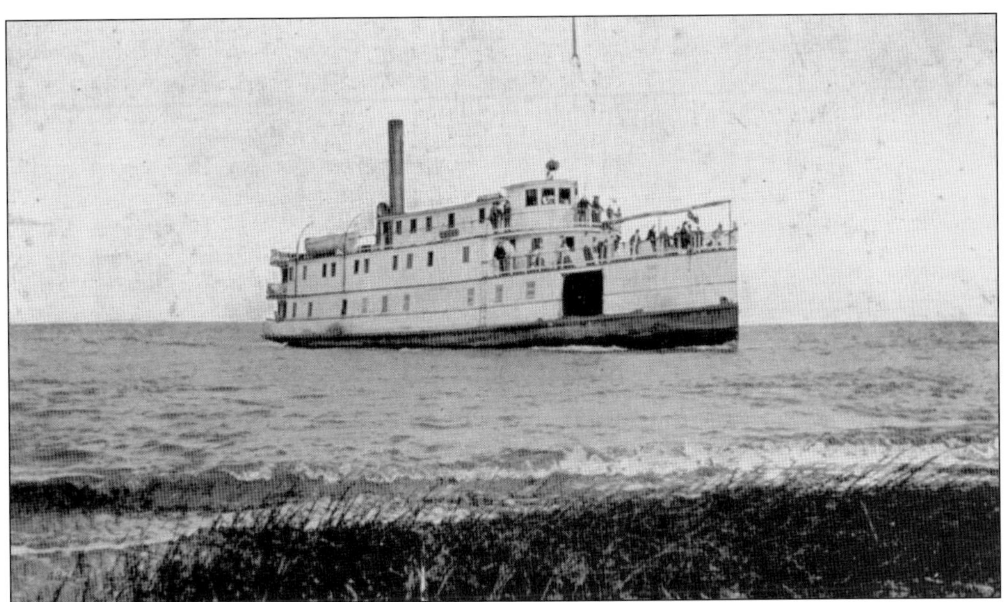

***ST. FREDERICA* PLYING THE WATERS BETWEEN FREDERICA, WEBBS LANDING, BOWERS, AND PHILADELPHIA.** Its location on the Murderkill River made Frederica, founded in 1772, the shipping center for the surrounding area. The town declined after the railroad bypassed it, but until 1929, steamers transported passengers and freight from Frederica to Philadelphia.

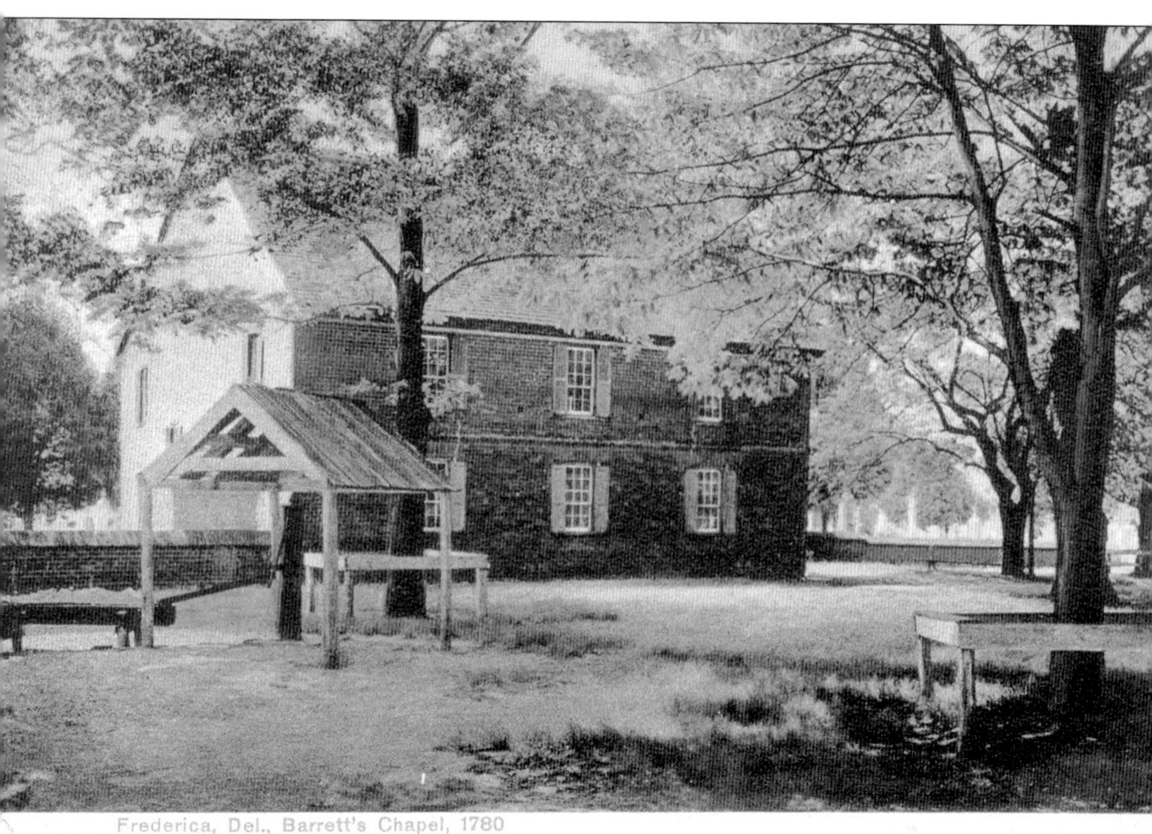

BARRETT'S CHAPEL, FREDERICA, 1908. Barrett's Chapel, erected in 1780, is known as the "Cradle of American Methodism." Methodism began as a movement within the Church of England and not a separate denomination. In November 1784, Thomas Coke and Francis Asbury administered Holy Communion during a service at the chapel. That act marked the beginning of Methodism as a separate church. Barrett's Chapel is now a museum of the Methodist Church.

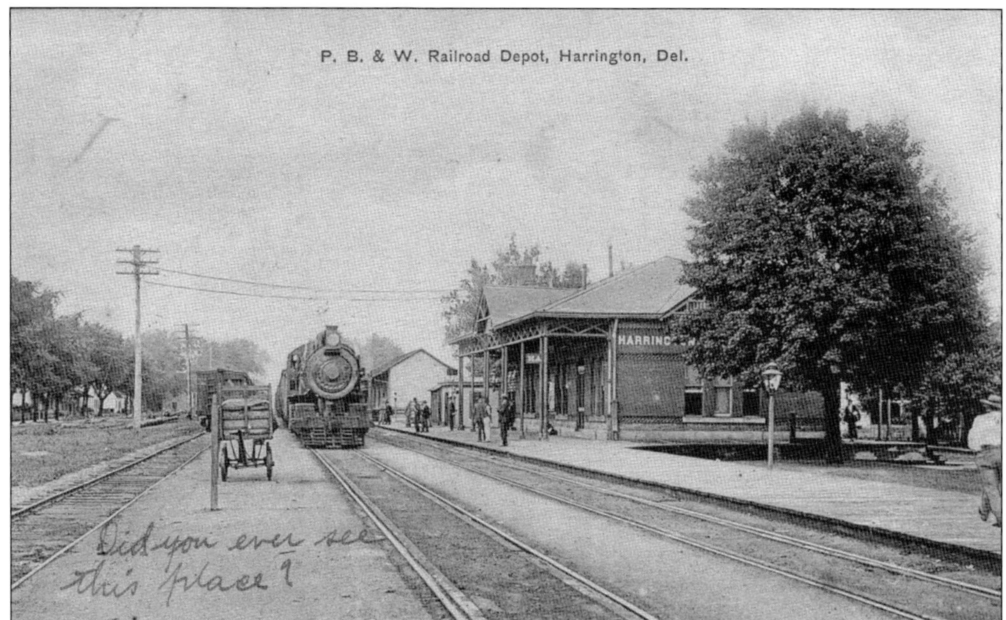

PHILADELPHIA, BALTIMORE & WASHINGTON RAILROAD DEPOT, HARRINGTON, 1909. Two railroads served Harrington: the Delaware, completed in 1856, and the Junction and Breakwater, completed in 1869. From 1855, the Delaware Railroad was leased to the Philadelphia, Wilmington & Baltimore Railroad. In 1902, further railroad consolidation made the Delaware Railroad part of the Philadelphia, Baltimore & Washington Railroad.

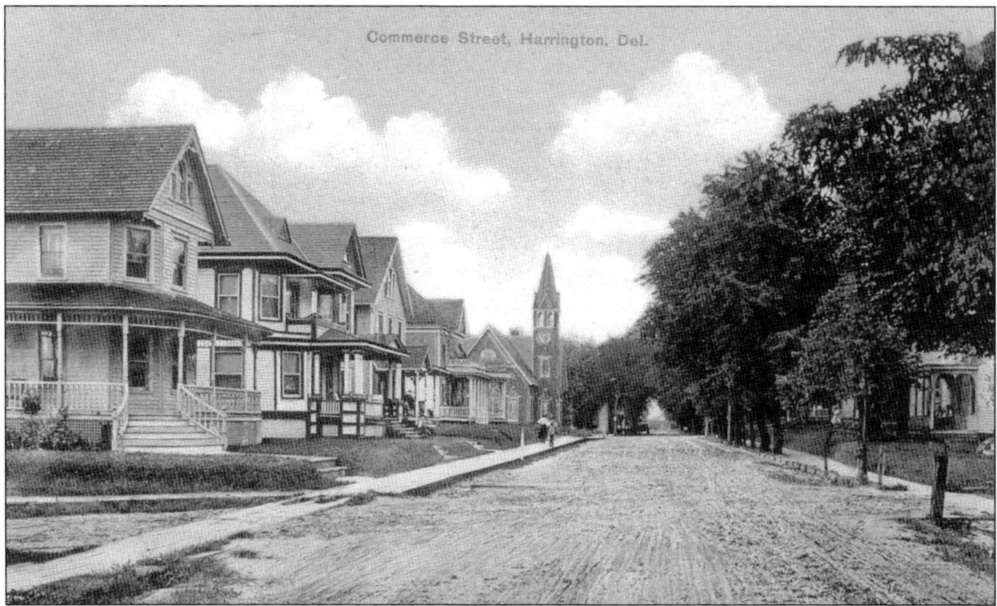

COMMERCE STREET, HARRINGTON, 1909. When the Delaware Railroad came in 1856, the hamlet of Clark's Corner grew into a town. It was renamed in honor of Samuel Maxwell Harrington, the Delaware Railroad's first president, in 1862. Comfortable frame houses line Commerce Street. Trinity Methodist Protestant Church, founded in 1880, stands in the distance on the left-hand side of the street. The building in the picture was constructed in 1904.

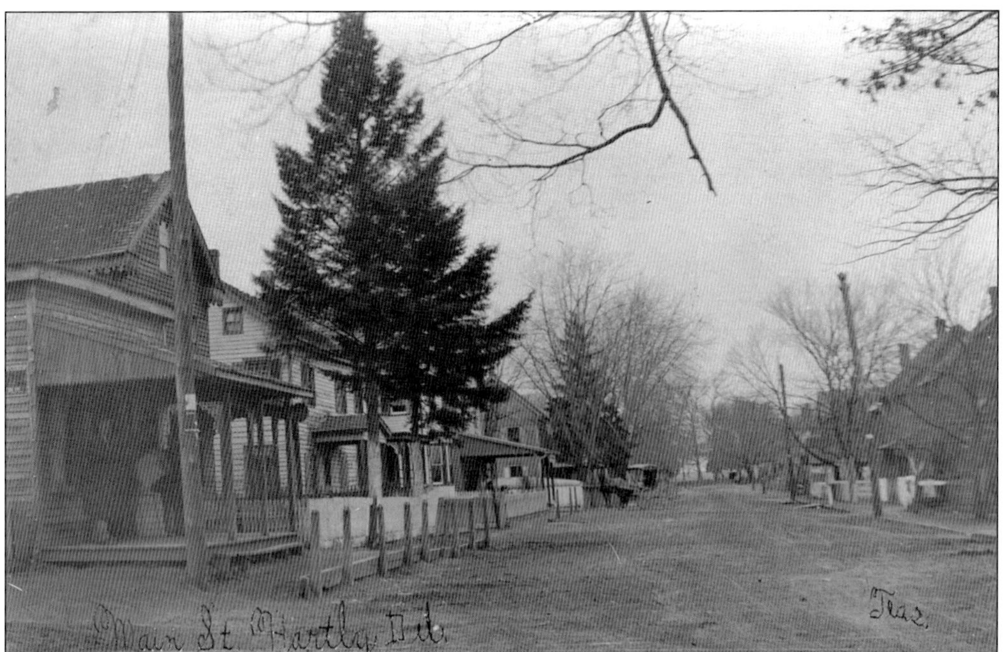

MAIN STREET, HARTLY, BEFORE 1910. Before acquiring its present name, Hartly was called Arthurville or Butterpat. In 1883, the village became a stop on the Delaware and Chesapeake Railroad and was renamed Hartly in honor of a Mr. Hart, who was influential in having the station located there. This view shows a quiet street with modest frame houses.

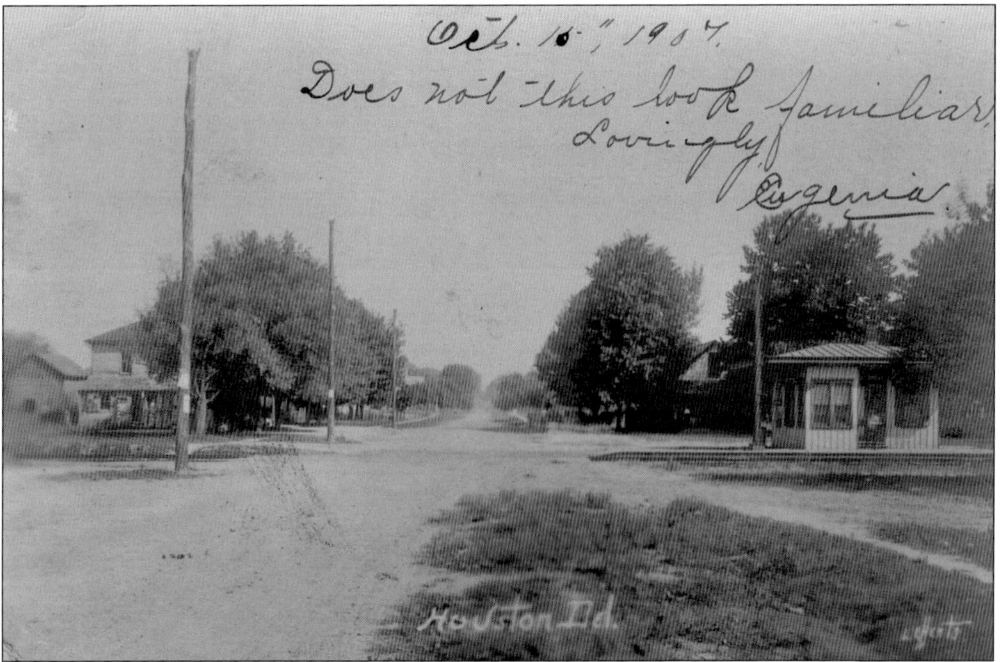

HOUSTON, c. 1910. Lefferts, a local photographer, took this view of Houston and its railroad station. The Libby, McNeil, Libby Cannery and the Delaware, Maryland, and Virginia branch of the Pennsylvania Railroad formed the heart of this small town.

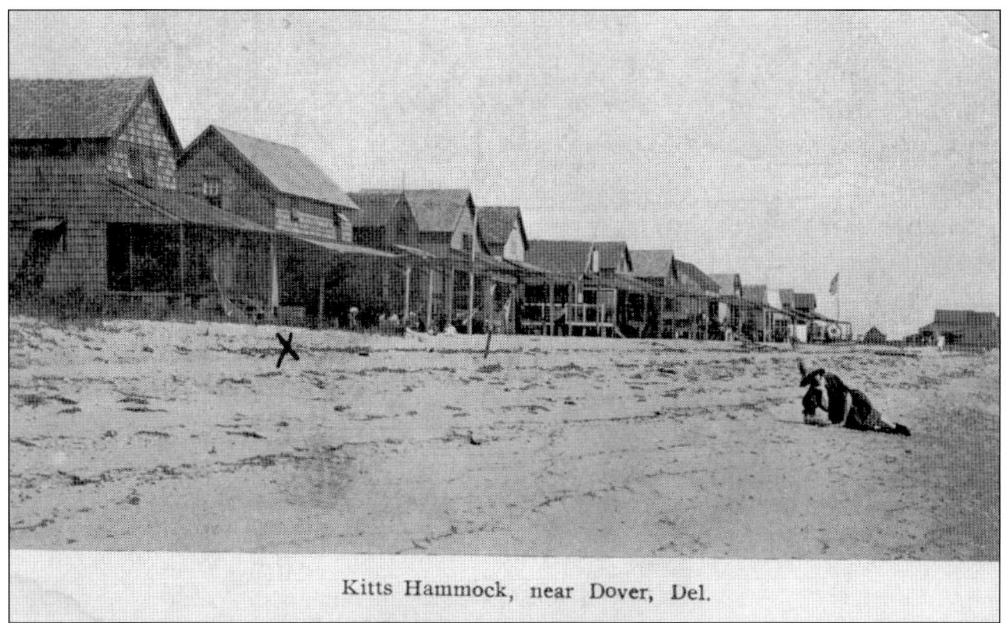

Kitts Hammock near Dover, 1909. Kitts Hammock began in 1738 when Jehu Curtis claimed 31 acres of high land. A hammock is a fertile area somewhat higher than its surroundings. For years, stories of Captain Kidd's buried treasure circulated about the area. During the Civil War some thought it the chief resort of Kent County secessionists. Kitts Hammock is located just north of the Ted Harvey Conservation Area.

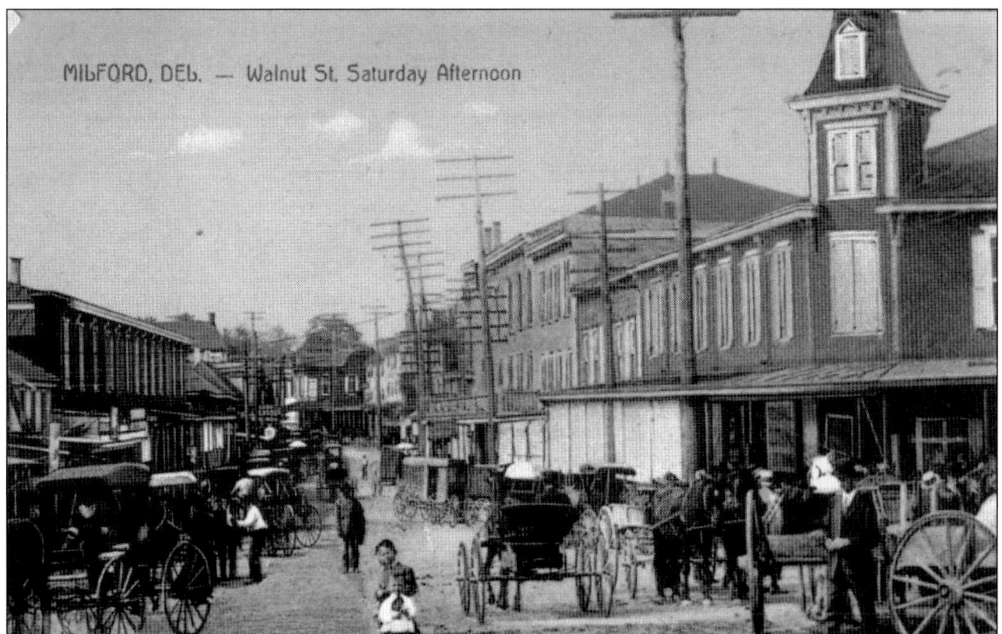

Walnut Street, Milford, 1906. Founded in 1785 by Joseph Oliver and Sydenham Thorne, Milford was chartered in 1807. This view of the business district shows the intersection of South Walnut and Front Streets. On Saturdays everybody from town and the surrounding area did their shopping.

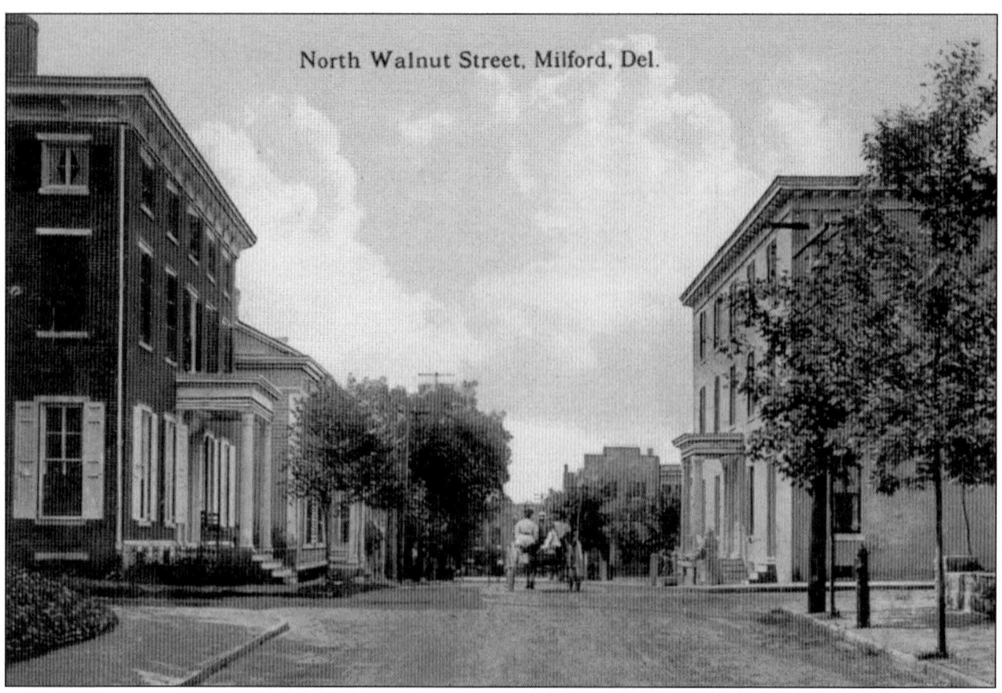

North Walnut Street, Milford, *c.* 1917. North Walnut Street is seen here from below Second Street. At the far left is 119 North Walnut Street, built as the Bank of Milford. Unfortunately the bank failed before the building was ready to open.

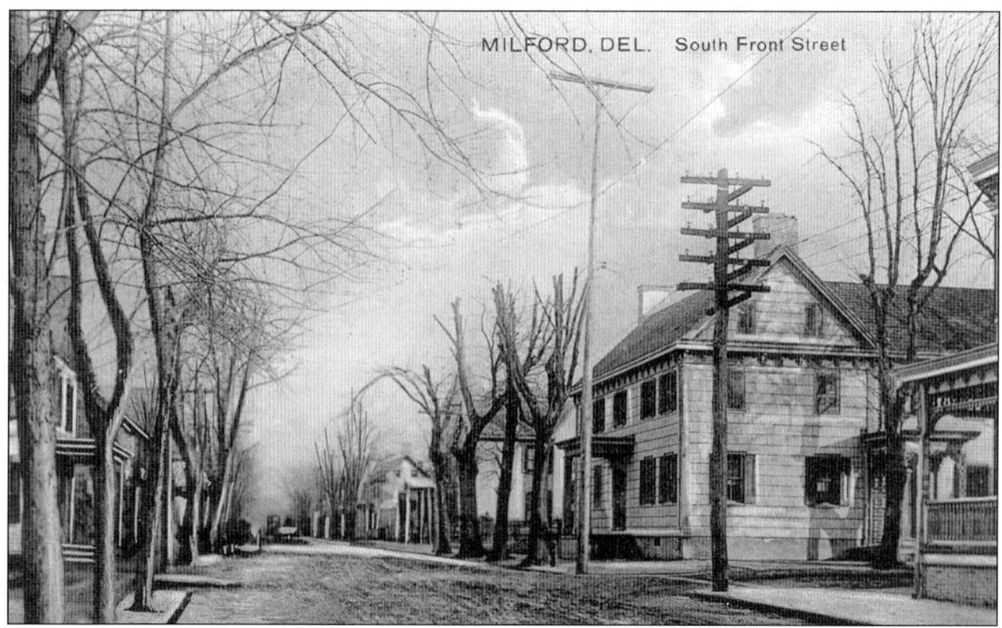

South Front Street, Milford, 1909. This is a pretty street scene at South Front Street and the intersection of Washington Street. The first house on the right was owned by a shipbuilding family, the Scribners. It is no longer standing.

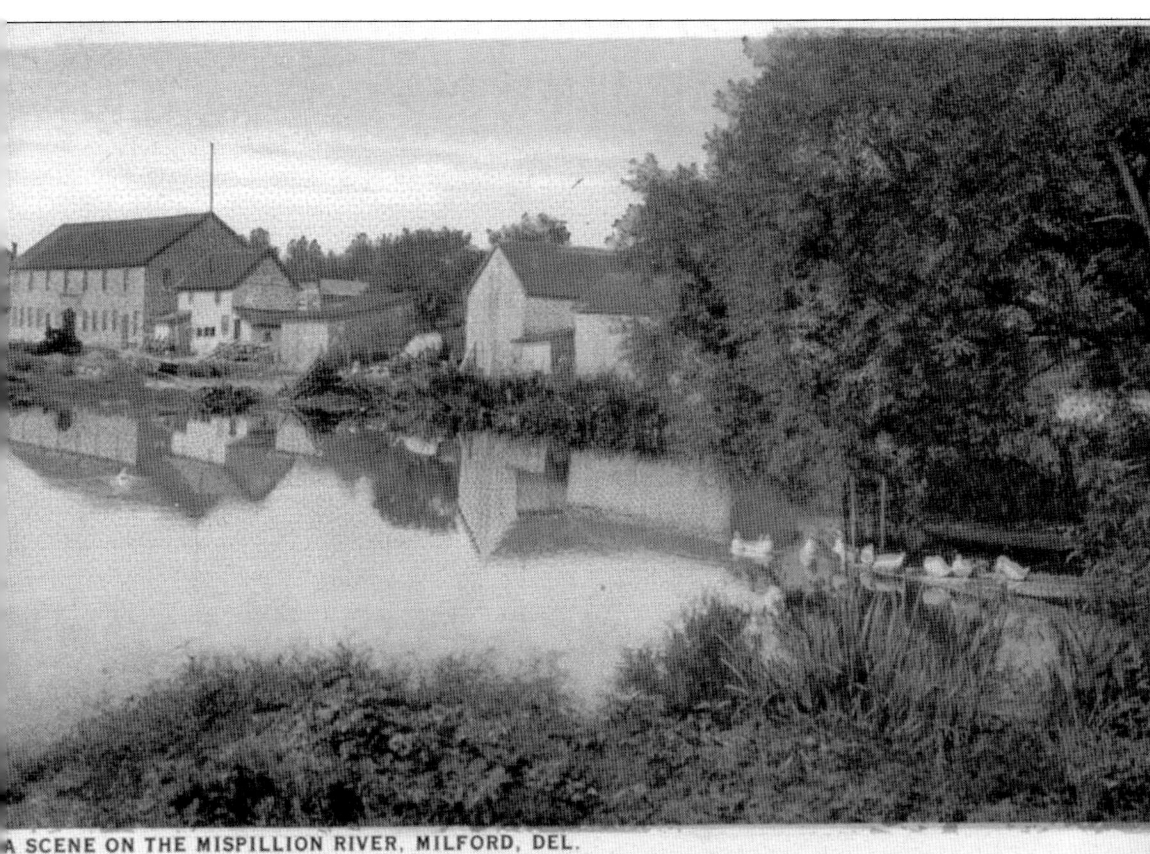

A SCENE ON THE MISPILLION RIVER, MILFORD, *c.* 1914. Milford developed on both the north and south sides of the Mispillion River, the widest and most navigable river in central Delaware. Connected by the Mispillion and Delaware Rivers to Philadelphia and New York, Milford was a prime spot for shipbuilding. Until the 1930s passenger steamers provided service to Philadelphia and to Lewes, where travelers boarded a coastal steamer to New York City. Freight boats made regular trips carrying farm produce, coal, lumber, and canned goods but were especially busy during the harvest time for watermelons, cantaloupes, baled hay, peaches, and tomatoes. Before the railroads as many as 45 schooners and sloops would winter at Milford wharves.

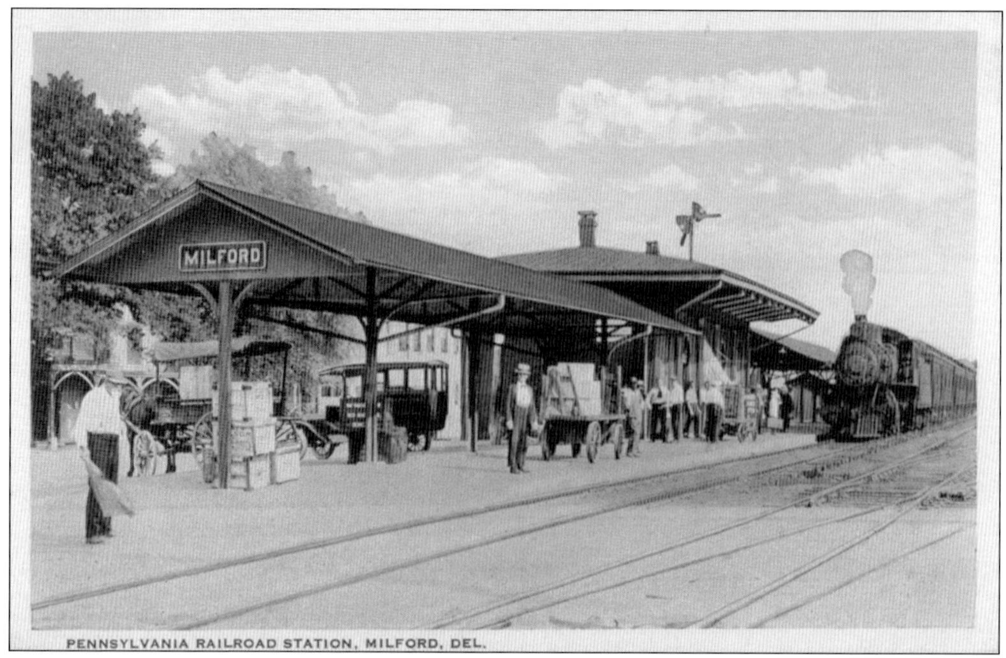

PENNSYLVANIA RAILROAD STATION, MILFORD, C. 1910. Trains began running north from Milford in 1859 and west to Harrington in 1869. A shipbuilding and shipping center, Milford's economy was diversified enough to avoid a collapse as the railroad eclipsed shipping. The center building of this station still stands near the post office, at 100 Lakeview Drive, the intersection of Maple and Causey Streets with Lakeview Drive.

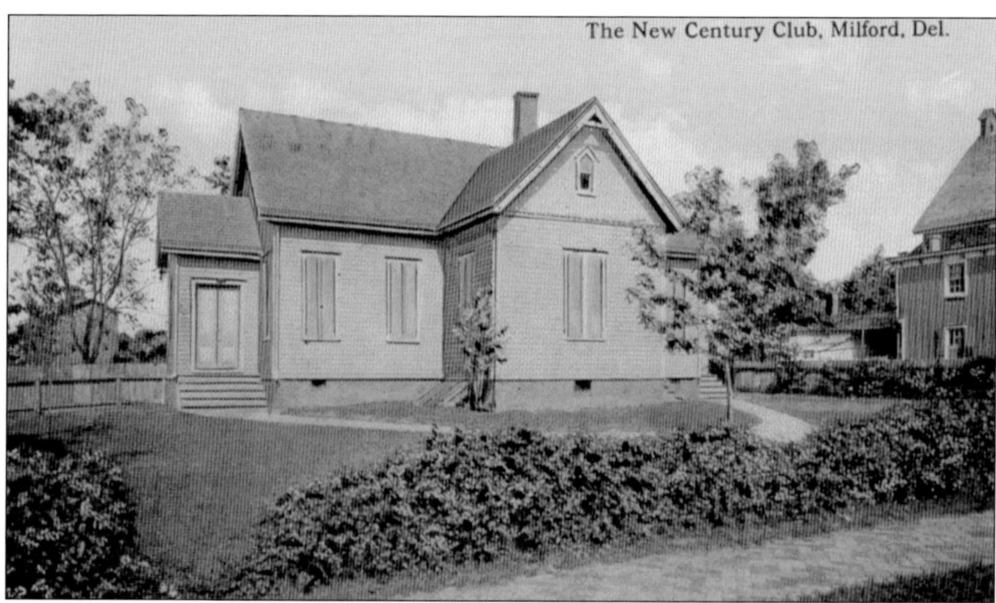

THE NEW CENTURY CLUB, MILFORD, 1910. The club was organized on February 14, 1898, to provide women with social and cultural opportunities. Involved in civic affairs, they also campaigned for improved sanitation. In 1899, the club began to meet in this building, the Old Classical Academy on Church Avenue, and purchased it in 1909 for $1,250.

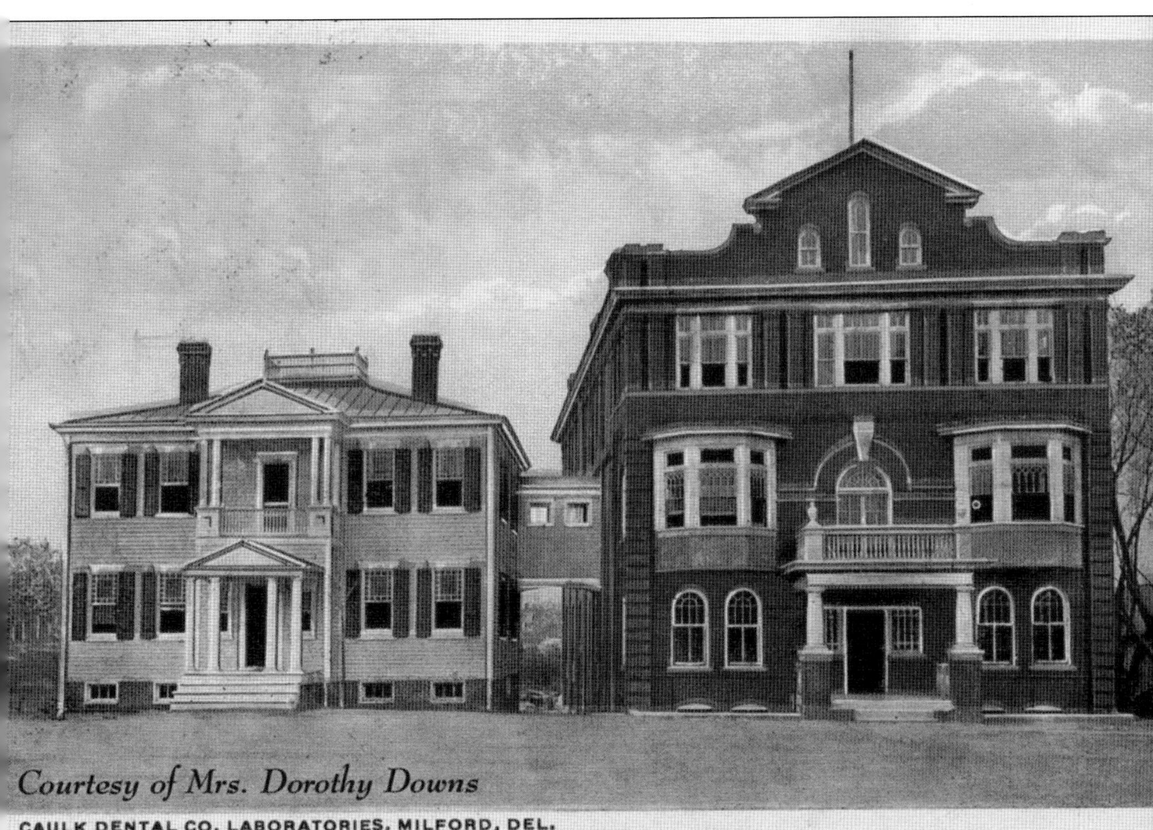

The Caulk Dental Co., Milford, 1910s. Dr. Lewis D. Caulk of Camden began manufacturing dental products in addition to running his practice. The business succeeded, and by 1900, Dr. Caulk had moved to Milford and built the two-story building on the left. Upon his death, a friend, Dr. G. Layton Grier, took over the business. Later, Grier and his brother Dr. Frank L. Grier, both dentists, bought the business. Today, Caulk is the world's largest professional dental products manufacturer. The Milford Masonic Lodge purchased the original building and moved it from this spot.

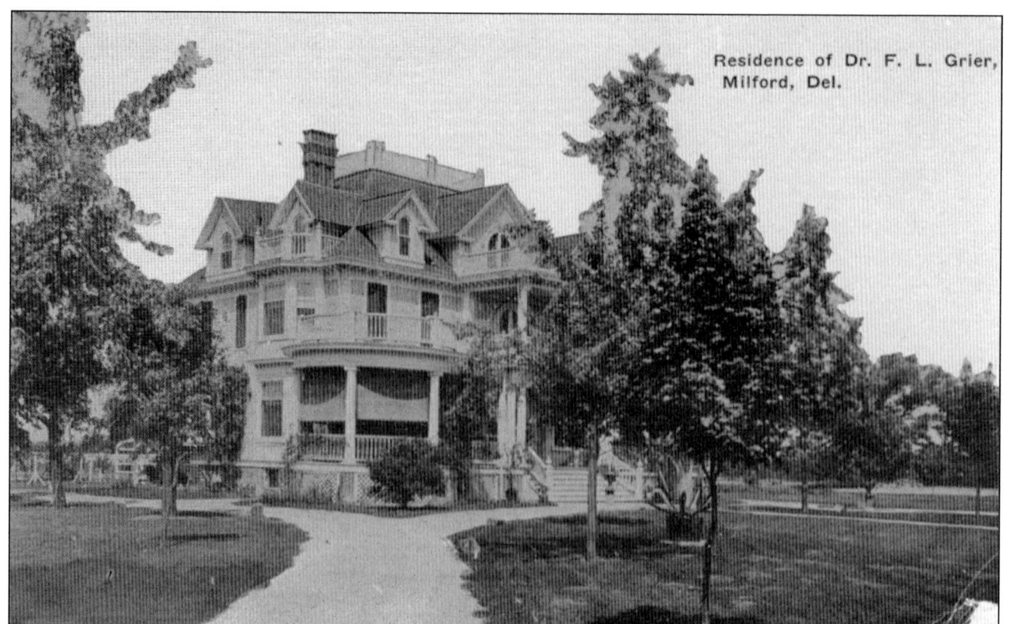

Residence of Dr. F.L. Grier, Milford, c. 1910. This was the home of Dr. Frank L. Grier, who married Florence Caulk, the daughter of Caulk Company founder Dr. Levin D. Caulk.

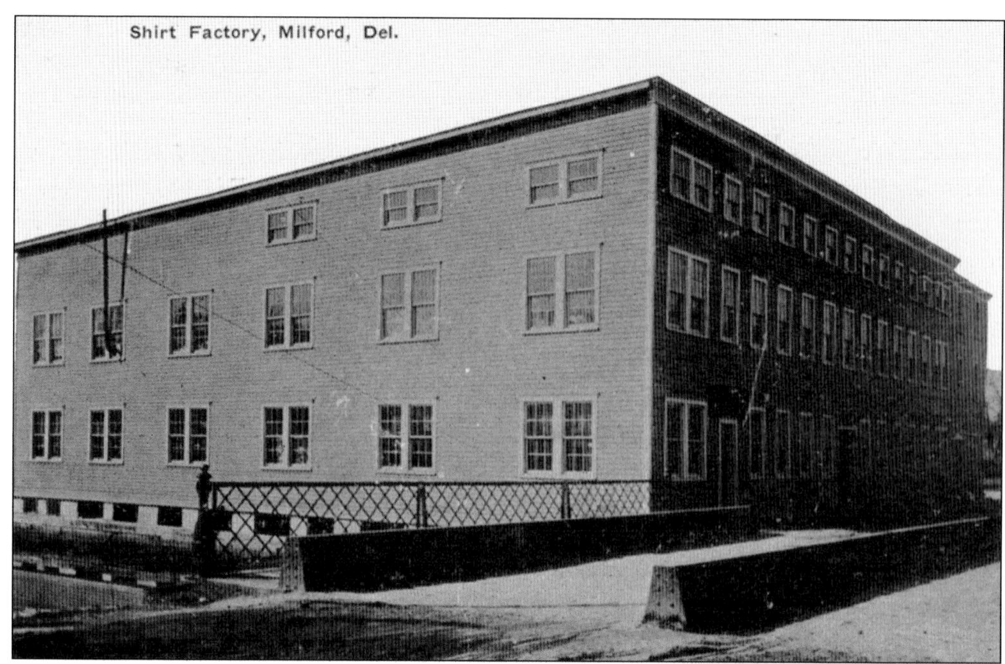

Shirt Factory, Milford, 1911. The Milford Shirt Factory opened for business in 1911. Located at Southwest Front Street and Church Avenue, the Barto Shirt Factory offered employment to Milford's young women, employing about 60 people full time. The building burned in 1920 and never reopened.

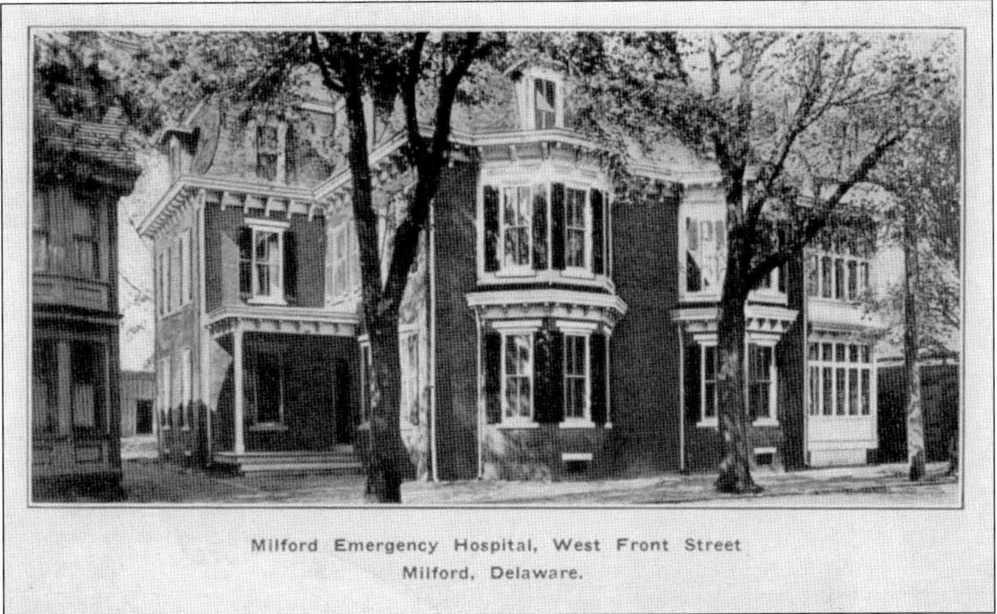

MILFORD EMERGENCY HOSPITAL ON WEST FRONT STREET, MILFORD, 1921. In the early 1900s Mary Louise Donnell Marshall and other women hosted a doll bazaar to raise money for a new hospital. As a result, a short-lived, two-room hospital opened on the second floor of the Masonic Temple. In 1912–1913 the General Assembly passed an act incorporating the Milford Emergency Hospital. This hospital opened with 12 beds, a bathroom, and an operating room.

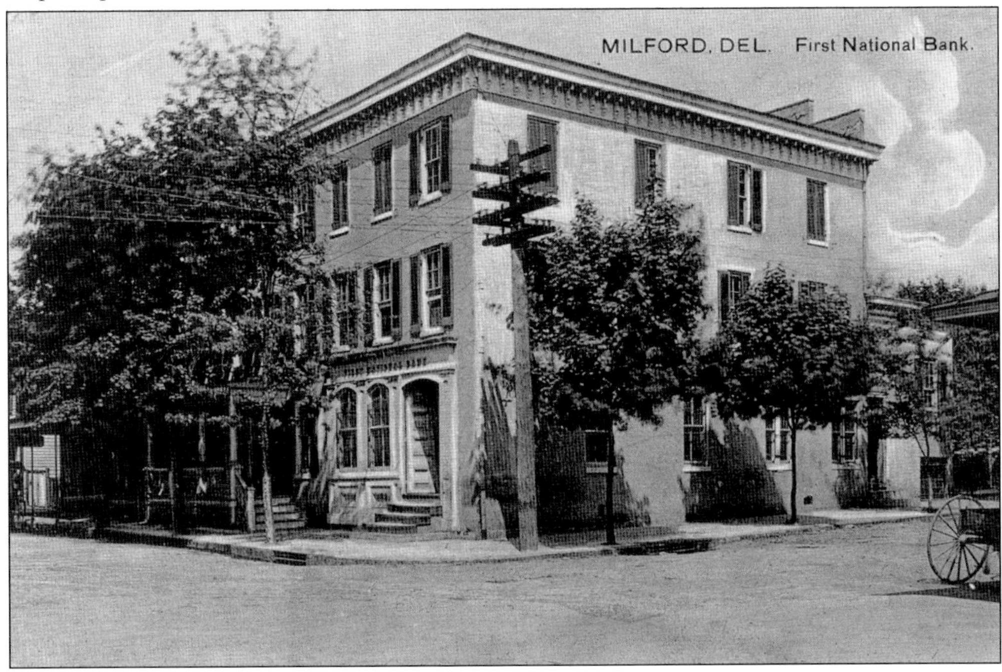

FIRST NATIONAL BANK, MILFORD, AFTER 1909. Built by Benjamin Wadhams, a merchant, the First National Bank opened in 1876. It was reported to be very elegant and fit to rival any big-city bank, complete with handsome gas fixtures, pink walls, and a cream-colored ceiling with gold trim.

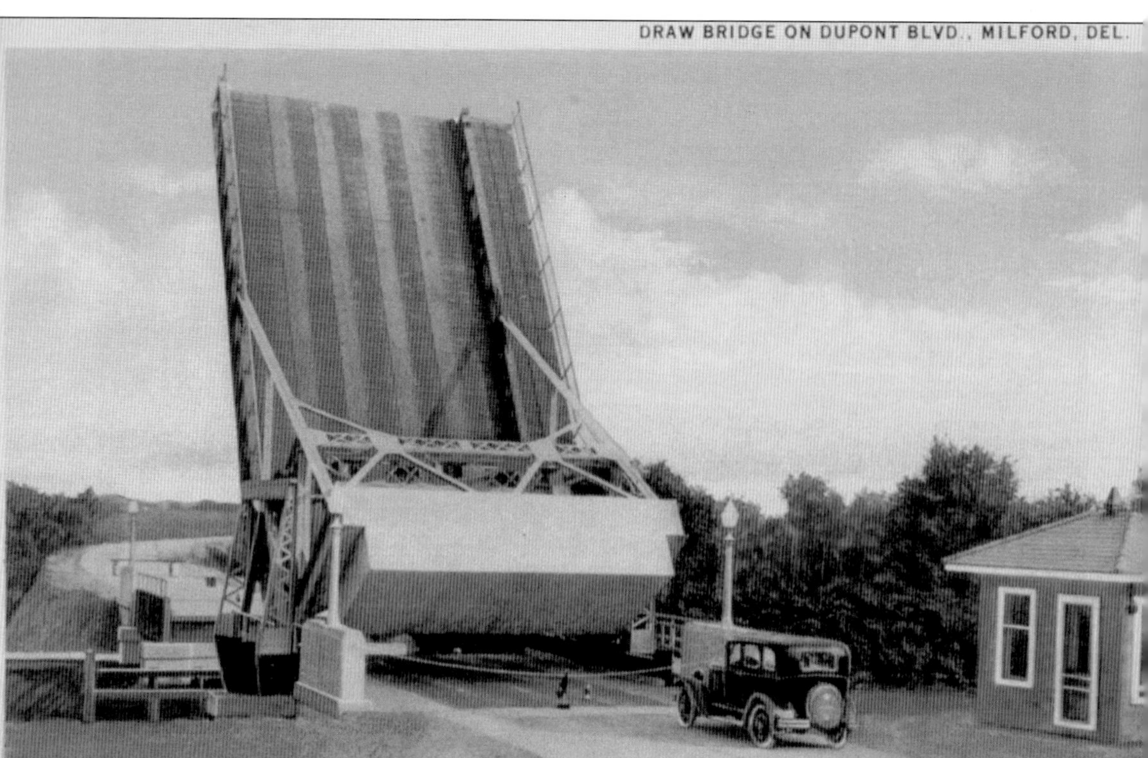

DRAW BRIDGE ON DU PONT BOULEVARD, MILFORD, *c.* 1925. This opening span bridge is located on the Rehoboth Highway, Business Route 1, just south of the intersection with Route 14. Today a large sign reading "Mispillion River" spans the top of the bridge.

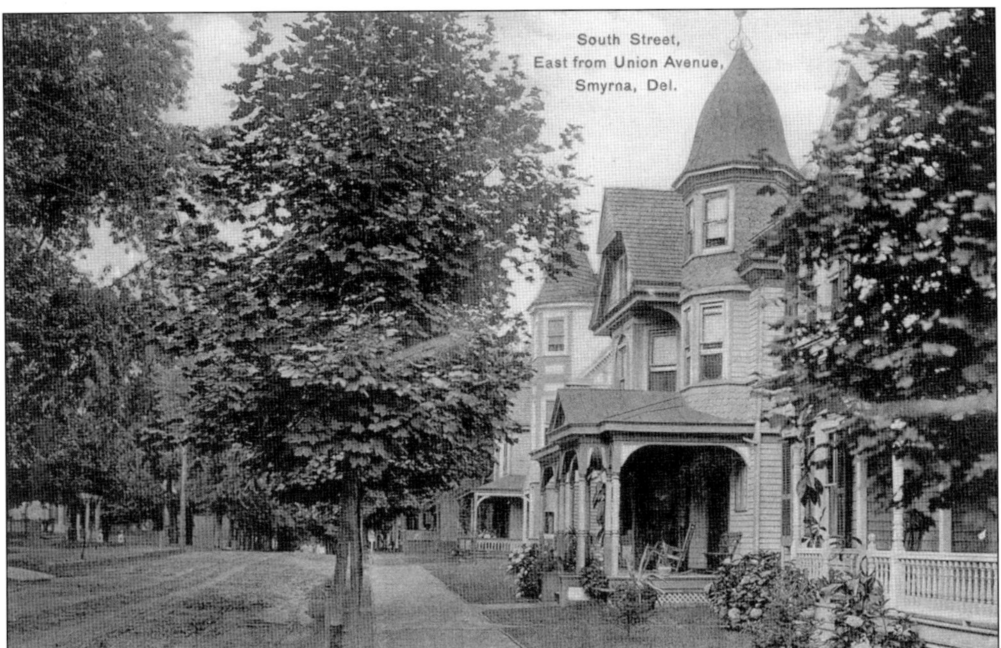

South Street, East from Union Avenue, Smyrna, 1910s. In 1890 a building boom started with the extension of South Street westward. Within 10 years, 18 commodious houses were built "up the hill." It is easy to see why they were the pride of the town.

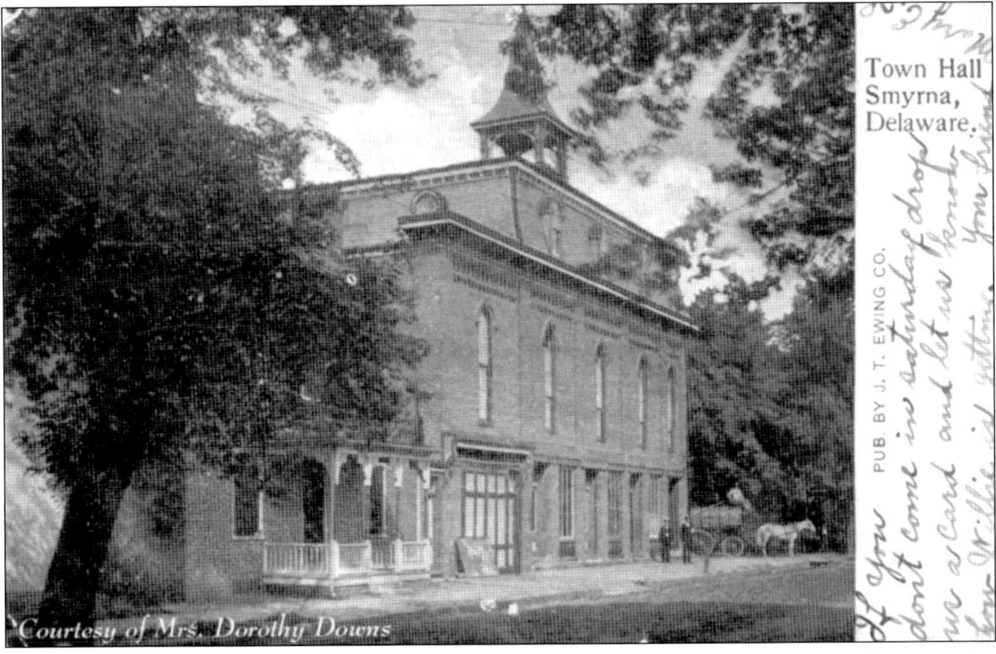

Town Hall in Smyrna, 1908. Built in 1869 on the southwest corner of Main and South Streets, this building was enlarged in 1886 to include an opera stage and volunteer fire company. Ironically, a fire badly damaged the building in 1948. It was repaired but lost its clock tower, bell, and "opera house glamour." In 1977 a new hall was built but did not fully replace this one.

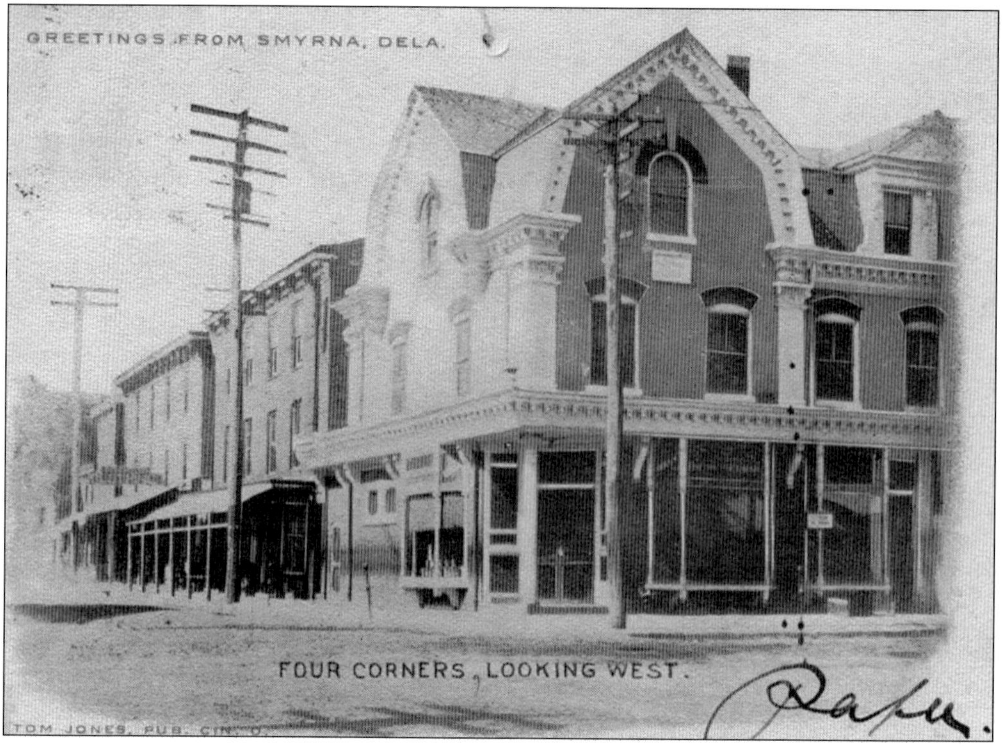

Four Corners Looking West, 1907. Over the years, the people of Smyrna have called the corner buildings by various names, usually associated with the owner. The building in the view above was built about 1824 by Jacob Raymond. Over the years, its first floor has held many businesses, and the upper levels served as living quarters. The building on the postcard below was built *c.* 1820 by R. Patterson. It was completely renovated about 1890 and given what one local historian called a treatment of "a riot of colors."

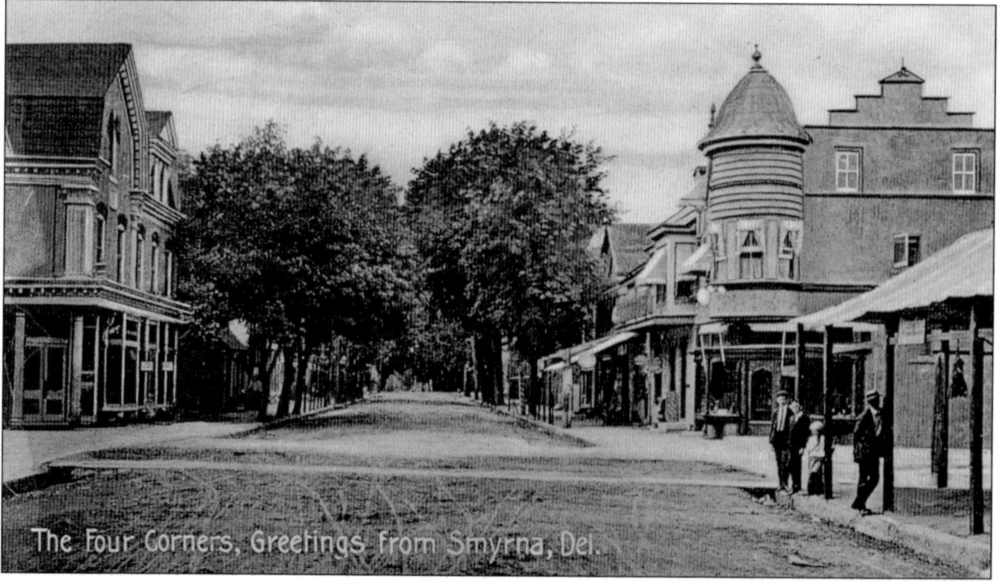

Four Corners, Greetings from Smyrna, 1908.

The Stand Pipe, Greetings from Smyrna. Located near the railroad station, the electric light plant, water works, and standpipe are curiously represented by two postcards in the Historical Society of Delaware collection.

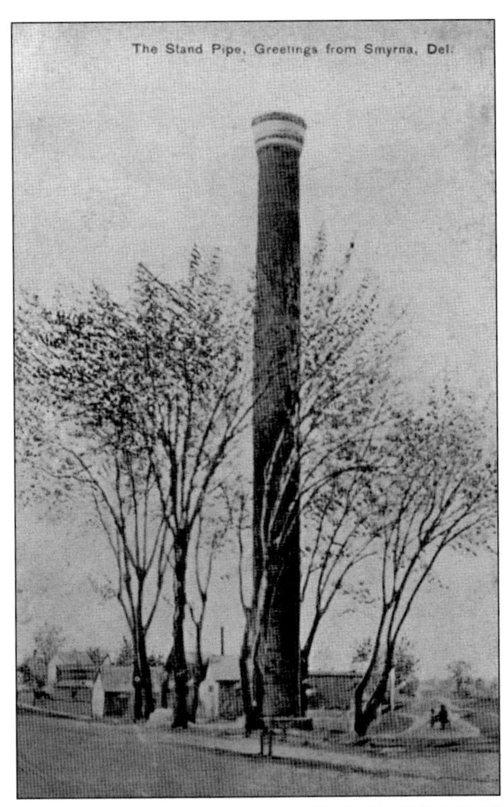

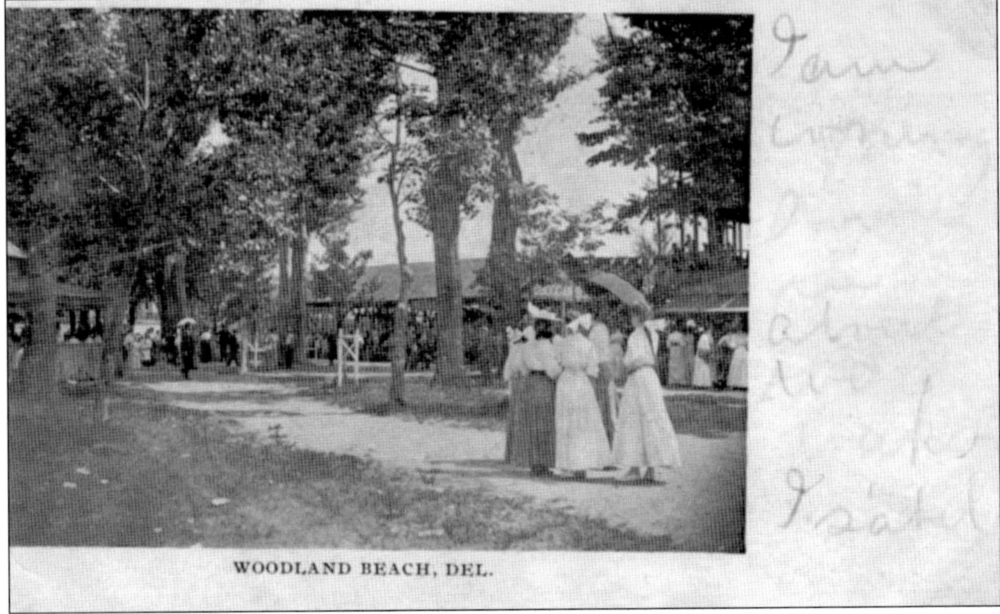

Woodland Beach, c. 1909. No longer a popular beach resort and picnic area, the land around Woodland Beach has been designated the Woodland Beach Wildlife Area to the north and the Bombay Hook National Wildlife Refugee to the south. A fishing pier remains at the site of the former pavilions shown here.

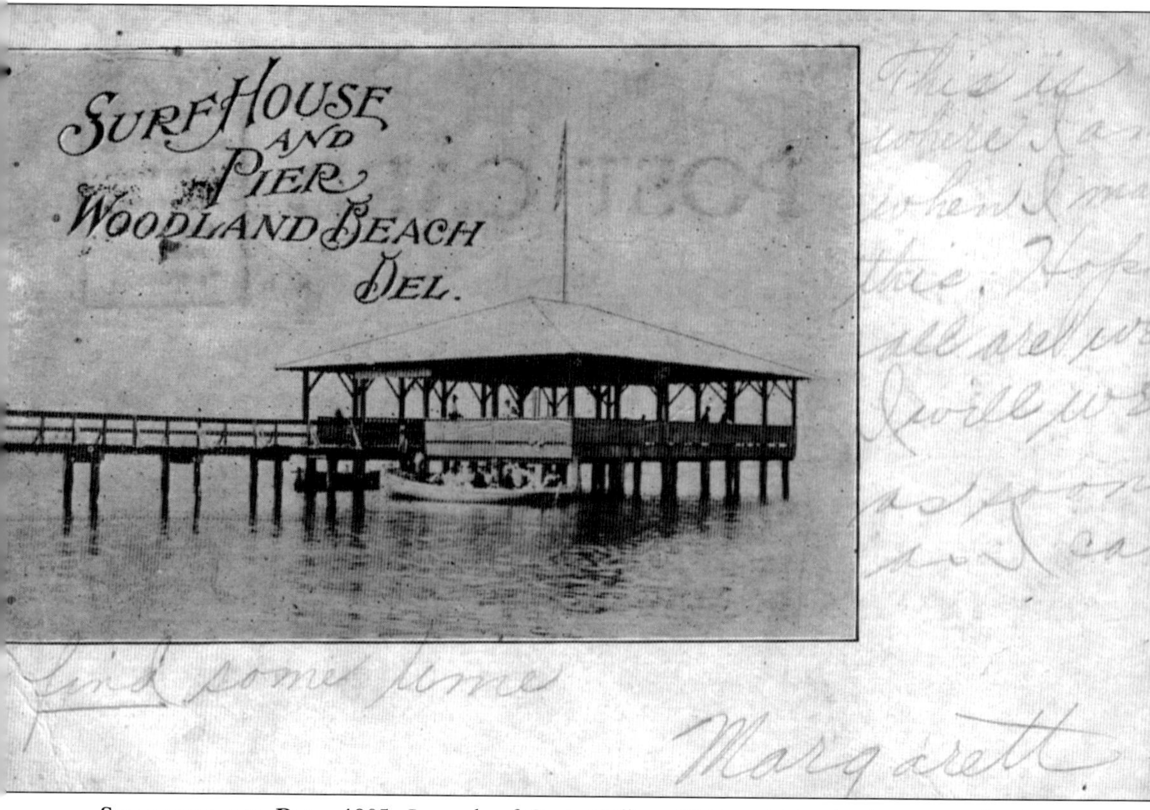

Surfhouse and Pier, 1905. Legends of Capt. William Kidd and his plunder surround this spot. Unfortunately no one has been able to prove the legend's truth. After the Civil War, Woodland Beach became a popular spot as steamers from Philadelphia and Wilmington dropped excursionists off at the pier. Some travelers boarded other ships for journeys further south to Cape May, while others stayed at the Woodland Beach Hotel.

Four

AGRICULTURE

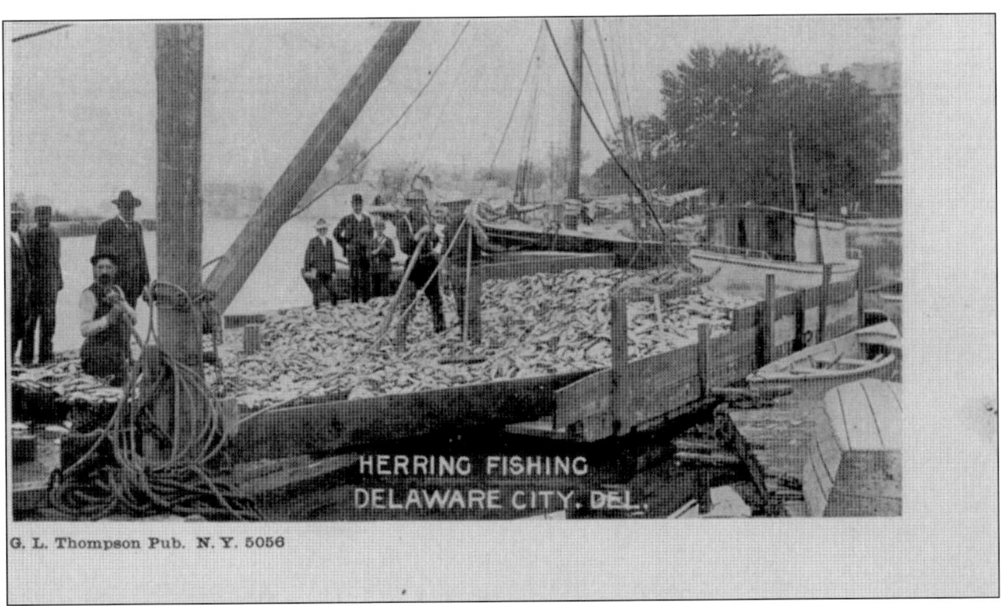

HERRING FISHING, DELAWARE CITY. During the late 1800s and early 1900s, Delaware City, like other river towns, was a major commercial fishing center. The spring fishing season began with herring, and vast quantities were caught. The back of this postcard bears a notation that reads, "Eighty-seven thousand at one catch."

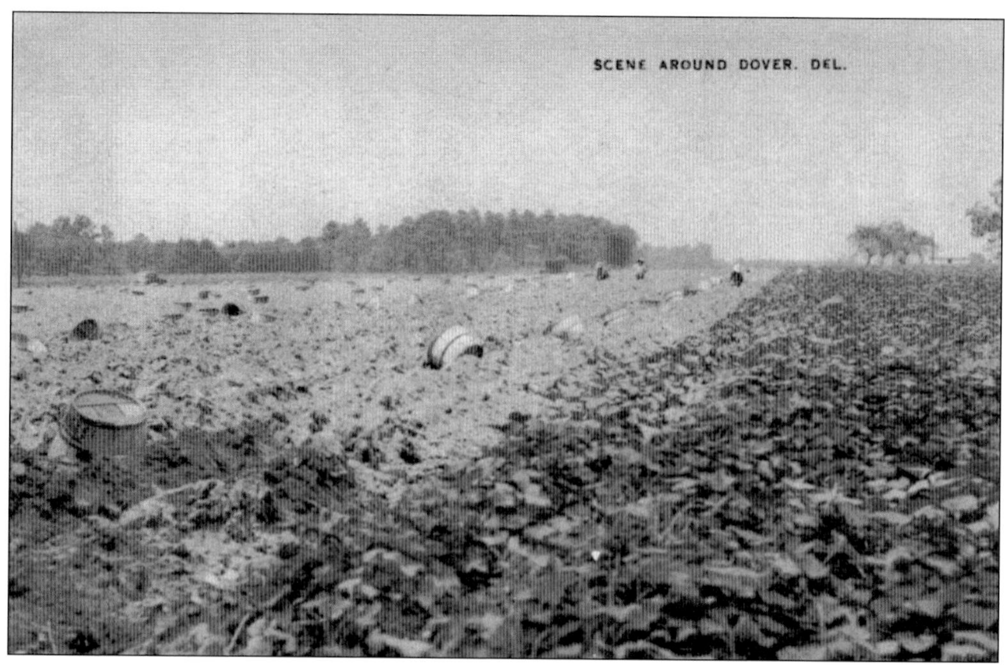

Scene around Dover, 1910s. In this typical farm scene in central Delaware, workers pick crops in the hot sun.

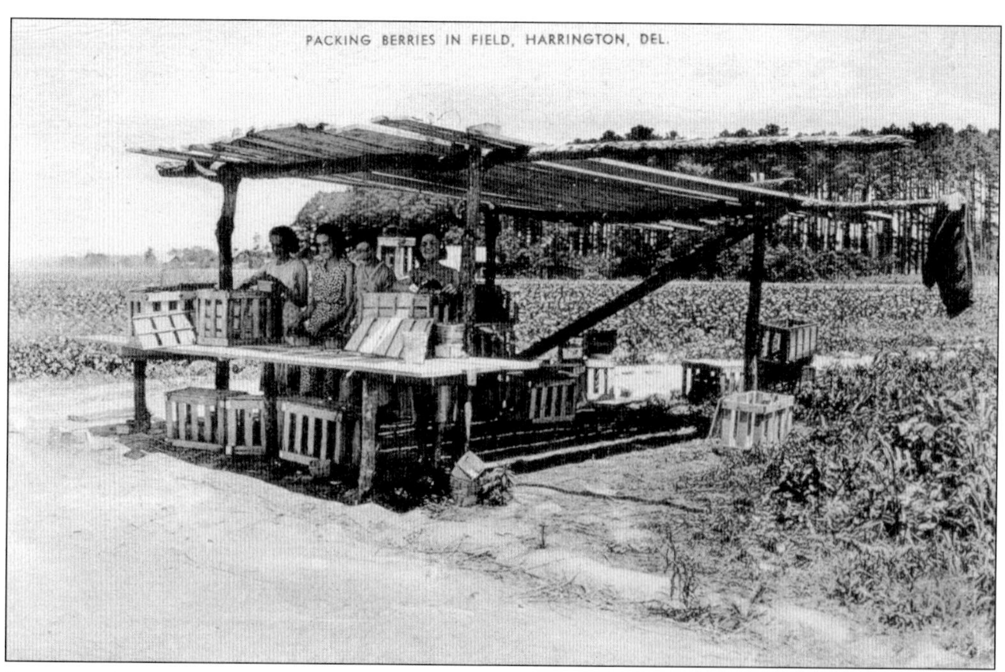

Packing Berries in Field, Harrington, c. 1910s. A shed provides a bit of shelter for women packing berries. The delicate fruit had to be packed quickly and gently to be rushed to urban markets. From the 1900s until World War II, Delaware was a leading producer of strawberries.

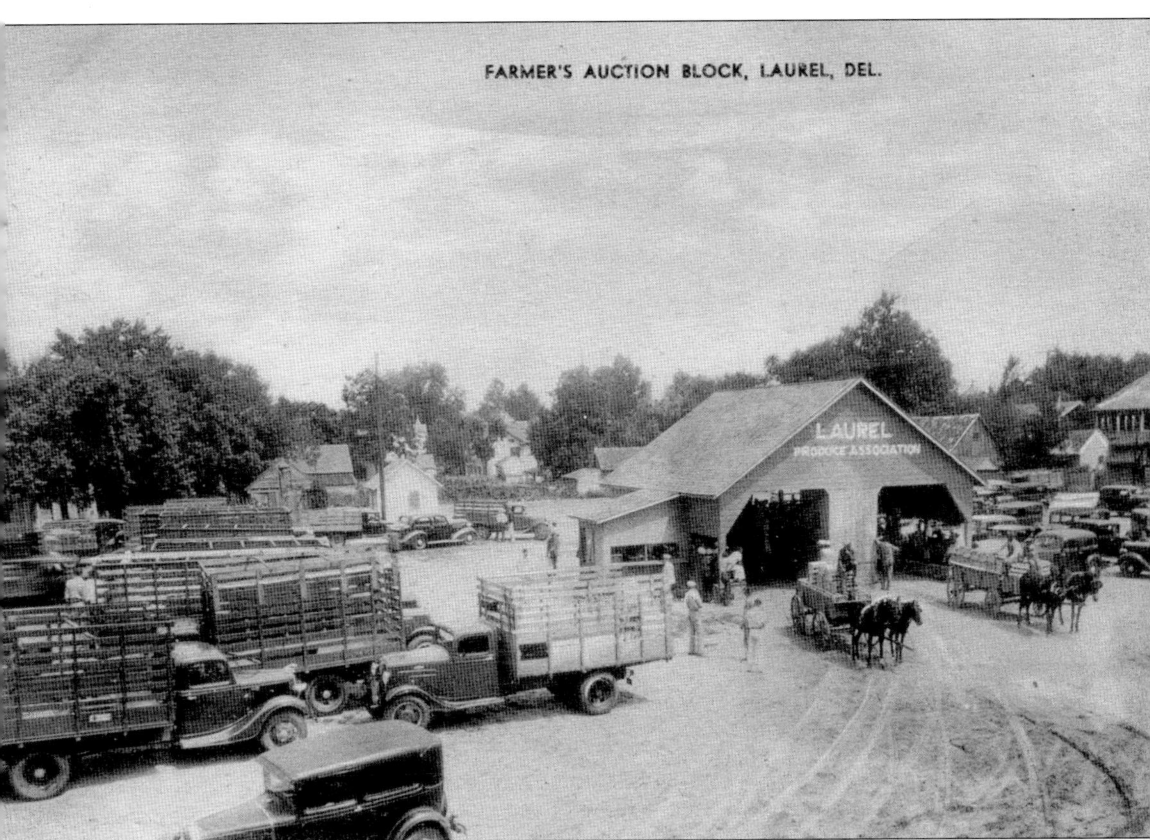

Farmer's Auction Block, Laurel, c. 1925. The Laurel Produce Association, which began in 1925, kept busy from May through the fall auctioning a wide variety of fruits and vegetables. On busy days, hundreds of farmers lined up to sell their produce. In 1940, area farmers formed the Southern Delaware Truck Growers Association, which still handles the marketing of produce.

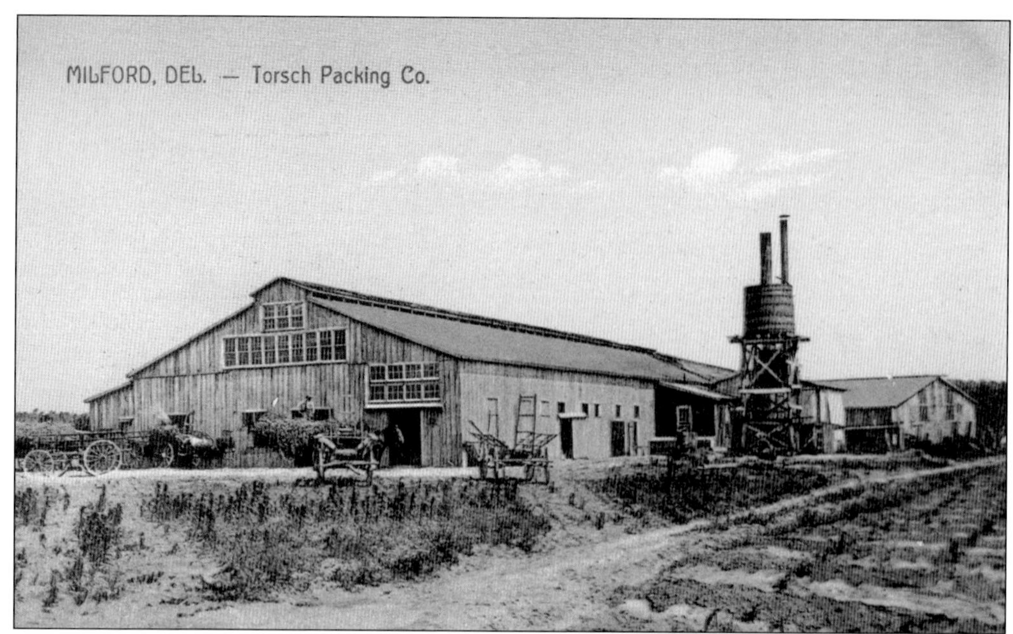

TORSCH PACKING CO., MILFORD, 1910S. Beginning in 1906 the Torsch-Stevenson Corporation ran this plant on the Mispillion River near Charles Street in the old Grier factory. In 1908 the plant was moved to East Front Street in South Milford.

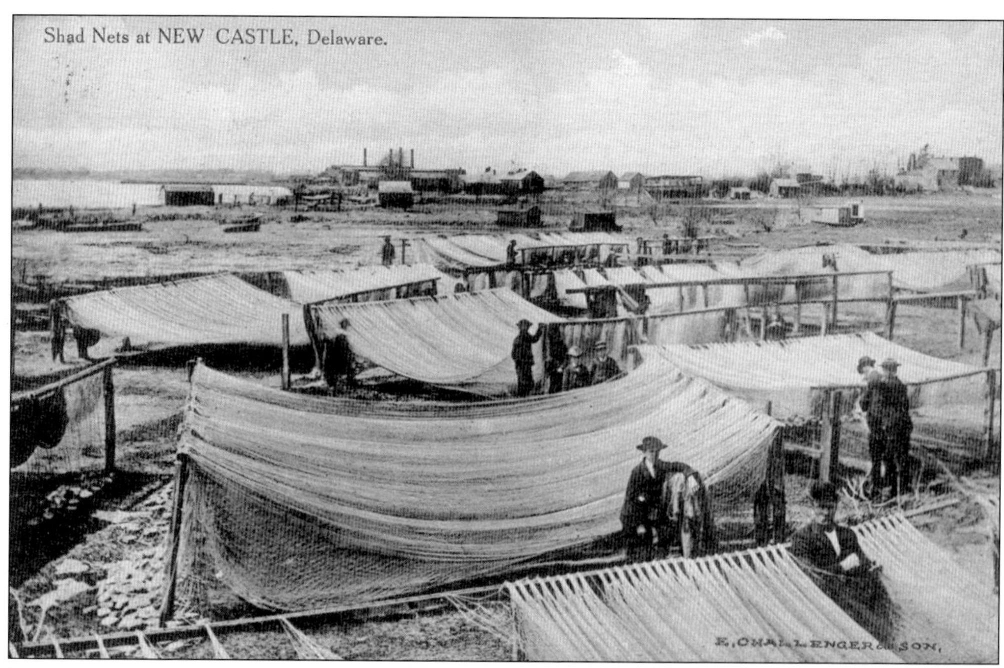

SHAD NETS AT NEW CASTLE, 1912. For many years Delaware River shad and shad roe were welcome spring delicacies, and shad fishermen sailed from ports all along the Delaware, including New Castle. In the early 1900s, as many as 20,000 shad were shipped to New York from New Castle each day. The catch of shad and other fish declined and finally ended due to overfishing and increasing pollution.

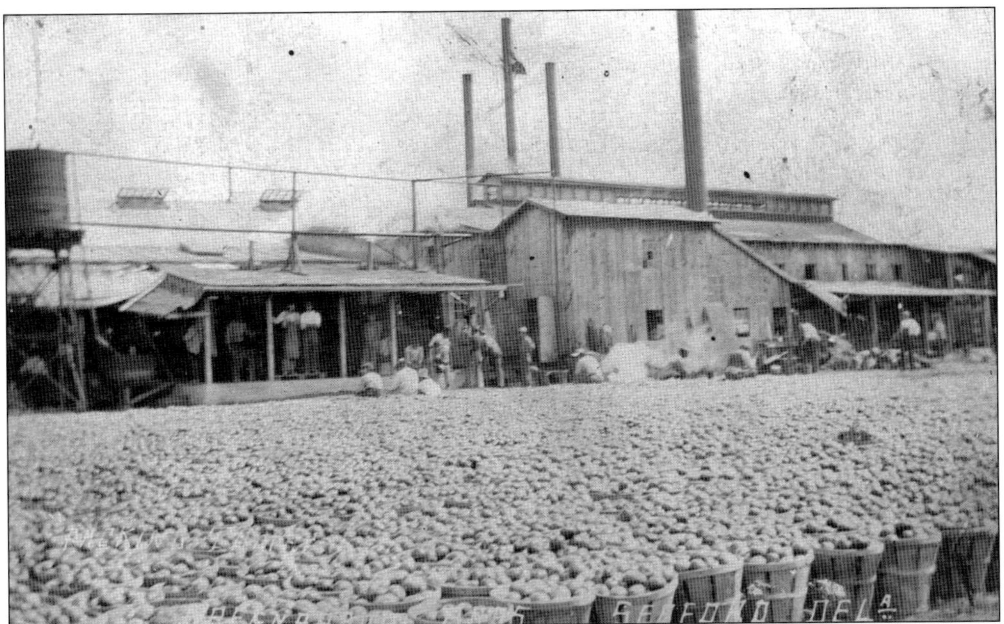

Packing Yams, Seaford, 1910s. The state began to keep production records for yams and sweet potatoes, an important crop, in 1868. By 1915, 7,000 to 10,000 acres were planted each year. But before modern day chemicals, about 40 to 50 percent of the crop was lost to disease after harvest. Greenabaum & Sons, seen here, was one of the largest canneries on the Eastern Shore.

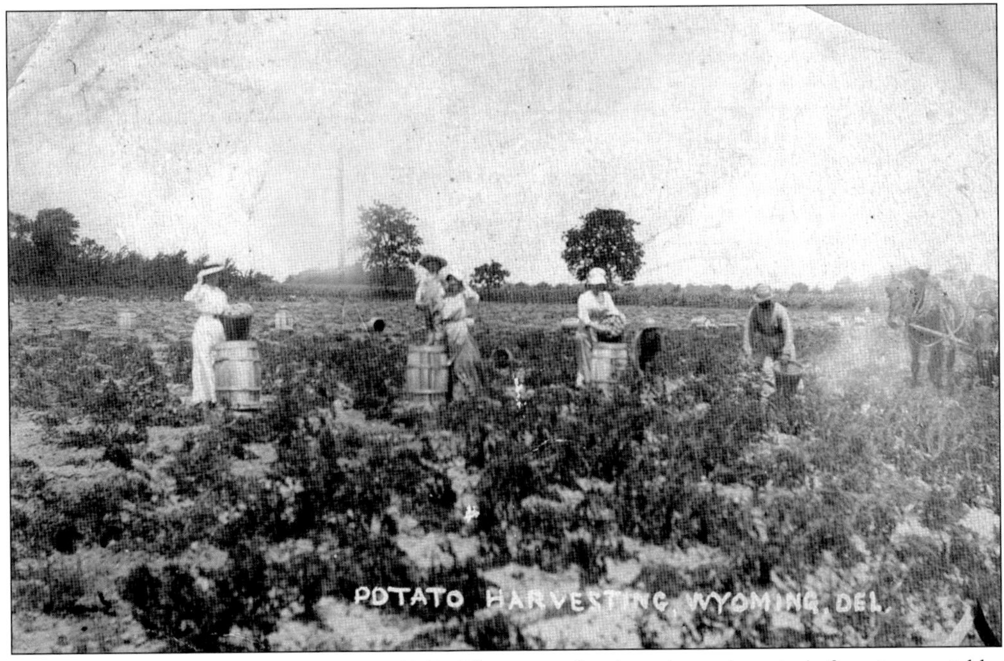

Potato Harvesting, Wyoming, c. 1910. The potato has long been America's favorite vegetable. About 6,000 to 8,000 acres were planted in potatoes in Delaware at the turn of the century, mostly between Middletown and Milford.

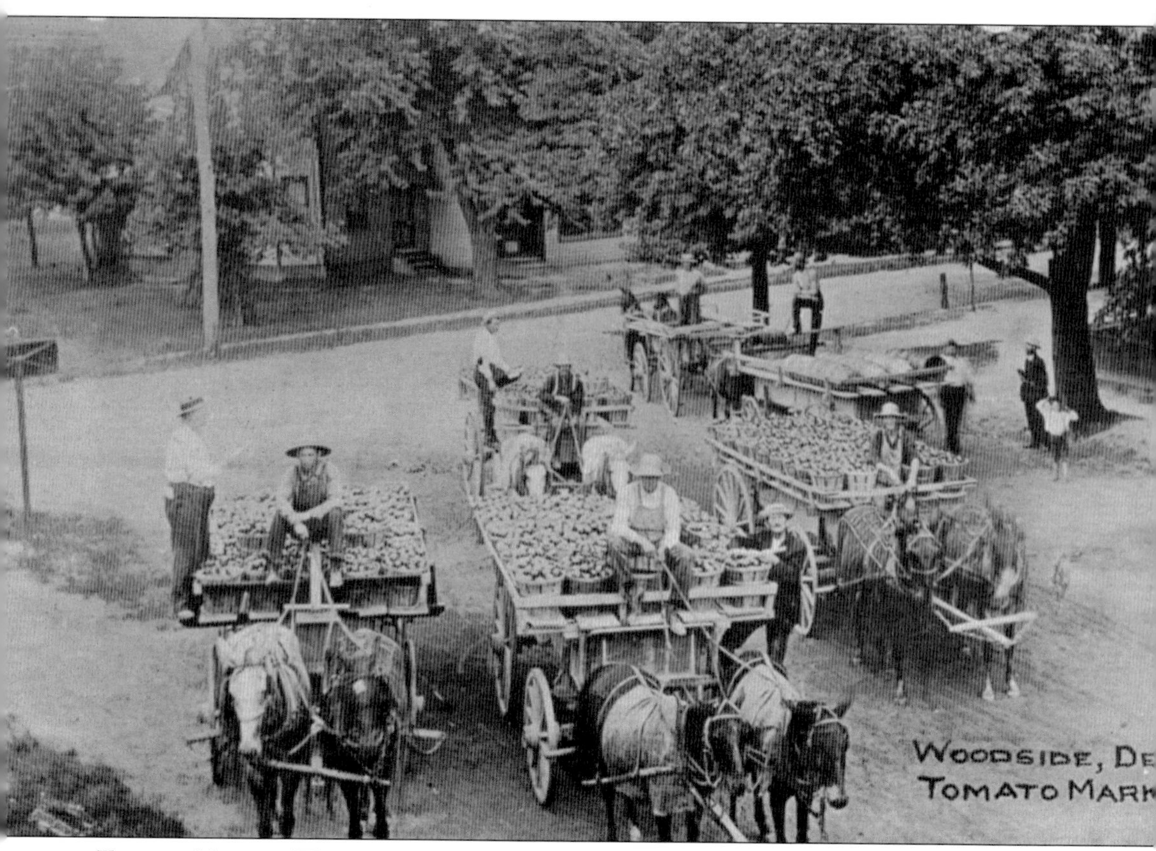

TOMATO MARKET, WOODSIDE, AFTER 1905. The village of Woodside was established in 1864 when a railroad station was built there, mainly through the efforts of Henry Cowgill. Situated in rich farming country, the station became a center for shipping fruits and vegetables. Here farmers arrive with wagons of tomatoes, which were probably shipped to area canneries.

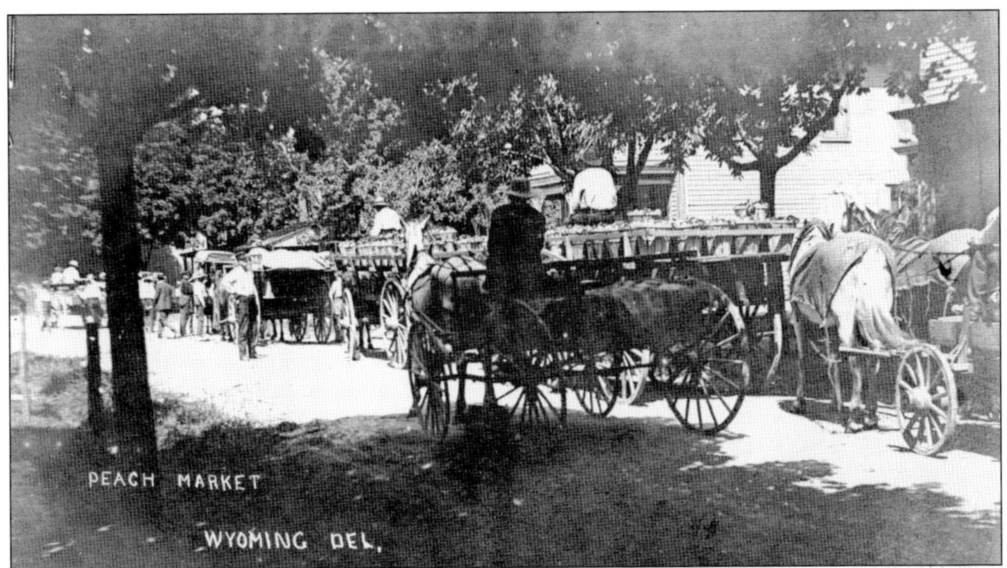

Peach Market, Wyoming, 1908. Wyoming owes its existence to Camden's refusal to allow the Delaware Railroad to go through the town in 1856. The railroad built the West Camden station instead, and the village that grew up around it was named Wyoming in 1865. The new town became a major shipping point for local produce, especially peaches. From the 1830s through much of the 19th century, Delaware was a major peach-producing state. However, the spread of disease and the development of large orchards in other states caused the decline of Delaware's peach crop. Even so, the state still had large orchards and produced 16,722 bushels in 1909. Wagons full of peaches line this street in Wyoming, waiting to be shipped on the Delaware Railroad.

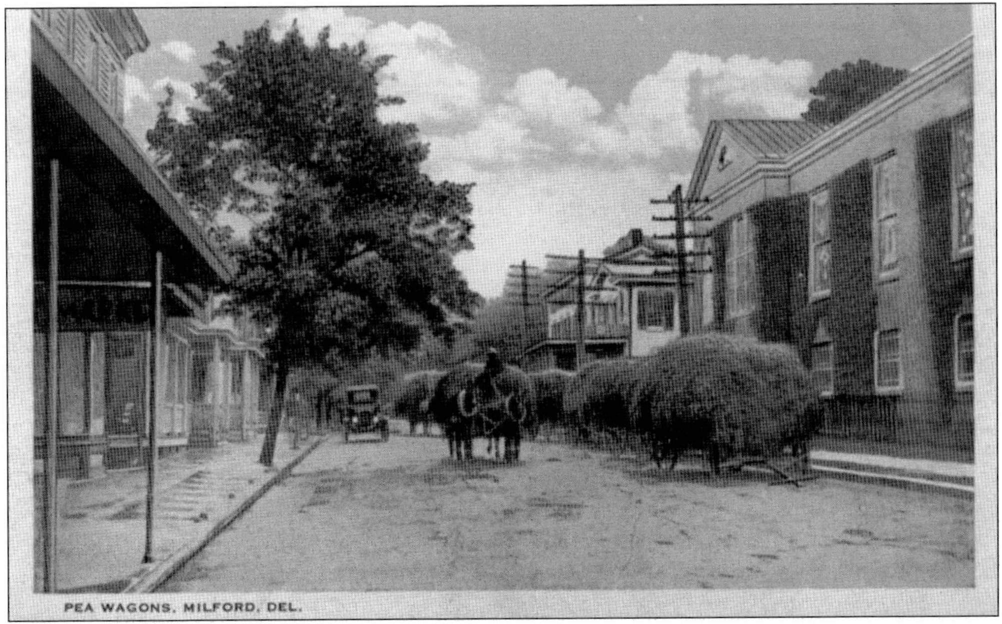

Pea Wagons, Milford, 1910s. Growing canning peas became popular in the late 1800s, though production records were not kept until 1918. On this postcard, a farmer transports his peas to the local cannery. By 1900 every small town had its own cannery, and there were about 300 statewide.

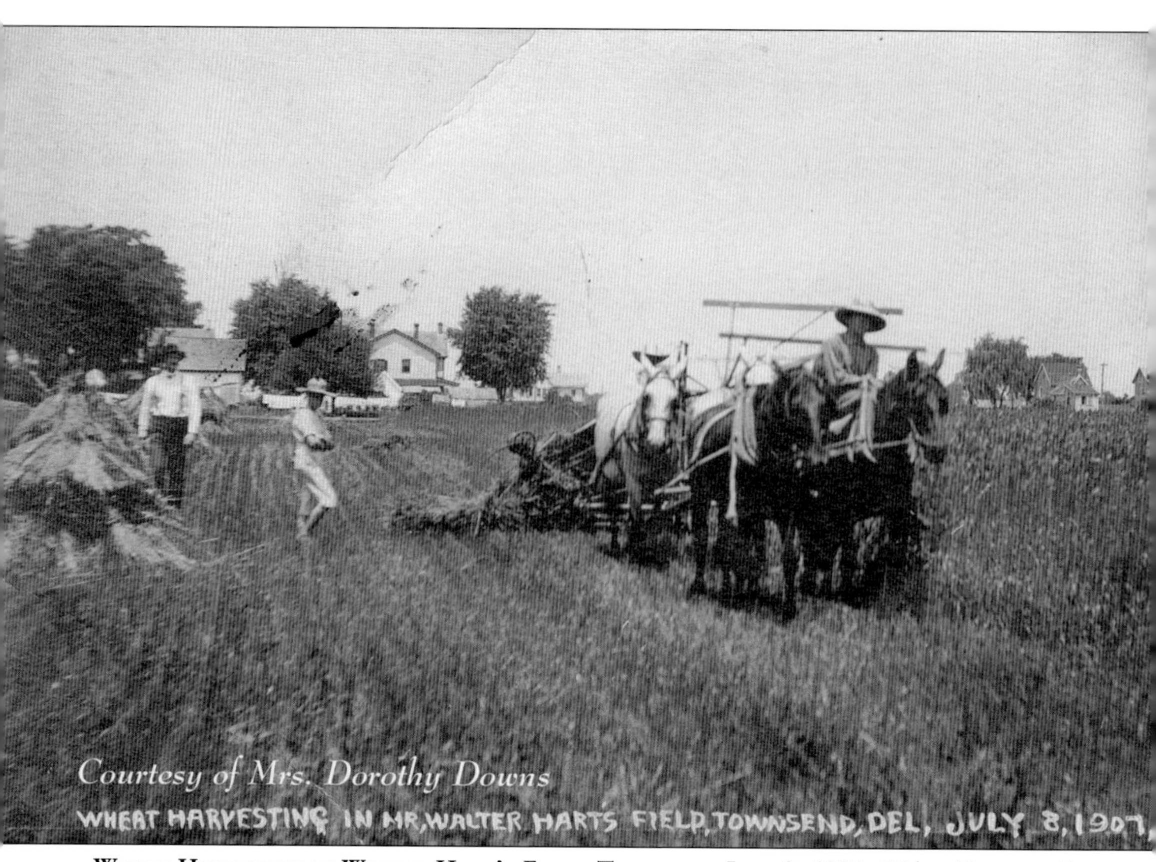

WHEAT HARVESTING IN WALTER HART'S FIELD, TOWNSEND, JULY 8, 1907. Walter Hart, age 49, preserved the memory of his 1907 wheat harvest by having a photograph of it made into a postcard. Cards like this were for personal use and were not sold. Although early 20th-century Delaware agriculture is best known for fruits and vegetables, the state's farmers also grew corn and wheat.

Five

New Castle County

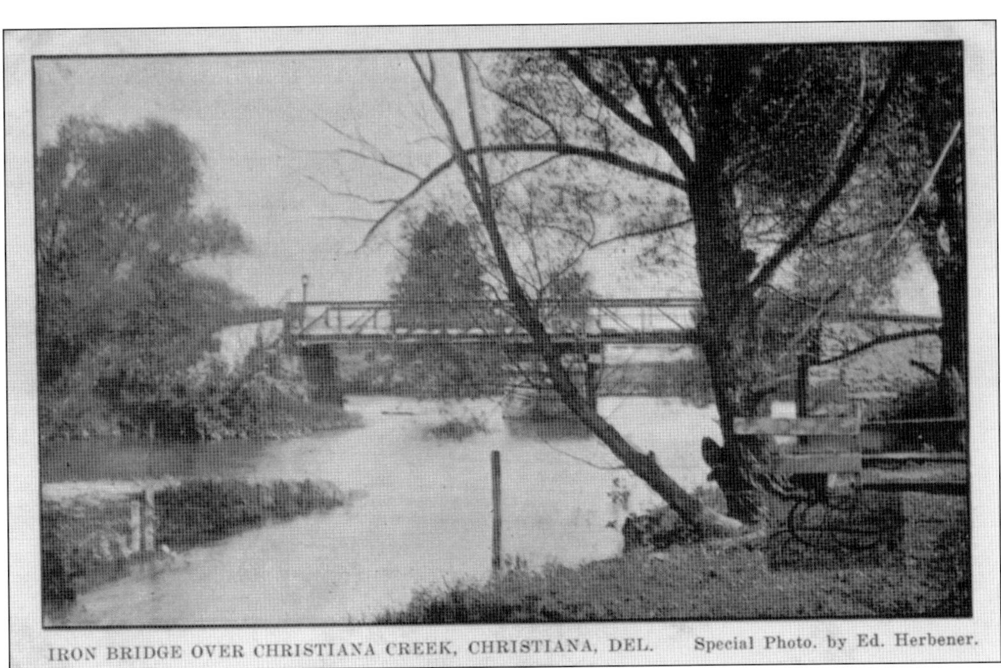

Iron Bridge over Christiana Creek, Christiana, 1907. A bridge has spanned the Christina River at Christiana since 1686. Although it is quiet today, Christiana was a busy place from the mid-1700s through the early 1800s. Many travelers passed through, and the town, at the head of navigation on the river, was an important grain-shipping port.

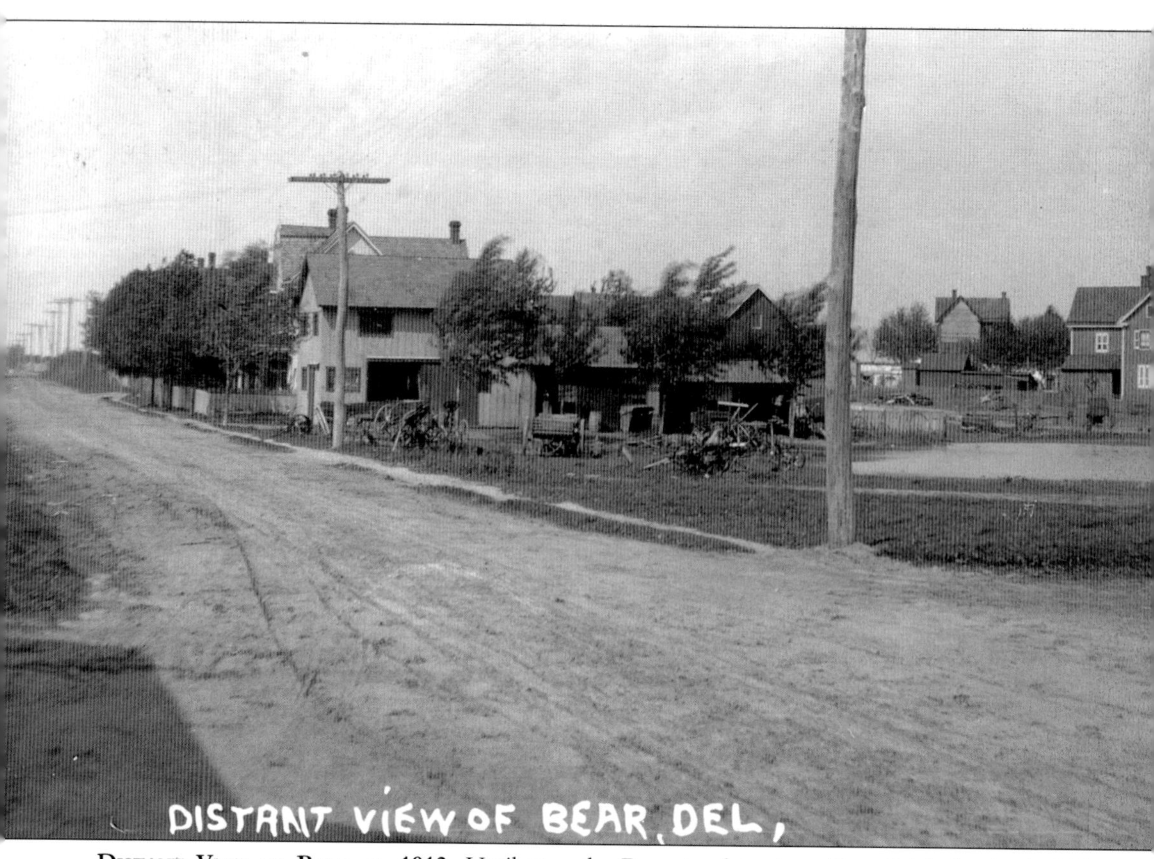

DISTANT VIEW OF BEAR, C. 1912. Until recently, Bear stood in the midst of rich farmland. Old Hamburg Road runs into the distance, while Bear-Corbit Road, now Route 7, goes off to the right in the foreground. Some of the buildings on the right are still standing, while an Odd Fellows Hall built in 1914 fills the open space on the right. The Eden Square Shopping Center and busy Route 40 are now just a short distance away from this location.

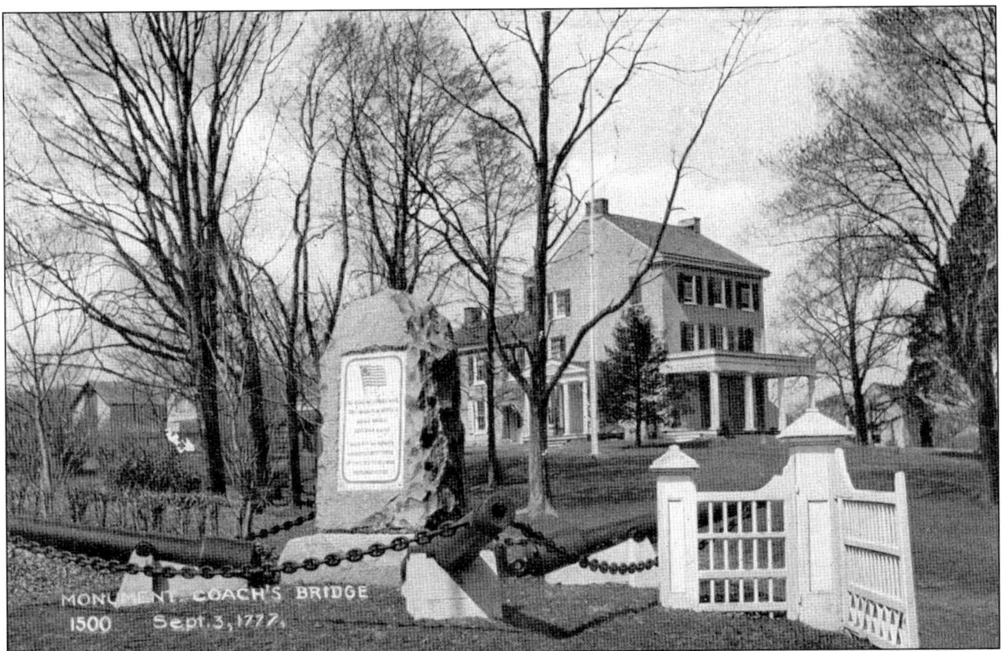

COACH'S [SIC] BRIDGE, SEPTEMBER 3, 1777. The only Revolutionary War military action in Delaware occurred at the Battle of Cooch's Bridge on September 3, 1777. Thomas Cooch owned the house, built in 1760, and mill that were the focal point of the skirmish. The British burned the mill and Lord Cornwallis occupied the house for several days. The monument, erected in 1901, is on Old Baltimore Pike.

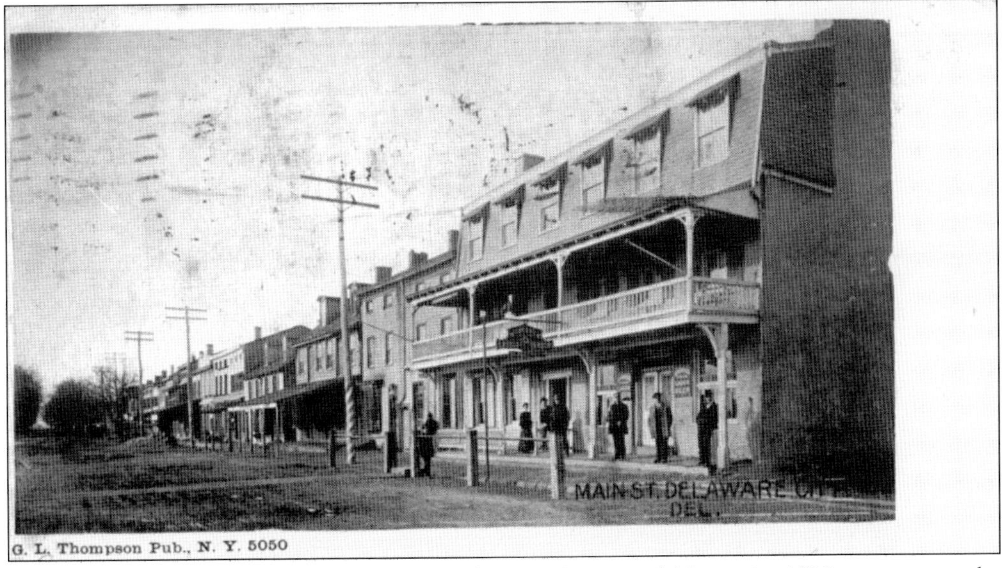

MAIN STREET, DELAWARE CITY, 1906. Delaware City was laid out in 1826 to serve as the eastern terminus of the Chesapeake and Delaware Canal. These buildings actually stand on Clinton Street, as Delaware City does not have a street called Main Street. The building in the right foreground is a tavern.

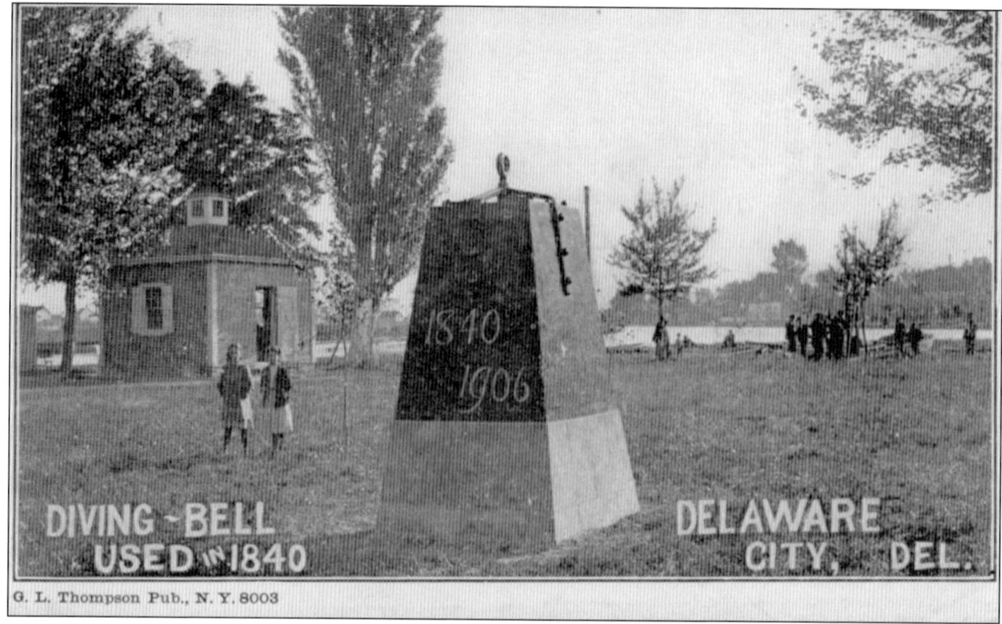

DIVING-BELL USED IN 1840, DELAWARE CITY, *c.* 1906. Employees of the Chesapeake and Delaware Canal went 15 to 20 feet underwater in this diving bell to clean and repair the gates in the canal's locks. The bell was placed in Canal Park around 1885 and can still be seen in Battery Park in Delaware City.

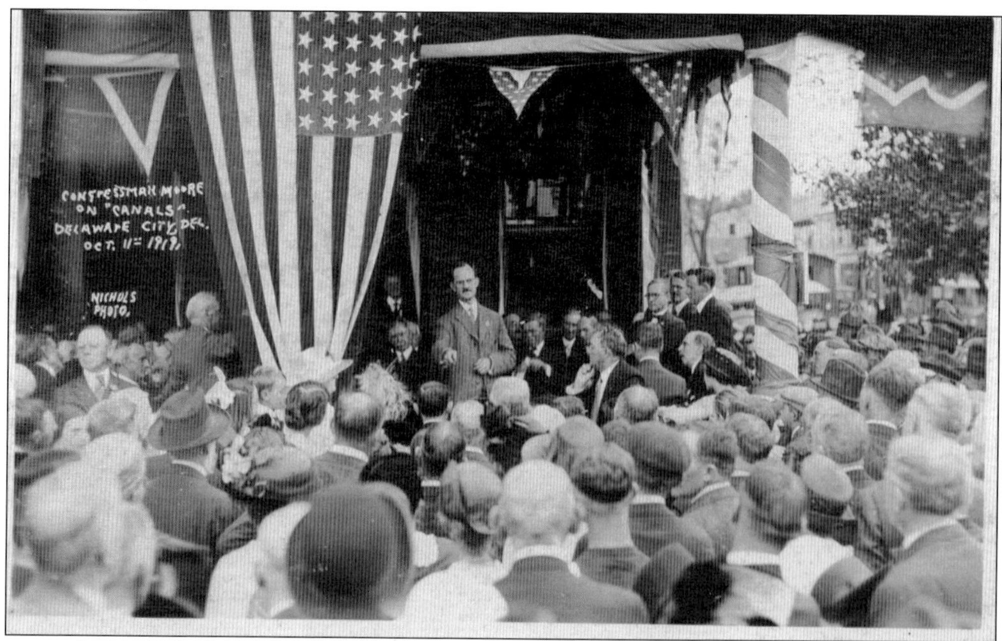

CONGRESSMAN MOORE ON "CANALS," DELAWARE CITY, OCTOBER 11, 1919. Congressman J. Hampton Moore of Pennsylvania speaks at the ceremony transferring the Chesapeake and Delaware Canal from private ownership to federal control. Since then the federal government has made improvements that allow the canal to accommodate ever-larger ships. Today the canal carries more tonnage than the Suez and Panama canals combined.

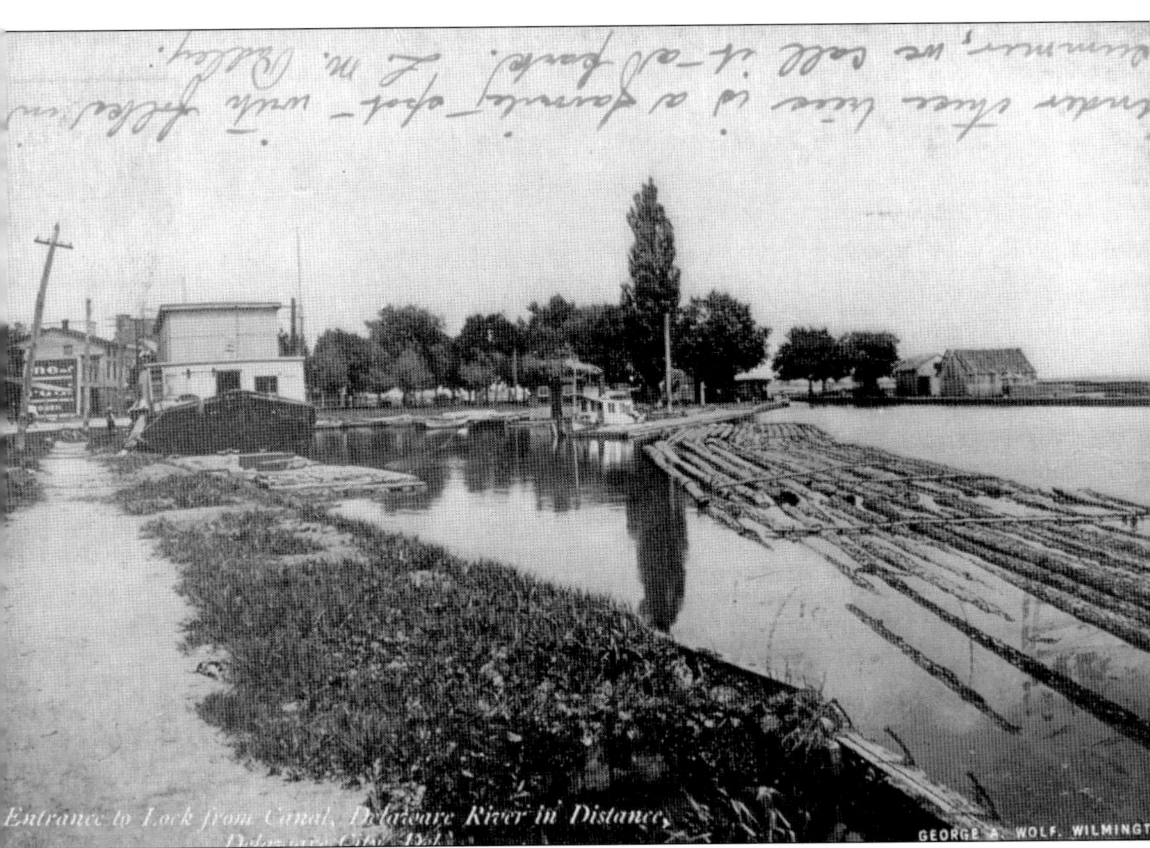

Entrance to Lock from Canal, Delaware City, 1907. Work on the Chesapeake and Delaware Canal, connecting the Chesapeake and Delaware Bays, began in 1824. The canal opened in 1827, was completed in 1829, and provided a welcome shortcut across the Delmarva Peninsula. Previously, ships going from the East Coast to ports on Chesapeake Bay had to sail all the way around the Peninsula. In addition to commerce, excursion boats like the steamer *Lord Baltimore* passed through on trips between Philadelphia and Baltimore. Here, the *Lord Baltimore* approaches the lock in Delaware City; the Delaware River is visible in the distance.

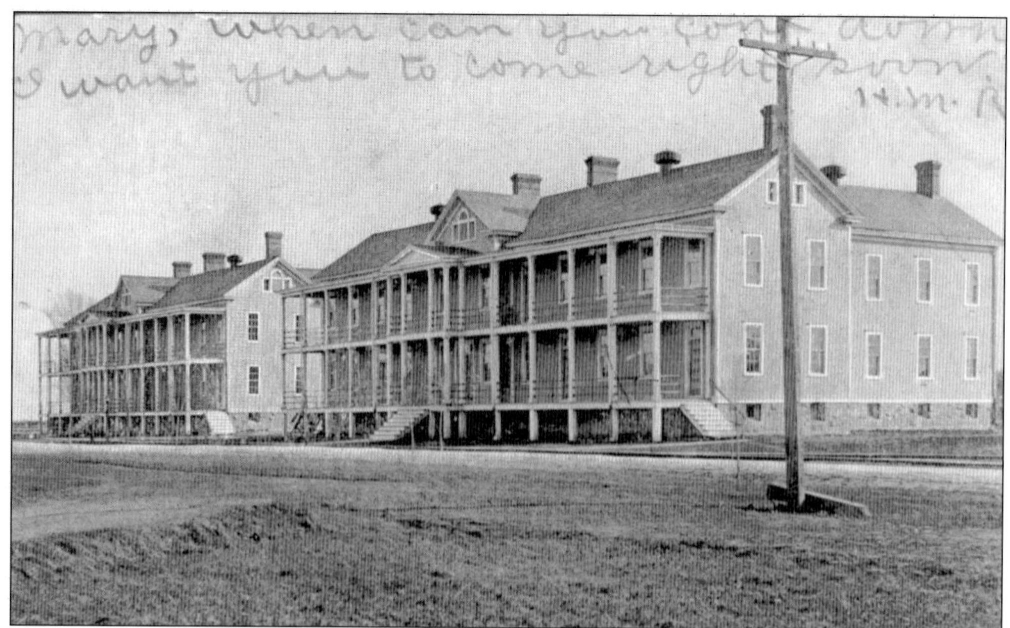

BARRACKS AT FORT DU PONT, DELAWARE CITY, 1907. Established in 1899 to defend the Delaware River and Bay, Fort Du Pont was named for Adm. Samuel Francis Du Pont. During World War II the fort housed American troops and 1,000 German prisoners of war. Fort Du Pont was turned over to the state of Delaware in 1947 and now serves as the Governor Bacon Health Center.

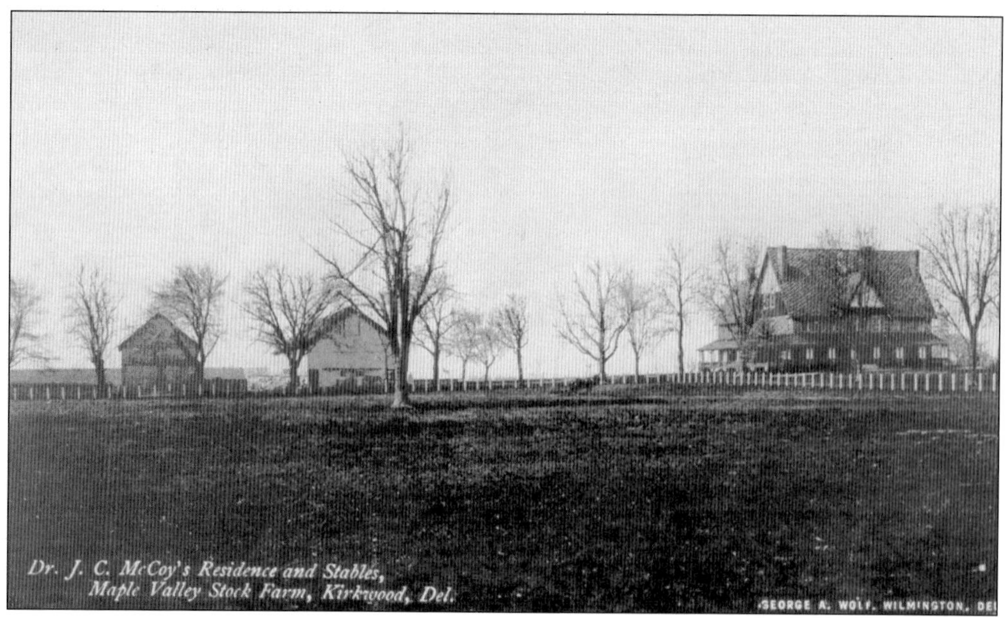

DR. J.C. MCCOY'S RESIDENCE AND STABLES, MAPLE VALLEY STOCK FARM, KIRKWOOD. Dr. J.C. McCoy was an officer for the Maple Valley Stock Farm. The town of Kirkwood, renamed in 1862 in honor of Delaware's Revolutionary War hero Capt. Robert Kirkwood, served as a shipping point along the Philadelphia, Wilmington & Baltimore Railroad. As more county roads were paved, the railroad lost business and Kirkwood's population declined.

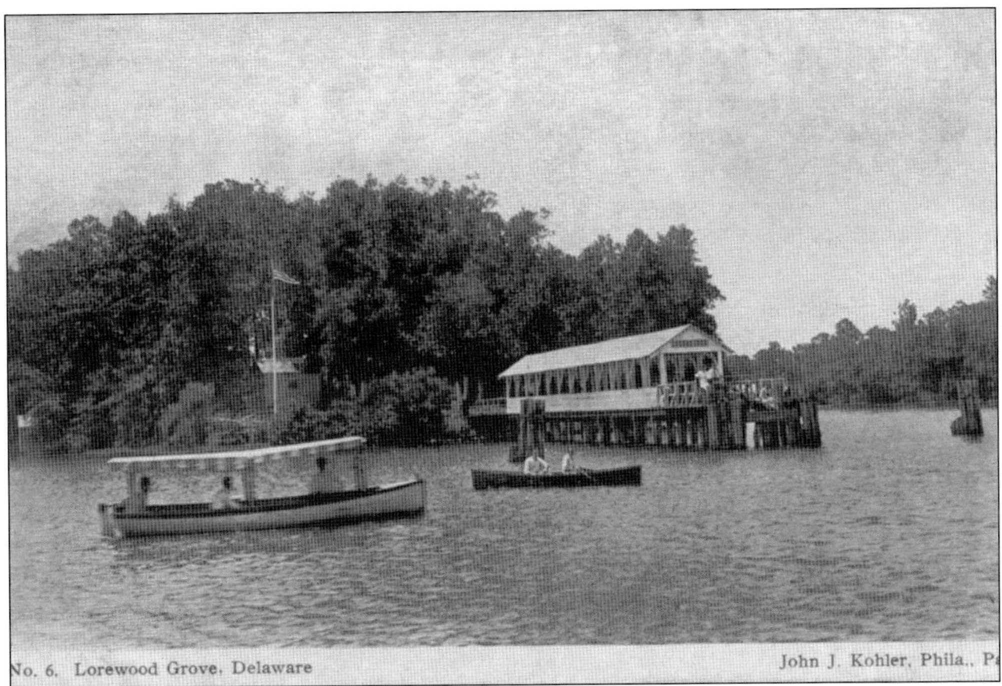

Lorewood Grove, c. 1912. Lorewood Grove was a stop along the Chesapeake and Delaware Canal for picnics, boating, fishing, and dancing. Also known as Lore's Landing, it was located near Summit Bridge along the south bank of the canal. Brochures for the Ericsson Line, which ran between Philadelphia and Baltimore, often included photographs of the picturesque site.

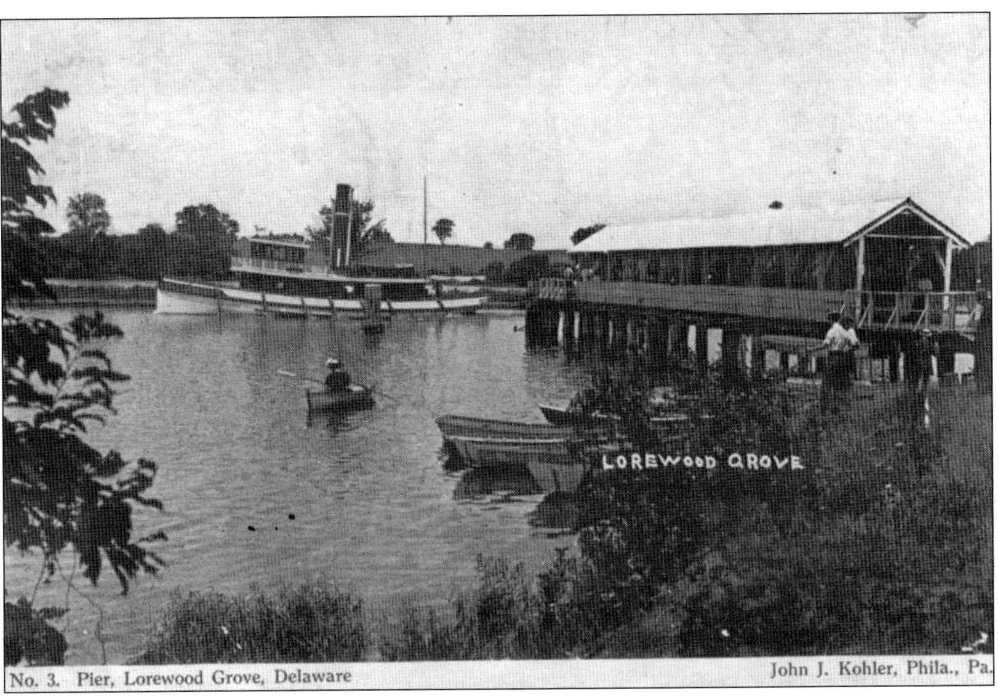

Pier, Lorewood Grove, 1912.

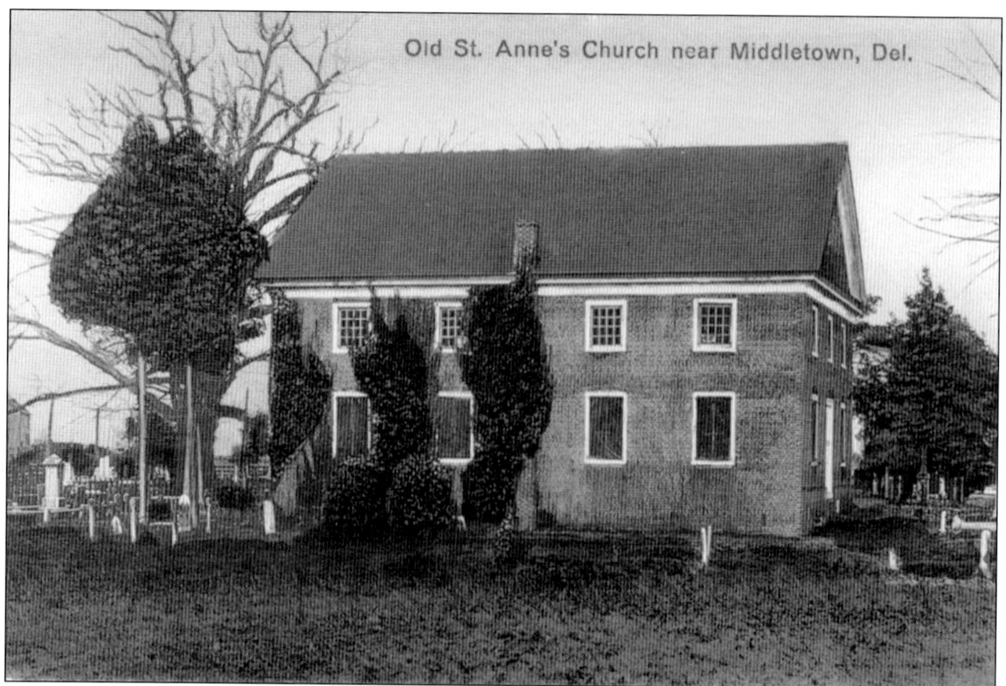

OLD ST. ANNE'S CHURCH NEAR MIDDLETOWN, 1910S. This church, just outside Middletown on Route 71, was built in 1768. It was the second building of the Anglican congregation started by the Society for the Propagation of the Gospel in Foreign Parts. Situated in a pretty hillside setting, the building has a brick fence that surrounds the churchyard and cemetery. The church is open for services between June and Labor Day.

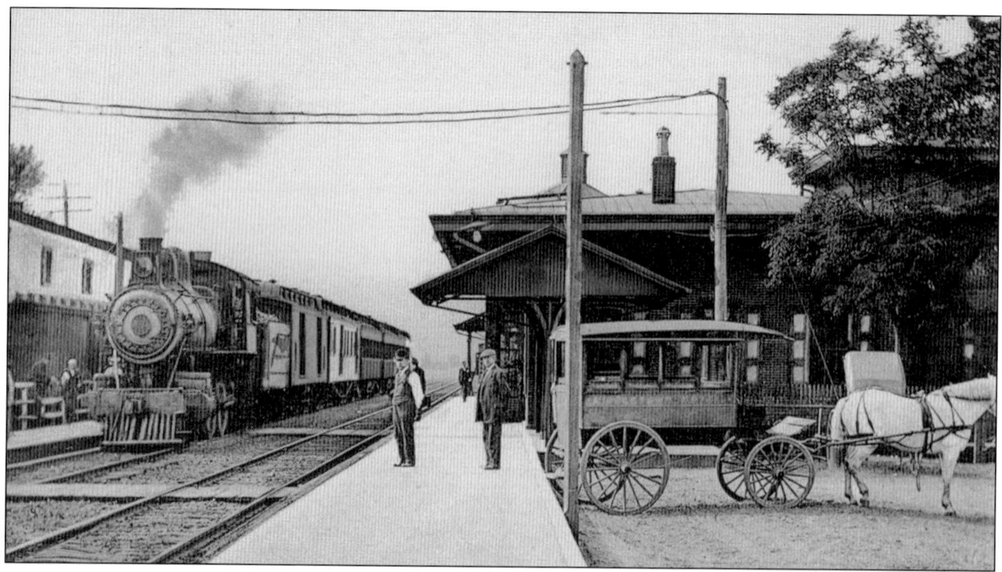

PENNSYLVANIA RAILROAD STATION, MIDDLETOWN, 1900. The Middletown depot, built in 1855, was torn down in the 1960s. Railroad developers originally planned the tracks to run through Odessa, but the people of Odessa did not want the railroad so the line was rerouted through Middletown instead.

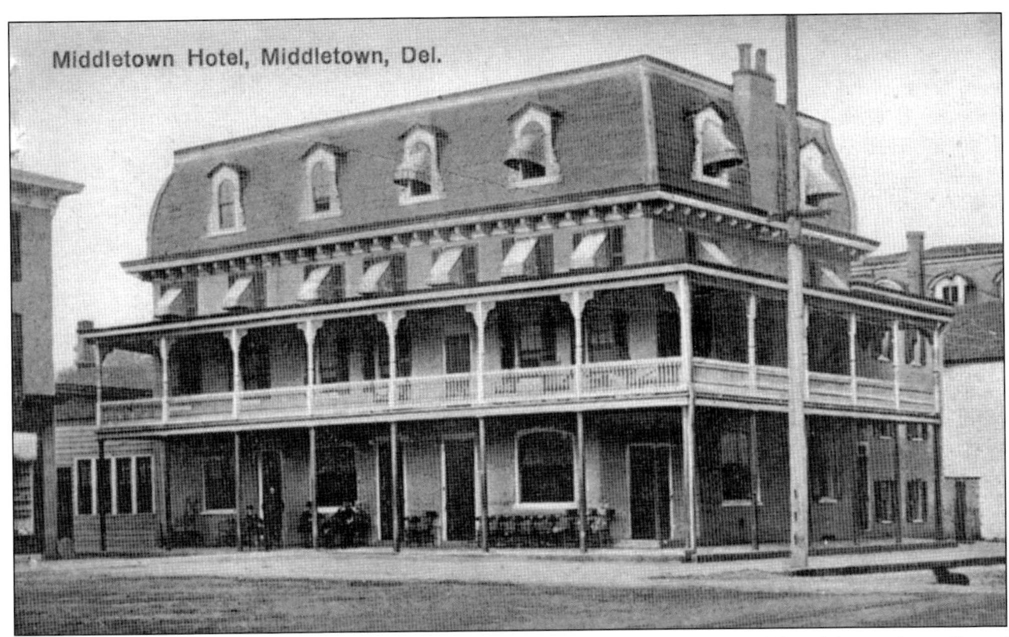

MIDDLETOWN HOTEL, MIDDLETOWN, 1916. This beautiful and substantial hotel located on Broad Street, just north of the square, was torn down after 200 years of service. It stood on the current site of Captain Witherspoon's Tavern. Built in 1761, the hotel served travelers on their way between Wilmington and Dover, and before the Chesapeake & Delaware Canal was built in 1829, it served those going east and west across the peninsula.

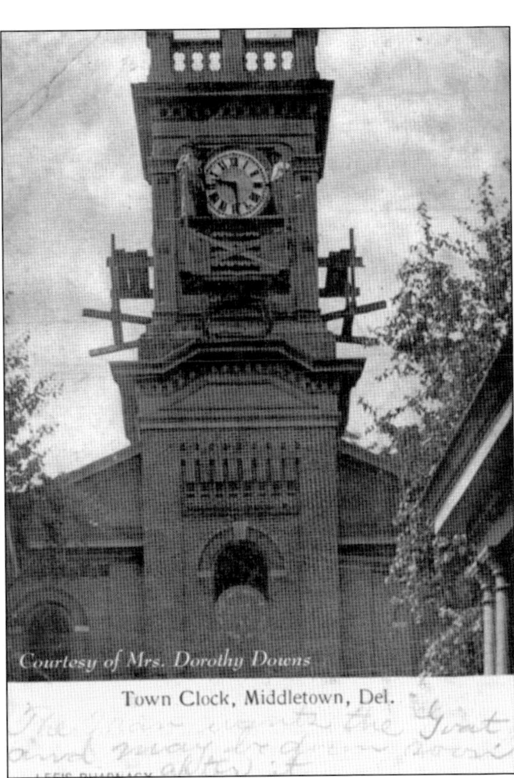

TOWN CLOCK, MIDDLETOWN, 1917. Middletown's town clock sits atop the First Presbyterian Church on West Main Street. The church was built in 1851 and remodeled a decade later. During the 1880s a further renovation was completed. The clock tower was probably erected then but the clock was not purchased and installed until 1906, when Frances Cochran Comegys gave it as a memorial to her parents.

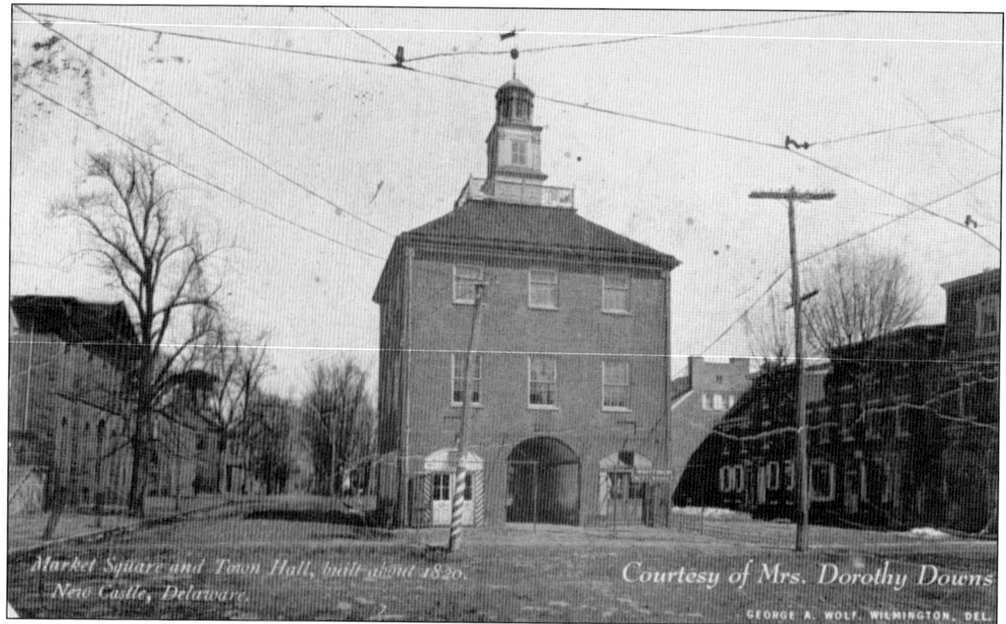

MARKET SQUARE AND TOWN HALL, NEW CASTLE, 1909. Built next to the New Castle County Courthouse on Delaware Street in 1823, this building served as New Castle's town hall for many years. The archway led to a wooden market house that extended behind the building, where area farmers sold fresh produce. Old Town Hall was completely restored in 2000.

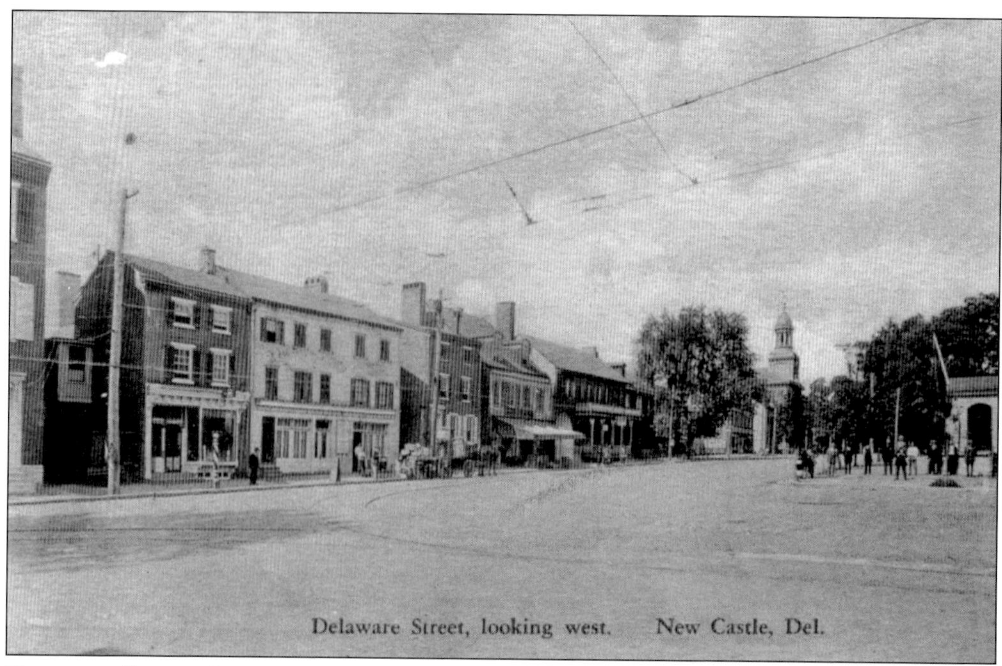

DELAWARE STREET LOOKING WEST, NEW CASTLE. Stores and businesses occupy the first floors of the buildings on the left side of the street. The cupola (since removed) of the Opera House, erected in 1879, is in the far distance. After 1881, New Castle, no longer the county seat, was a quiet town surrounded by industry. The buildings in this view are all still standing.

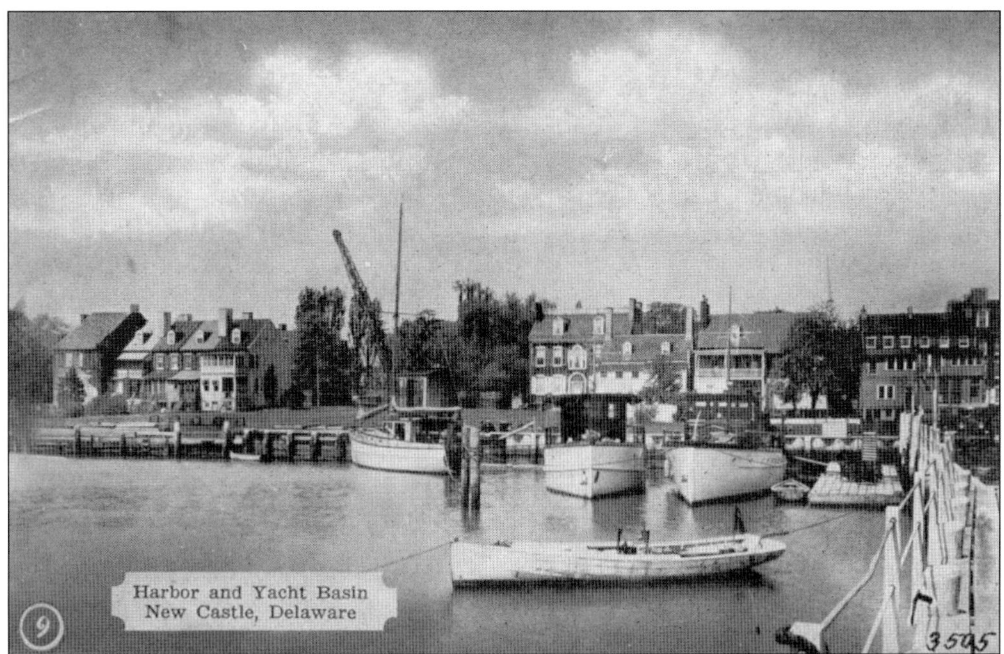

Harbor and Yacht Basin, New Castle. New Castle's harbor has a long history. Many colonial immigrants landed at New Castle, and in the 1700s and early 1800s, passengers bound from Philadelphia to Baltimore frequently sailed to New Castle for the first leg of the journey. As transportation changed, New Castle's port became less important, and by the time of this view it hosted mainly pleasure boats.

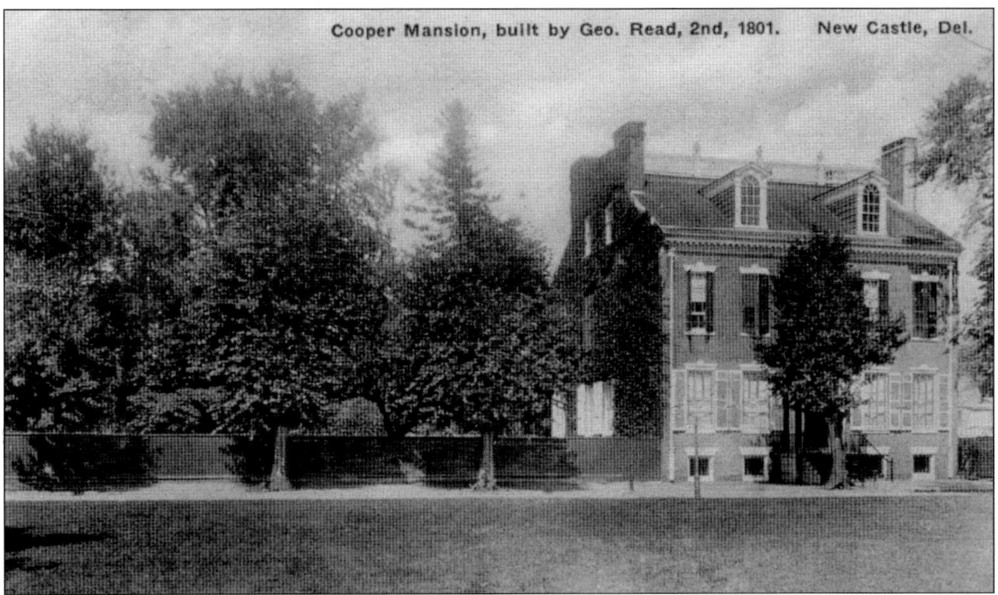

Cooper [sic] Mansion, New Castle, c. 1910. George Read (1765–1836) built this 22-room mansion, the grandest in New Castle, between 1797 and 1803. William Couper purchased it from the Read family in 1846 and installed the Victorian garden to the left of the house. The Read House and Gardens are now open to the public as a museum of the Historical Society of Delaware.

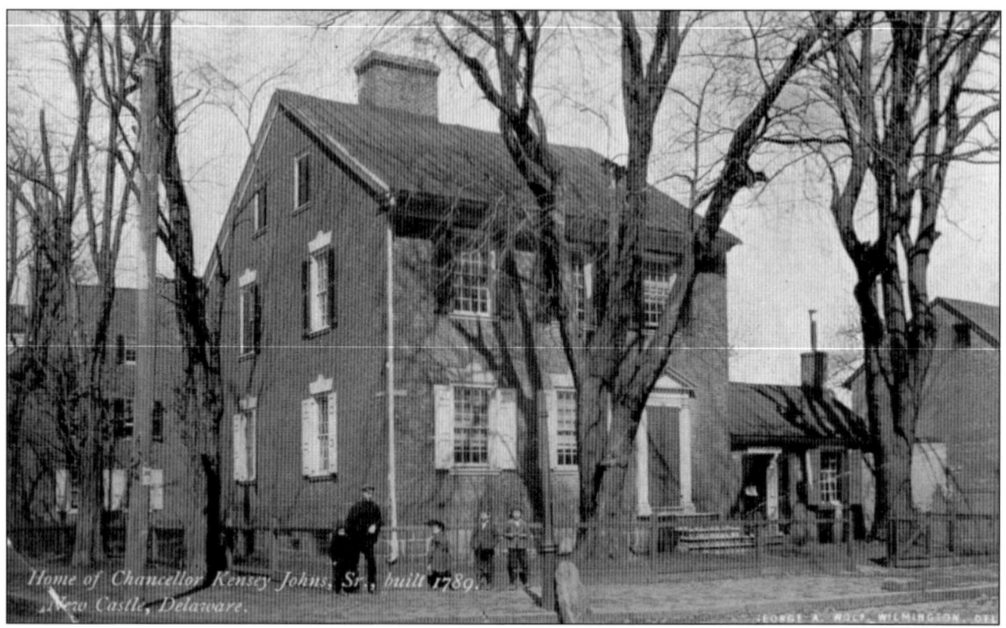

Home of Chancellor Kensey Johns Sr., New Castle, before 1910. Kensey Johns Sr. (1759–1848), a prominent attorney, served as chief justice and chancellor of Delaware. He built this handsome brick house at the corner of East Third and Delaware Streets in 1789–1790. The small wing to the right served as his law office. Many of New Castle's houses date from the late 1700s and early 1800s.

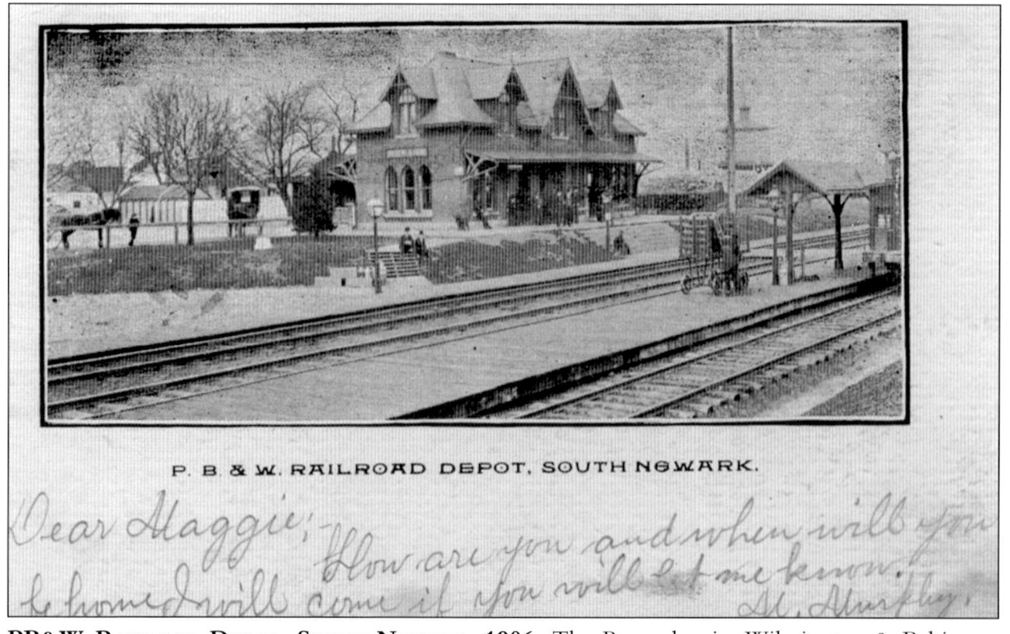

PB&W Railroad Depot, South Newark, 1906. The Pennsylvania, Wilmington & Baltimore Railroad provided service to Newark in 1836. This elegant brick station was built just off south College Avenue in 1877 and replaced a wooden station at Main and Chapel Streets. Restored to its Victorian splendor, the station is now the headquarters of the Newark Historical Society.

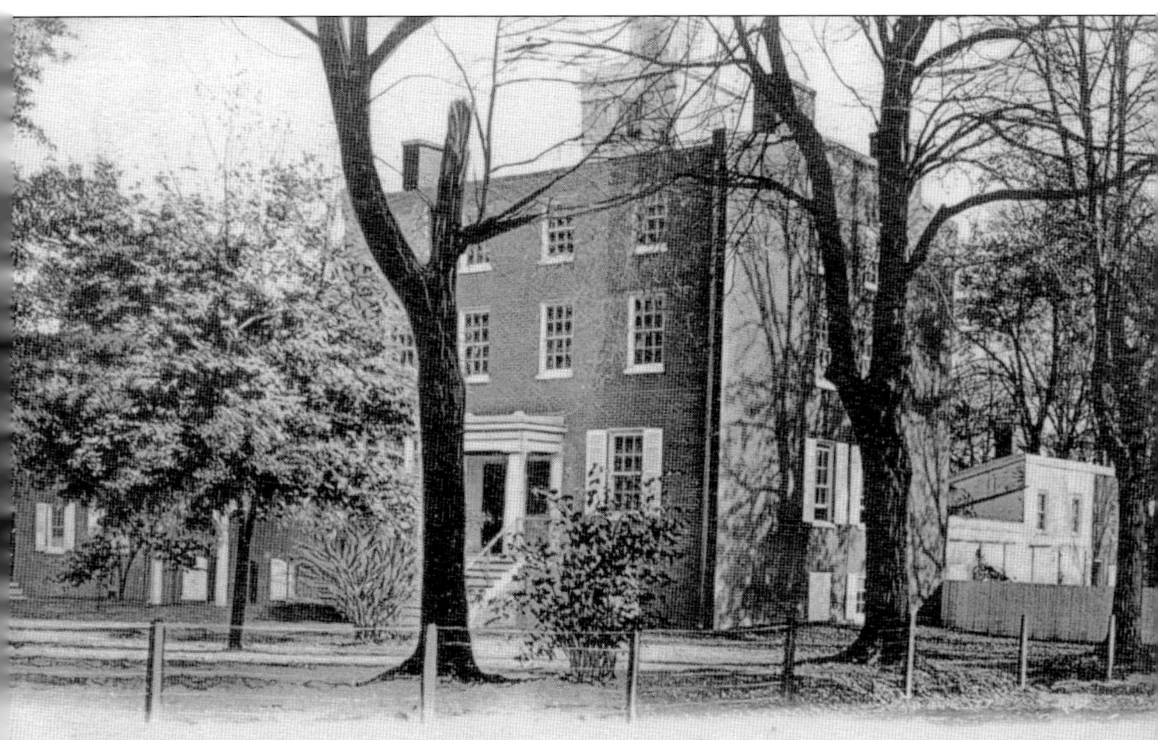

NEWARK, DEL. ACADEMY (FOUNDED 1769), 1906. Francis Alison, a Presbyterian minister, began a boy's school in New London, Pennsylvania, in 1743. The school moved to Newark in the early 1760s, and Delaware College, now the University of Delaware, grew out of Newark Academy in 1834. The academy continued to operate and built two Greek Revival buildings on the town square at Main and Academy Streets in the early 1840s. Operated as a private school until 1898, the building then housed Newark's public high school until 1925. After that, the structure served various civic purposes. In 1976, the trustees of the academy, who still owned it, turned the building over to the University of Delaware. The university restored the academy building and uses it as offices.

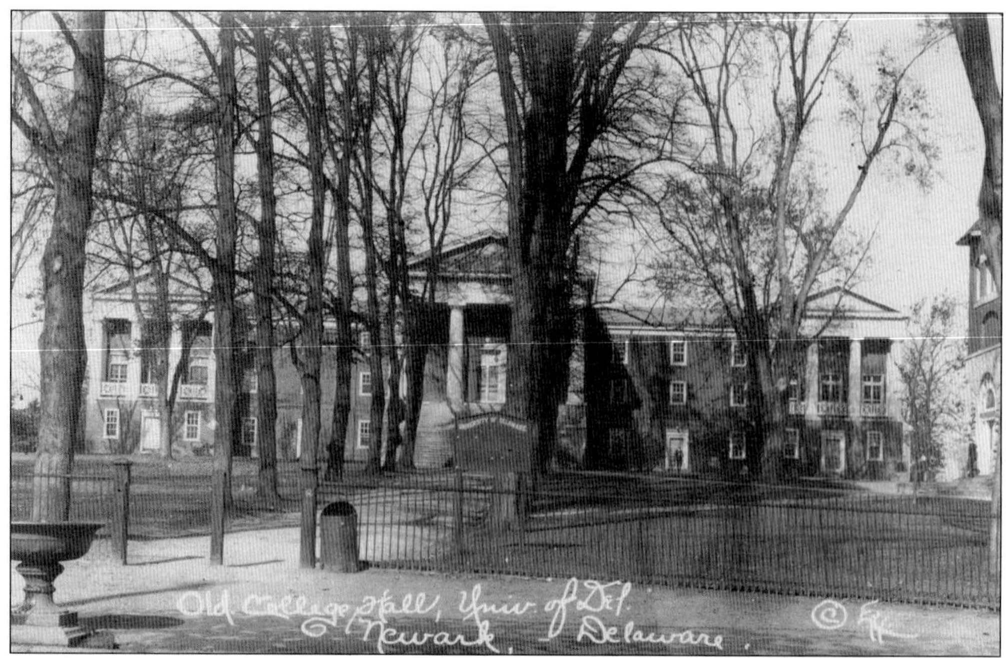

Old College Hall, University of Delaware, Newark, after 1921. The University of Delaware began as Delaware College, a small school for men founded in 1833. The school's first campus was at Main Street and North College Avenue. Old College, the school's first building, was designed in the Greek Revival style and completed, in a simpler form, in 1834. Recitation Hall stands to the right of Old College on the quadrangle. Built in 1891–1892, it was designed by Furness, Evans Company of Philadelphia. Both buildings still serve the university and its students.

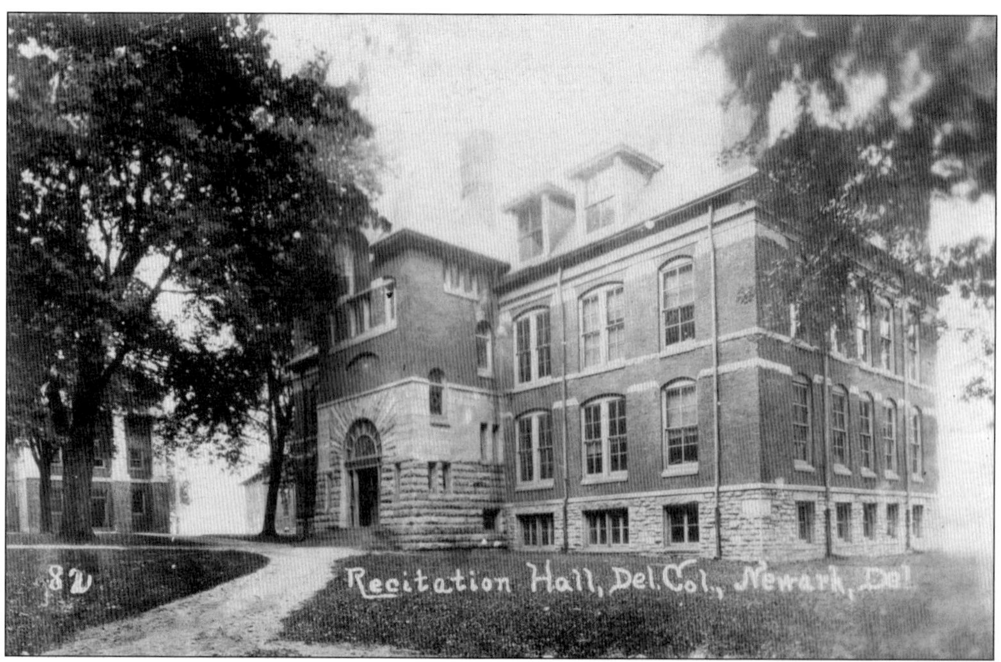

Recitation Hall, Delaware College, Newark, *c.* 1909.

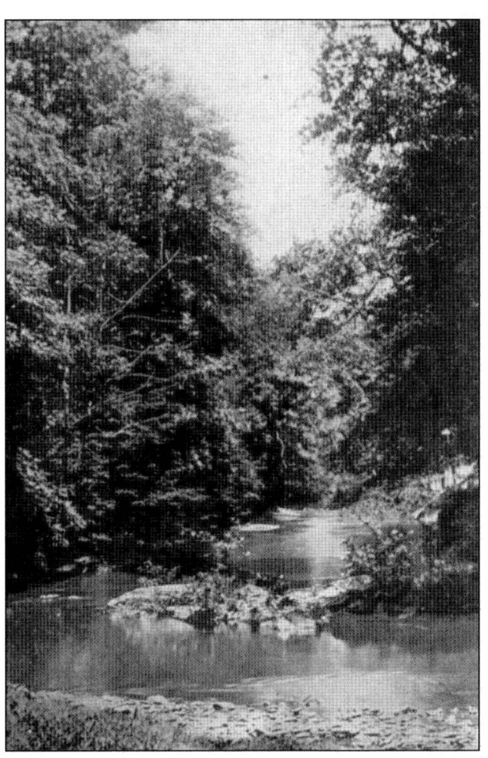

White Clay Creek at Lovers Retreat, near Newark, 1913. White Clay Creek flows down from Pennsylvania just above Newark and then runs eastward. This pleasant spot obviously had romantic associations for earlier generations.

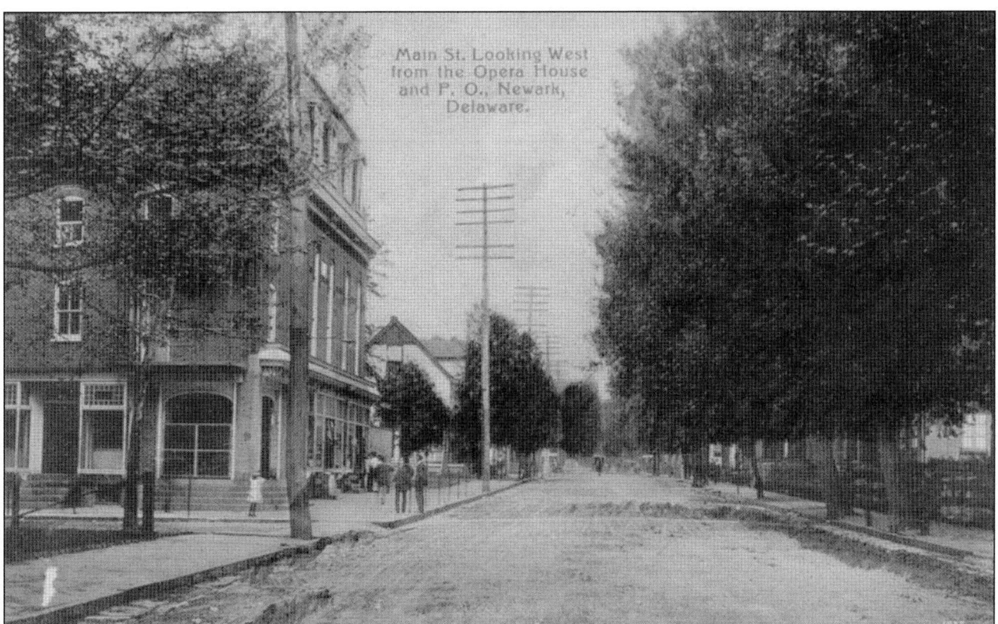

Main Street Looking West from the Opera House and Post Office, Newark, 1907. Newark began as a farming and milling village in the mid-1700s. Newark Academy and Delaware College made it an educational center as well. Only in the late 1800s did the town expand much beyond Main Street. The building on the left, which still stands at Main and Academy Streets, was probably built in the late 1800s.

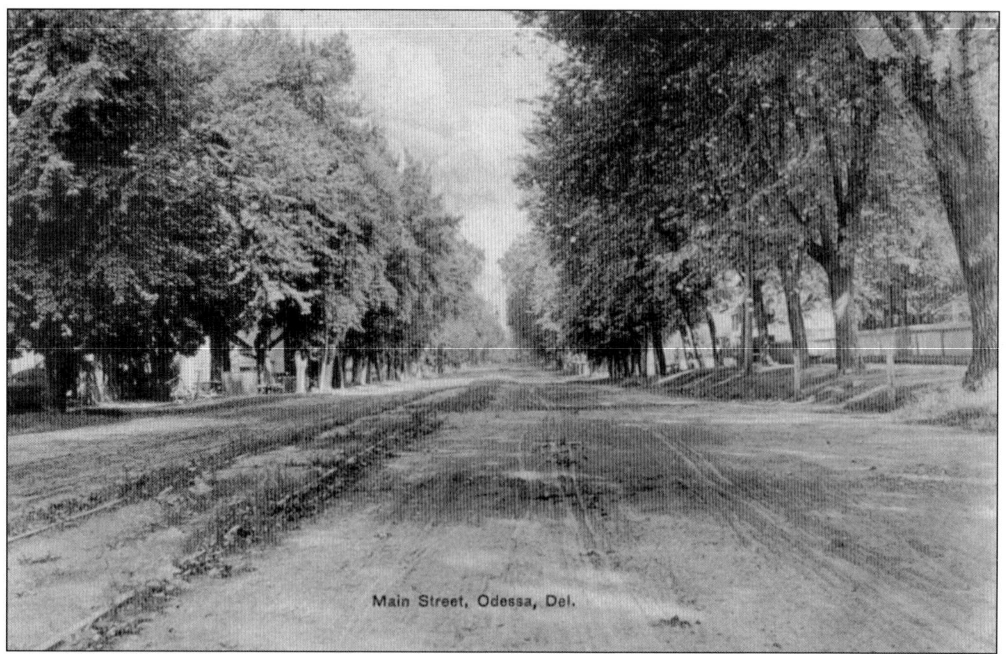

MAIN STREET, ODESSA, 1908. This is a quiet view on Main Street, also known today as Route 299. Nothing filled the economic void left by the decline of shipping and Odessa's refusal to allow the Delaware Railroad to go through town. At the left are the slightly overgrown tracks of the Odessa & Middletown Railway Company, which provided trolley service between 1903 and 1907.

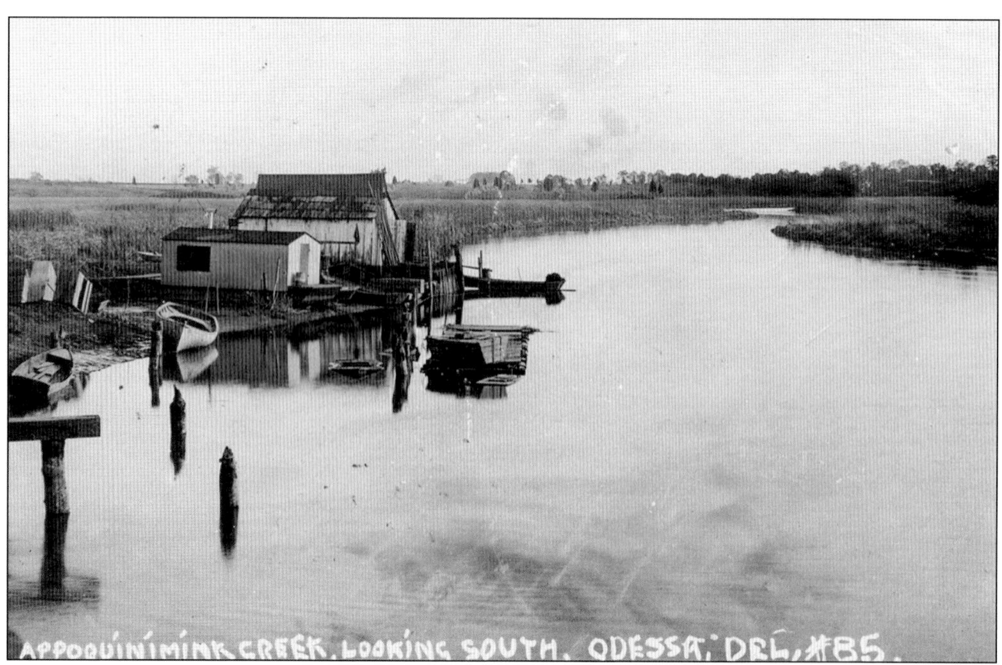

APPOQUINIMINK CREEK LOOKING SOUTH, ODESSA, 1909. Cantwell's Bridge, a grain-shipping port, grew up around the toll bridge begun by the Cantwell family in 1721. The town's name was changed to Odessa in 1855, after a major grain port in Russia, in hopes of reviving trade.

Old Drawyer's Church. Old Drawyer's Church near Odessa is a treasure of Georgian architecture. The congregation began meeting between 1671 and 1700; this church, built in 1773, is the second church at this site. The pulpit has two sets of stairs curving around the preceptor's box, and above the pulpit is a golden dove and a canopied sounding board. Weekly services were discontinued in 1861 but an annual service is held in June.

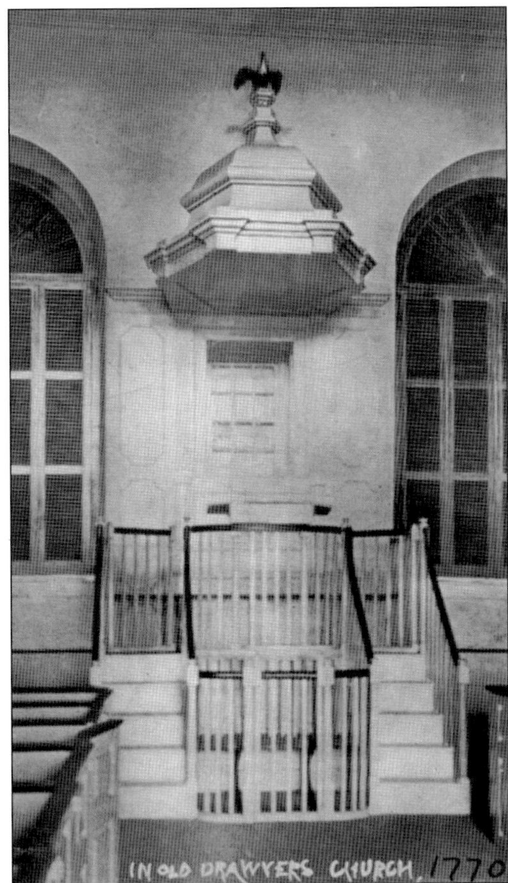

Reedy Island Rear Lighthouse Station, Taylor's Bridge, 1908. This light first shone on February 16, 1904, from atop a temporary, 100-foot-tall lantern post at the far right. The eight-room keeper's house, at far left, was built in 1906. The permanent light, which is still in service, was completed in 1910. The hamlet of Taylor's Bridge was several miles south of Port Penn, by the southern end of Reedy Island.

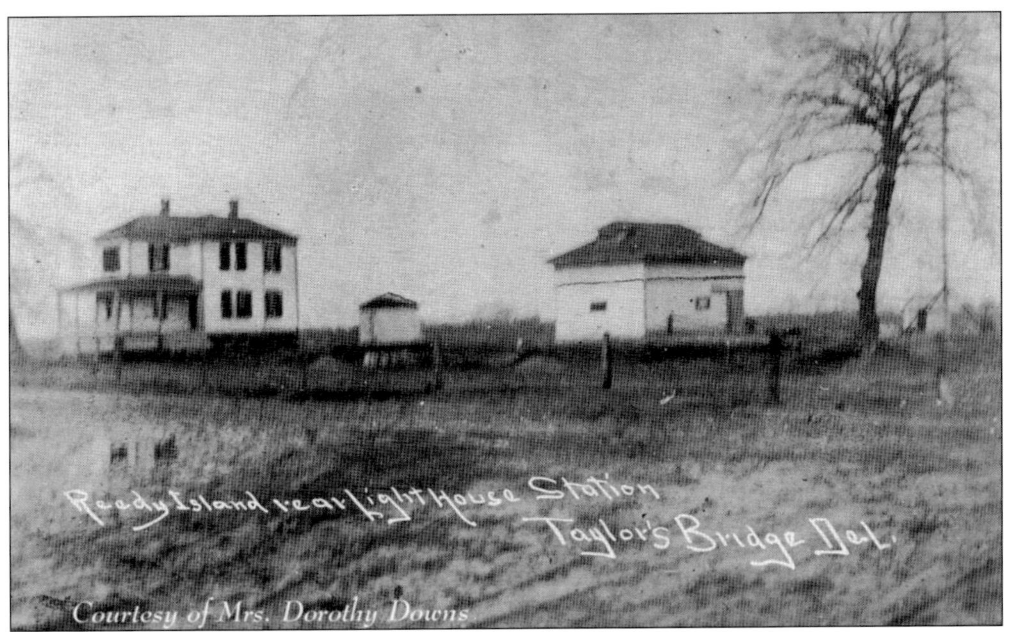

Courtesy of Mrs. Dorothy Downs

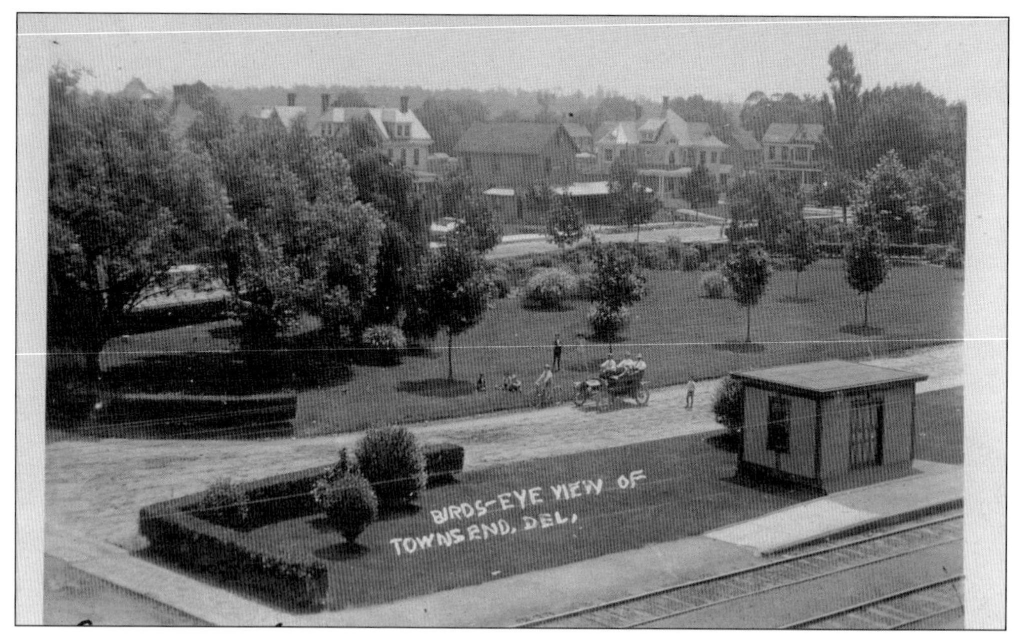

Bird's-eye View of Townsend, 1907. A well-landscaped park served as a buffer between the railroad and the comfortable homes on Commerce Street. Similar homes lined Main Street; Wyndfield Cottage stands on the left. The area that became Townsend was originally an African-American village called Charley Town, named for Charles Lloyd, a well-known resident. After the Delaware Railroad came through, Samuel Townsend, a prosperous farmer, succeeded in having the developing town named after himself. The railroad made Townsend a marketing center for local farmers.

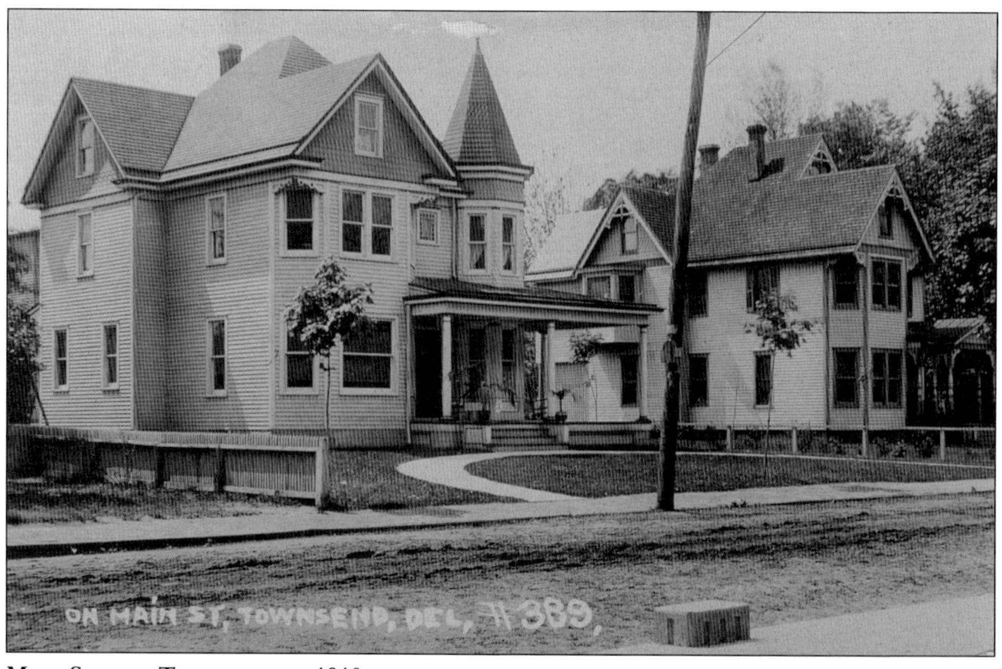

Main Street, Townsend, *c.* 1910.

Six

Suburban Wilmington

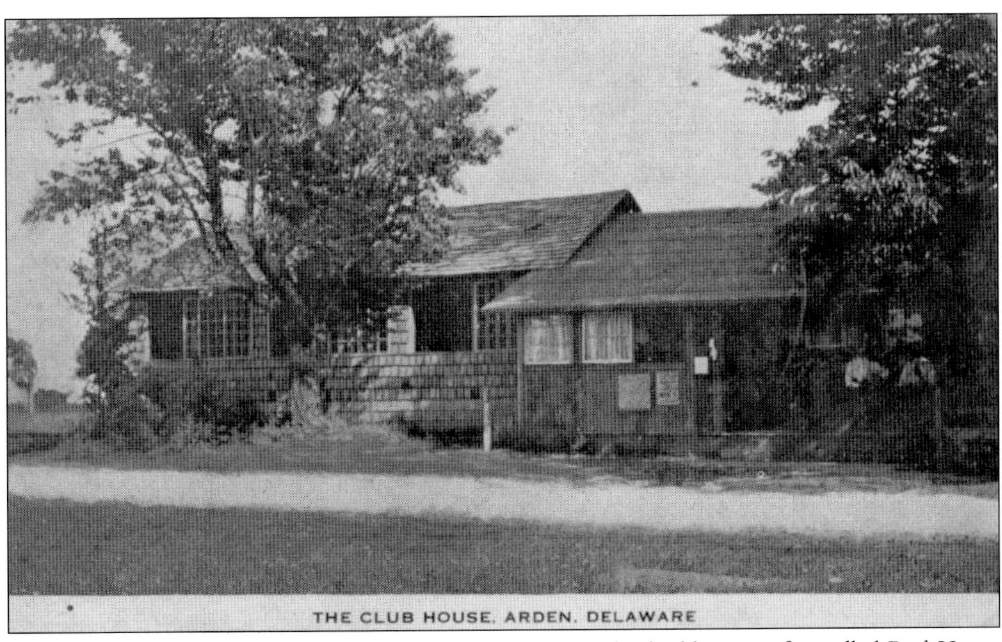

The Club House, Arden, after 1910. Erected in 1901, this building was first called Red House after the home of William Morris, the Englishman whose Arts and Crafts philosophy inspired Arden's founders. It served as Arden's first community center, and with a large addition in 1913, it became the Craft Shop. The building, at Cherry Lane and Miller Road, is now used as apartments.

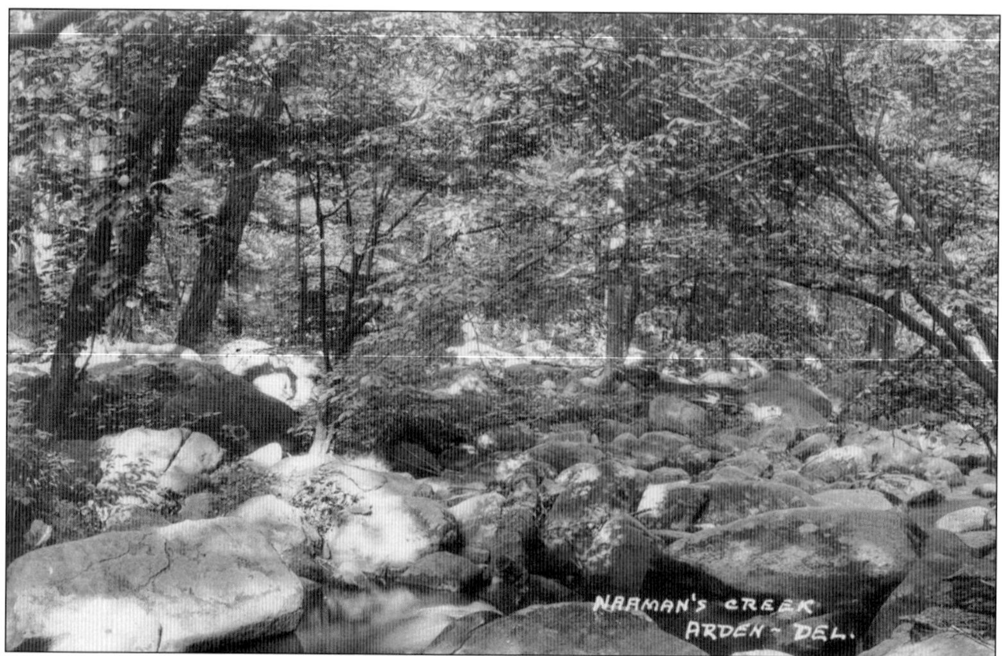

NAAMAN'S CREEK, ARDEN, 1950. Pictured here is a sylvan scene on Naaman's Creek, which Arden residents have enjoyed for generations.

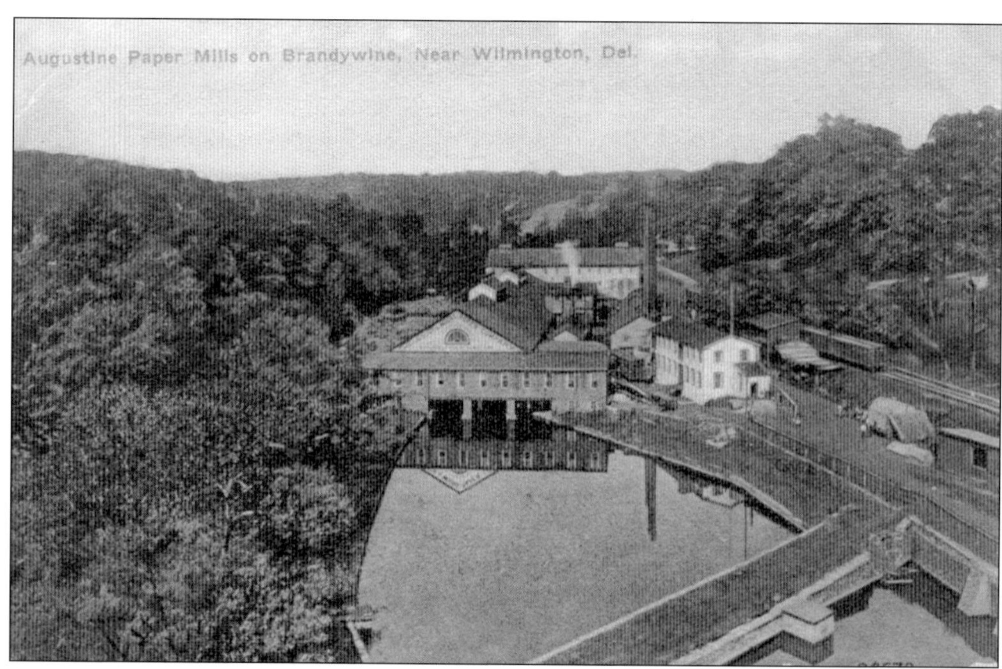

AUGUSTINE PAPER MILLS ON BRANDYWINE, NEAR WILMINGTON, 1910S. Joshua and Thomas Gilpin began the first paper mills on the Brandywine in 1787. In 1843 Augustus E. Jessup and his son-in-law Bloomfeld Hanes Moore began the Jessup and Moore Mill. In 1845 they converted an old snuff and flour mill to a paper mill, calling it Augustine Mill. Destroyed by fire, the mill was rebuilt in 1881.

ENTRANCE TO BRANDYWINE SPRINGS PARK, NEAR WILMINGTON, c. 1910. "Let All Who Enter Here, Leave Care Behind." Brandywine Springs hotel opened as an elegant resort in 1827 but lasted less than 20 years. Reopening in 1886, the amusement park was a beloved destination for Wilmington families. Encompassing theaters, arcades, pavilions, a pond, a carousel, a toboggan run, and a skating rink, there was something for everyone. The park closed in 1923.

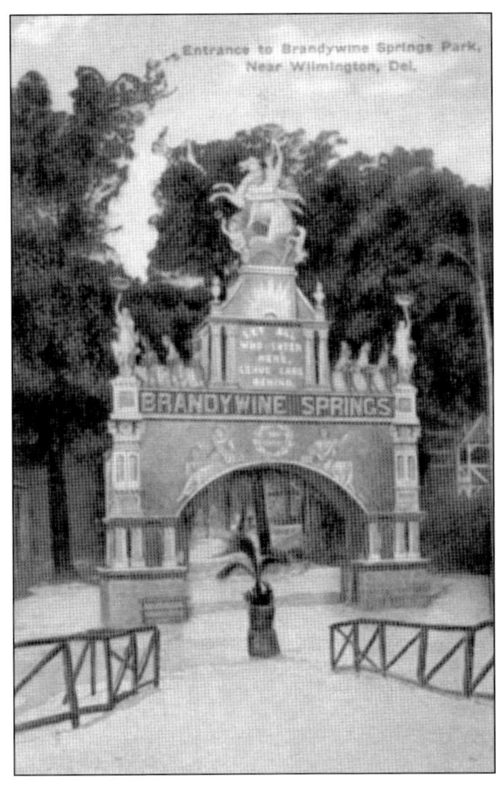

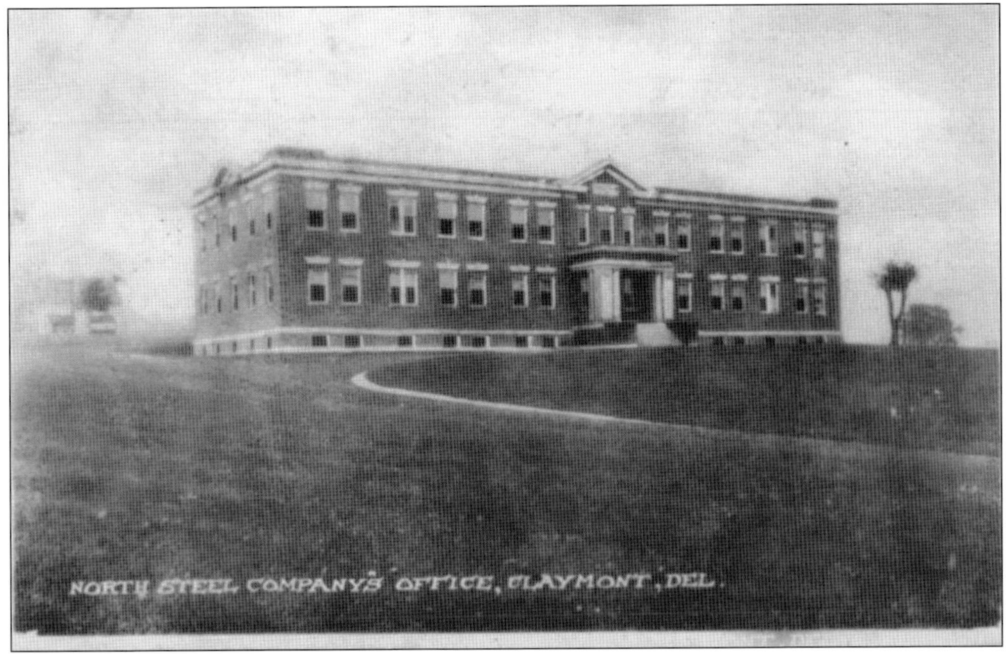

NORTH [SIC] STEEL COMPANY'S OFFICE, CLAYMONT, LATE 1910S. Located at 4001 Philadelphia Pike, the Worth (not "North") Steel Company began operating about 1916. The main office building, seen here, still towers over the Pike but belongs to CitiSteel.

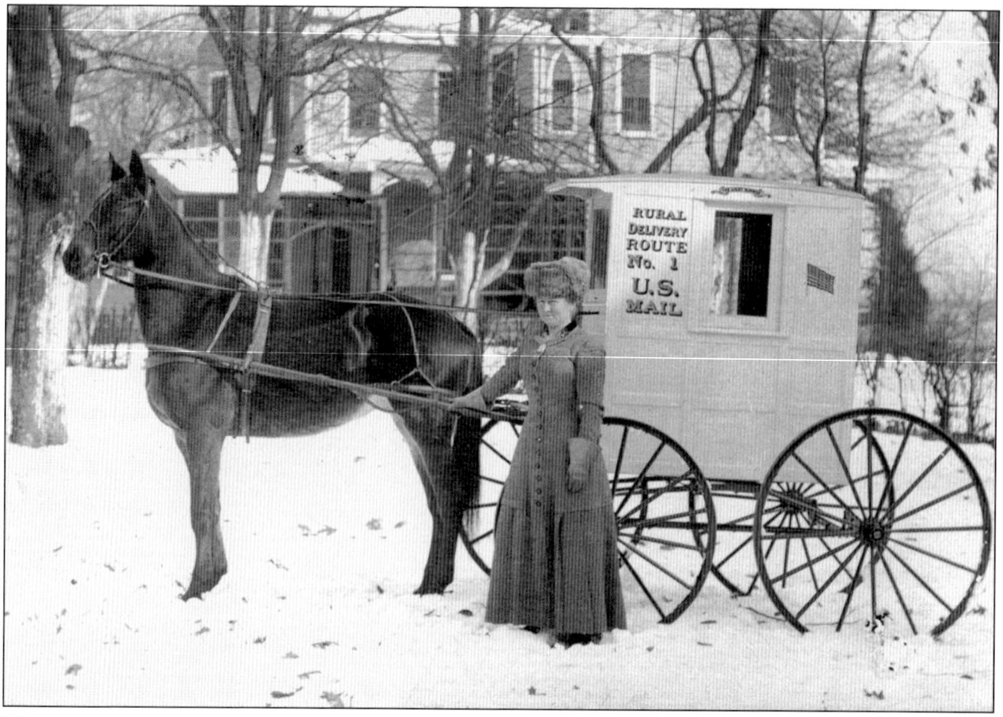

MAIL CARRIER, 1910. Neither snow, nor rain . . . In her horse-drawn carriage, Lillie Donohue, Delaware's first female carrier, delivered mail from Penny Hill to Arden from 1905 to 1910. She also served as an officer in the Rural Letter Carrier's Association. This postcard was Ms. Donohue's Christmas and New Year's greeting to her customers.

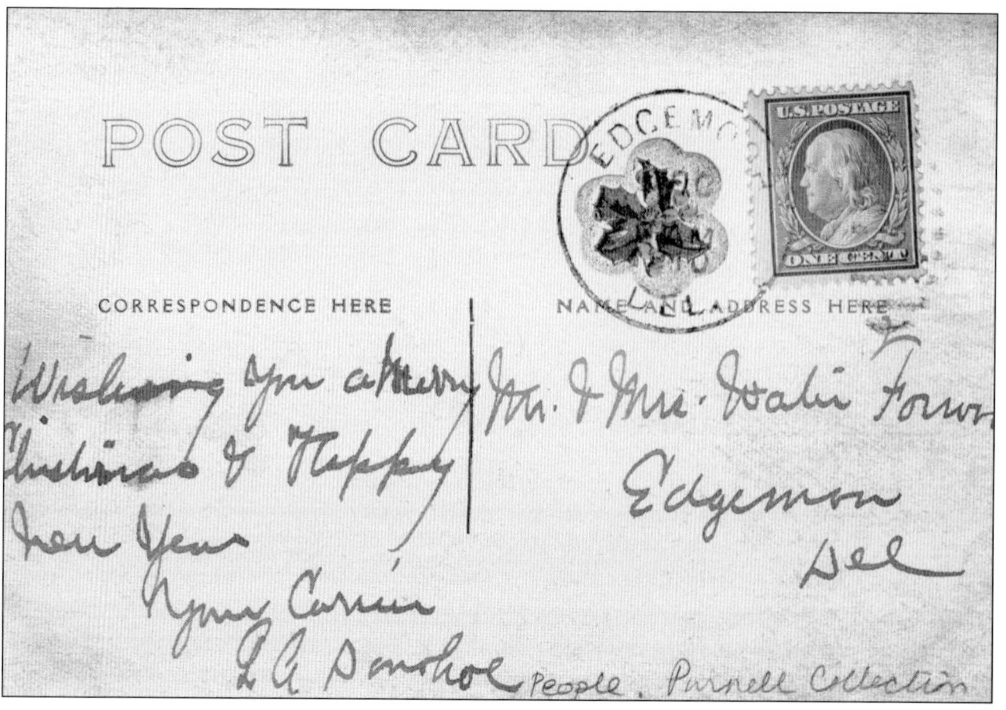

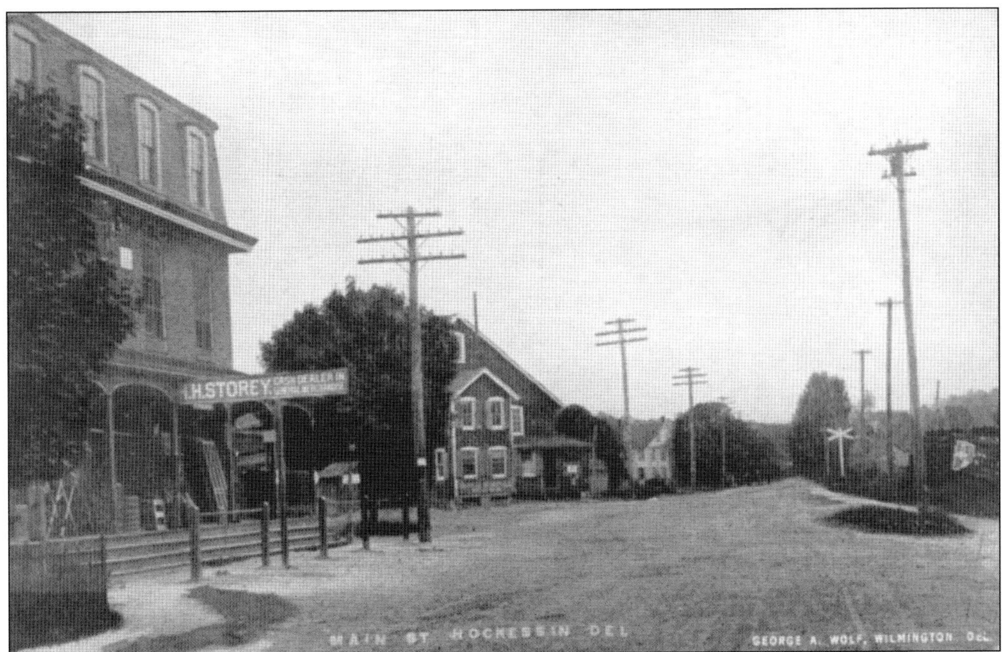

MAIN STREET, HOCKESSIN, C. 1905. This scene shows Hockessin as a quiet community whose main business interests were mushrooms and mining kaolin or china clay. Looking along Old Lancaster Pike, the building on the far left is now Henretty's Butcher Shop and Grocery. The building in the center stands today near the entrance to the Hockessin Corner shopping center.

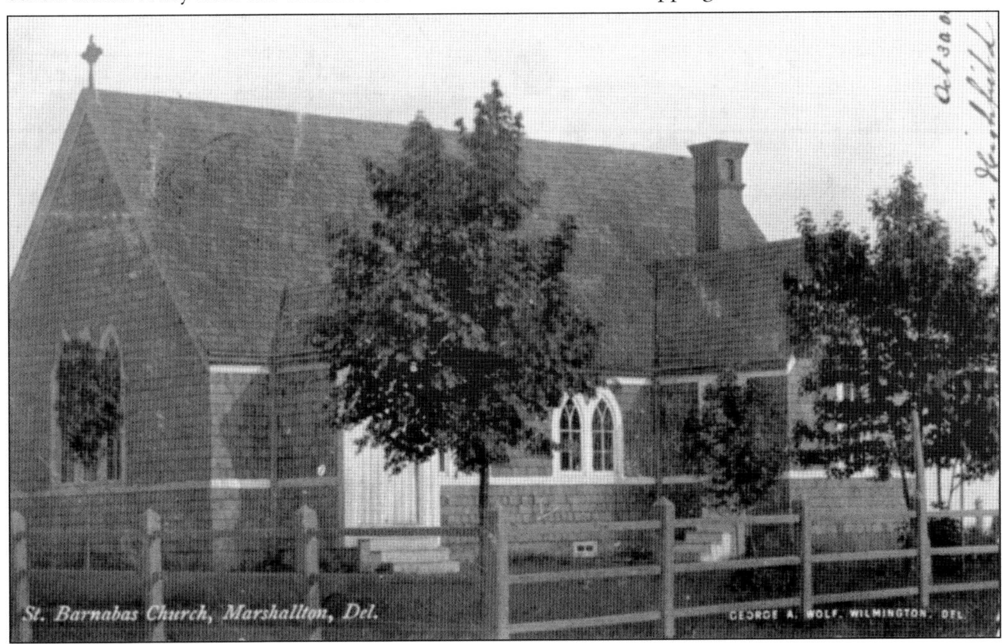

ST. BARNABAS CHURCH, MARSHALLTON, 1906. Named after the owner of the first rolling mill along Red Clay Creek, the Marshallton post office opened in 1878. St. Barnabas Episcopal Church organized in 1890, and eight years later, its first building burned on Christmas Day. This new church was consecrated in 1899.

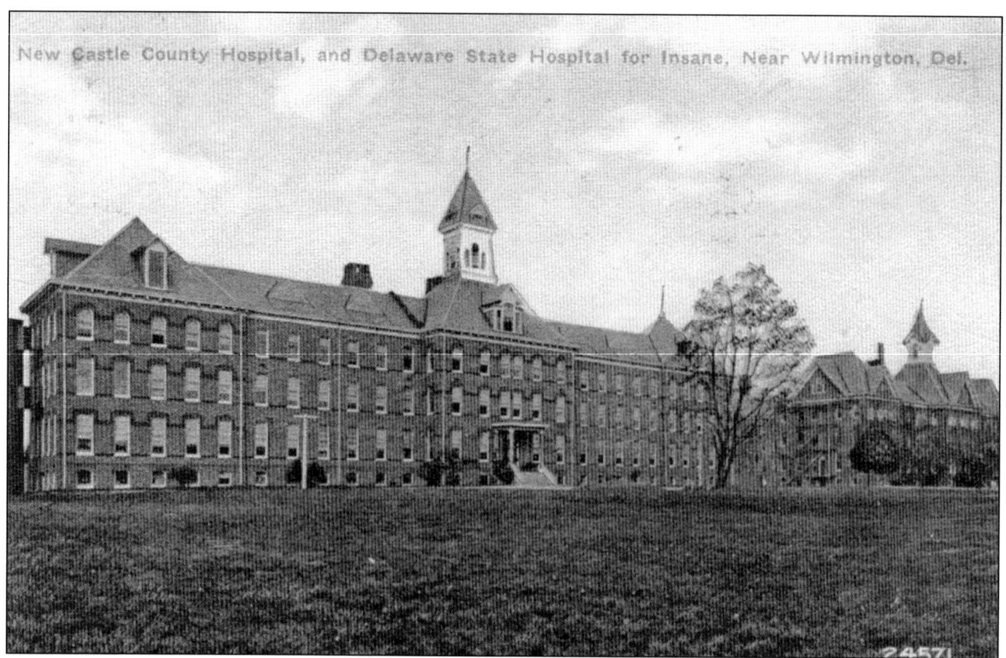

NEW CASTLE COUNTY HOSPITAL AND DELAWARE STATE HOSPITAL FOR THE INSANE, NEAR WILMINGTON, 1911. In 1889 the General Assembly established a State Hospital for the Insane, making Delaware the first state to assume obligation for complete care of the mentally ill. In 1891 it was named the Delaware State Hospital and was one of the first state mental institutions in the country to be approved by the American College of Surgeons and the American Medical Association.

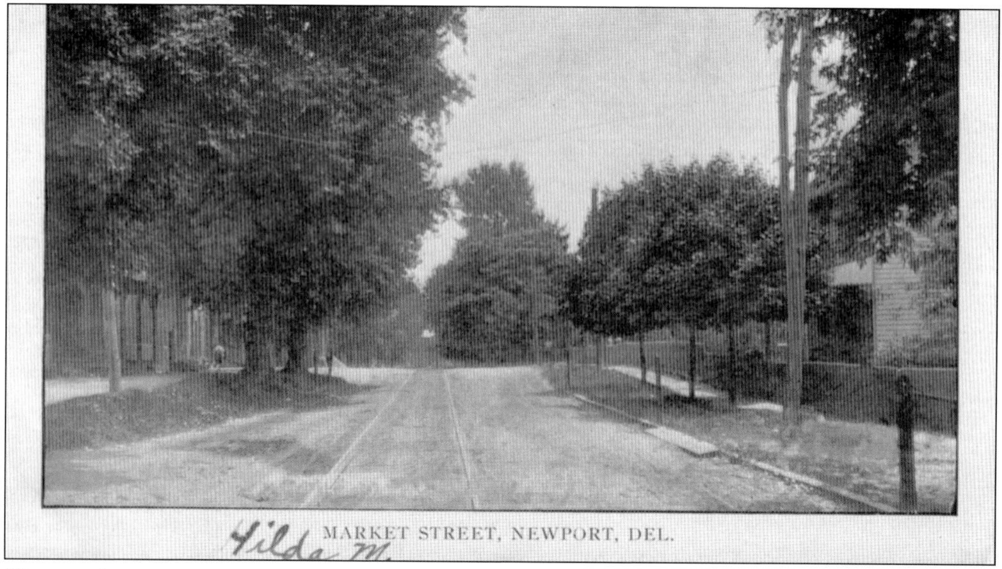

MARKET STREET, NEWPORT, 1912. Quiet Market Street is now busy Route 4. Newport, founded on the Christina River in 1735, prospered early on as a flour-milling and grain-shipping center. In time, it became a suburb of Wilmington. Trolley service, which used the tracks in the center of the street, came to Newport in 1901.

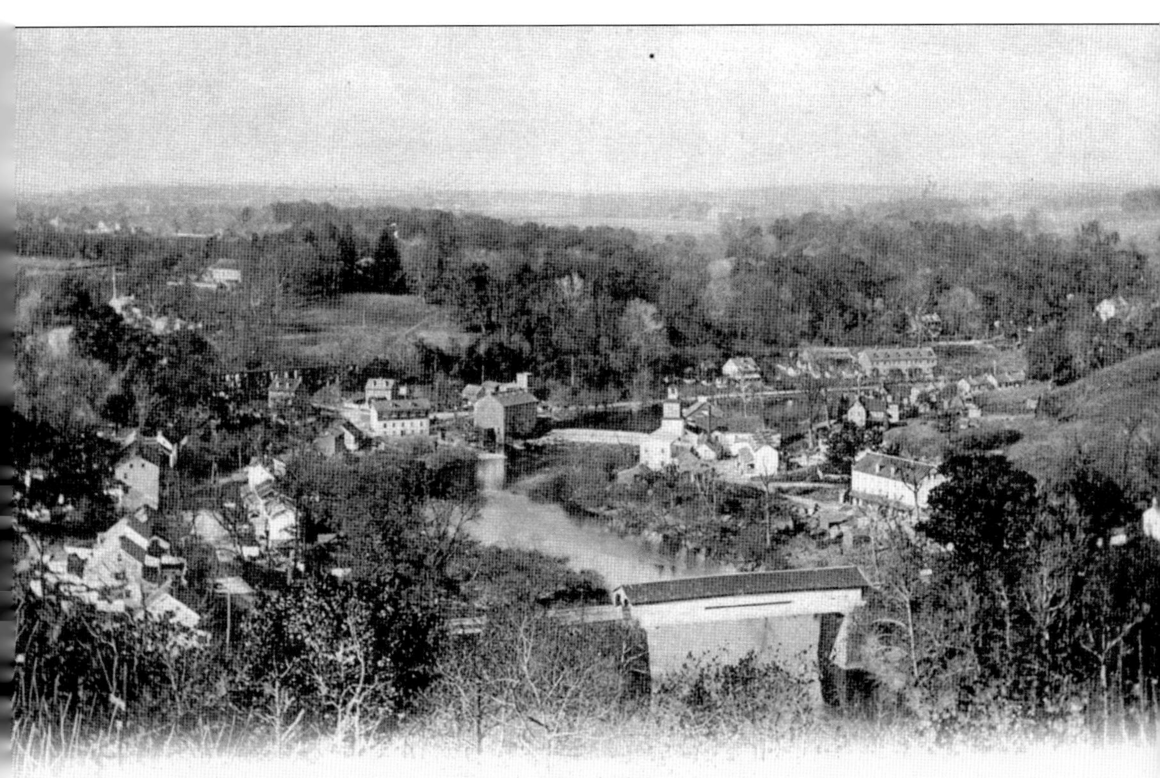

RISING SUN VILLAGE NEAR WILMINGTON, *c.* 1905. This is a view of the du Pont Company's original black powder yards at Henry Clay, or Rising Sun Village. The powder mills operated until 1921. This place has been known by many names, including Henry Clay Factory, Henry Clay, the du Pont Banks, Rokeby, Rising Sun, and New Bridge. The Rising Sun covered bridge in the foreground was built in 1833 and torn down in 1927.

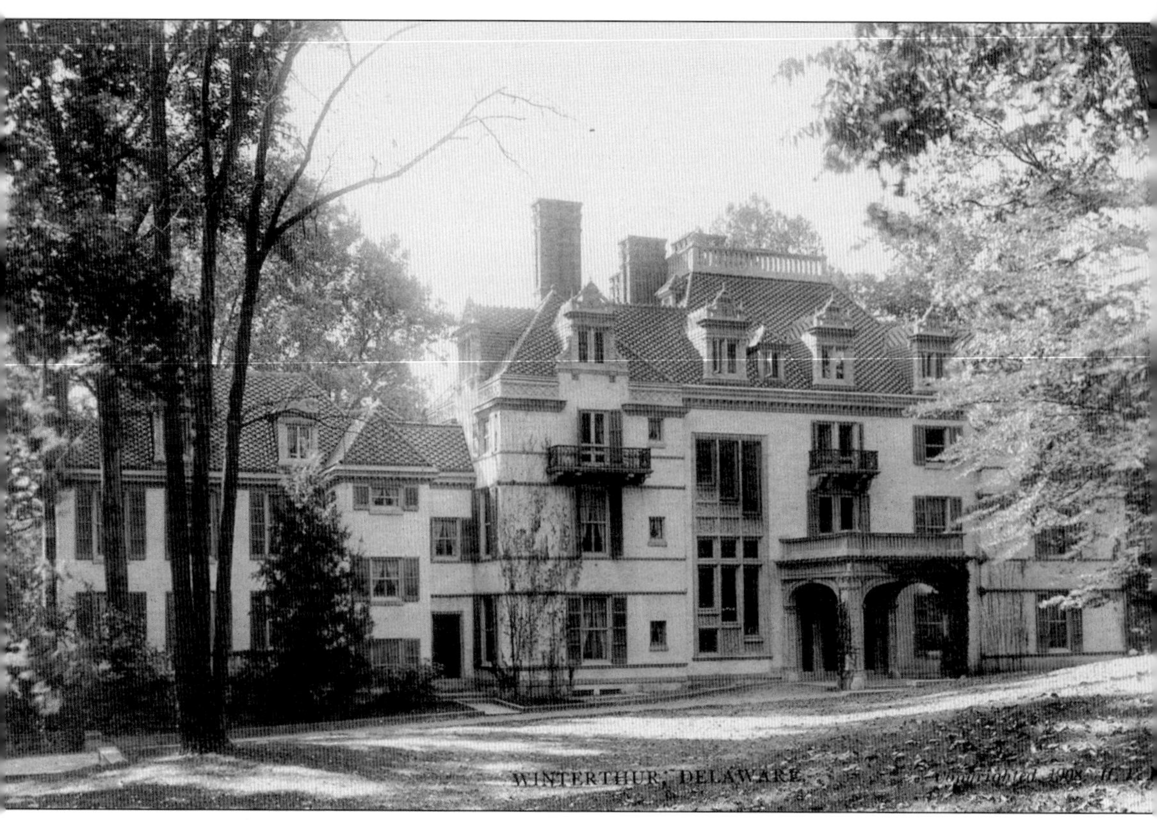

Winterthur, 1908. Today Winterthur is synonymous with its world-renowned collection of early American antiques, but until 1951, it was a du Pont family home. Built about 1838 by James Antoine and Evelina Gabrielle du Pont Bidermann, Winterthur was named for the Swiss village where Bidermann's father lived. In the 1910s, Henry Francis du Pont began collecting American antiques, sometimes rooms at a time, adding them onto the house. In 1951 the house opened as a museum.

Seven

WILMINGTON

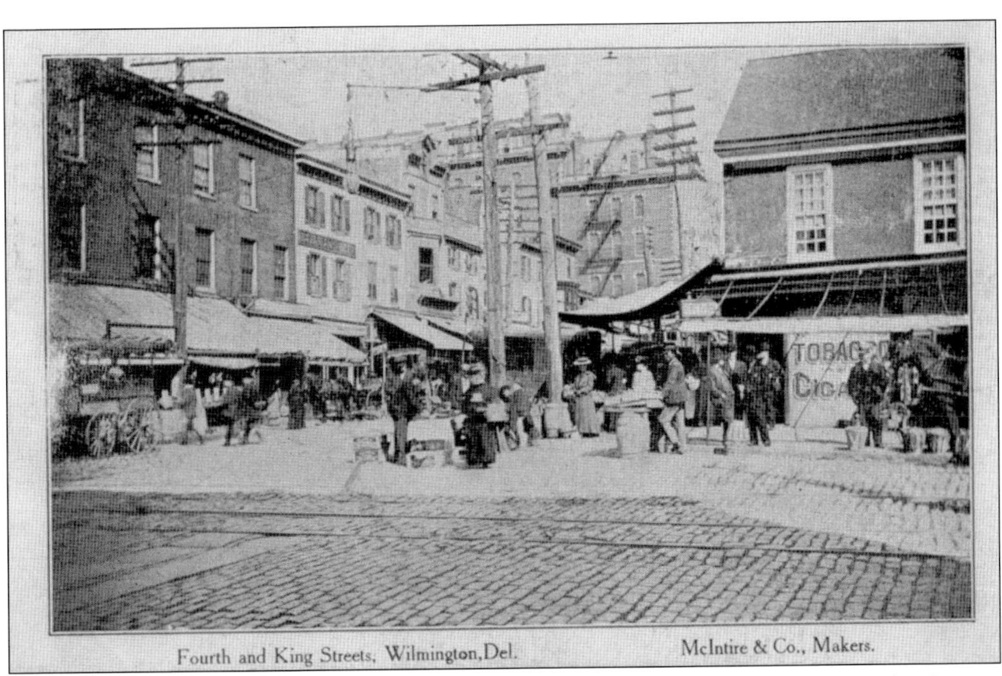

FOURTH AND KING STREETS, WILMINGTON, 1906. King Street's network of shops, market houses, and street markets was at its height in 1900—a busy, crowded place, full of sights and smells. This view was taken from Fourth Street looking north. The large building in the distance near the center of the postcard is the Clayton House, in its last years as a hotel. In 1915 the building reopened as the Queen Theater.

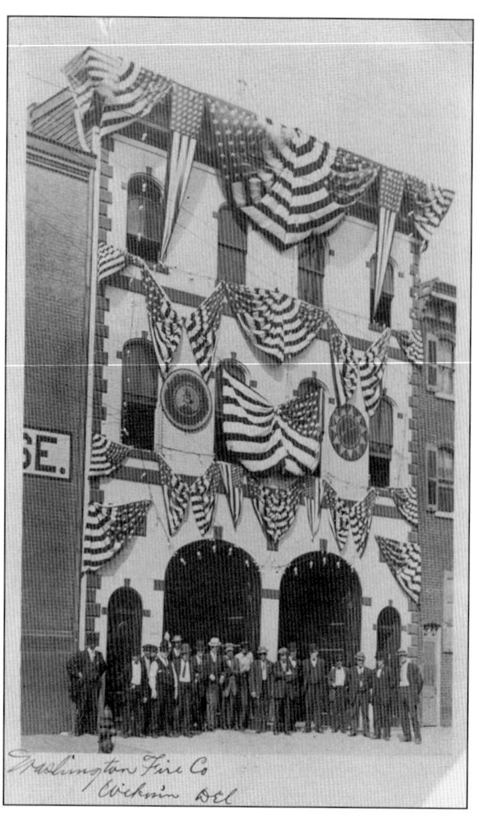

WASHINGTON FIRE COMPANY, c. 1910. Fire Company #7, or the Washington Fire Company House, is pictured here lavishly decorated with bunting and lights. The house, built in 1873, was located at 303 French Street, and the company was organized in January 1840.

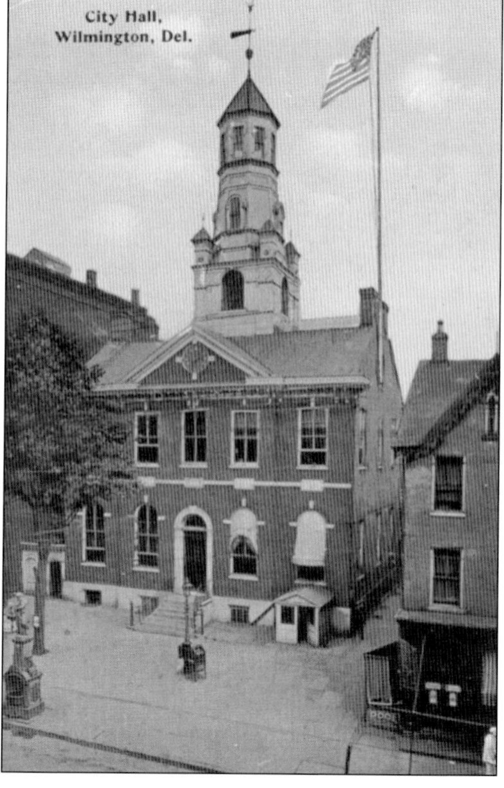

CITY HALL, WILMINGTON, c. 1910. Town Hall, built in 1798, served the city until 1916. In 1875, Victorian Wilmingtonians updated the building with a cupola, new cornice and balustrade, and wrought-iron hand railings for the front stairs. Purchased by the Historical Society of Delaware, the building was returned to its 1798 appearance in the 1920s.

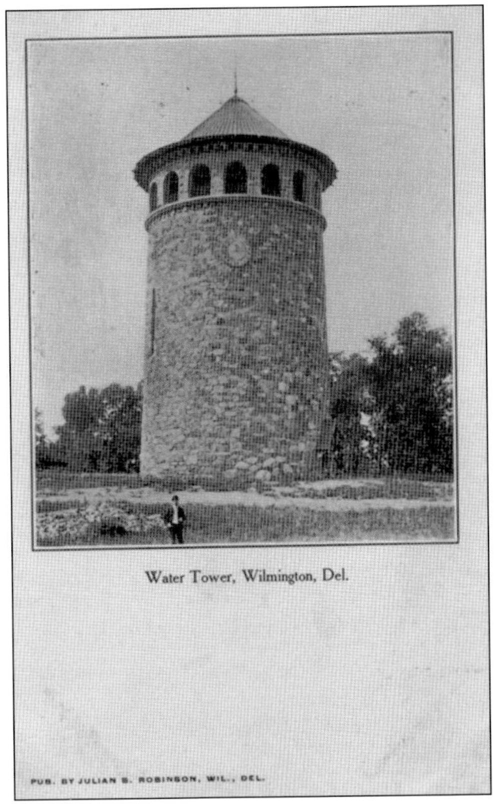

Water Tower, Wilmington, c. 1900. Built to blend into the park's setting and to provide a water supply for city residents, Rockford Tower was completed in 1901. Standing about 115 feet tall atop Mt. Salem Hill in Rockford Park, the tower took two years to build and cost $76,281. It encloses a water tank 40 feet in diameter and 60 feet high. Thick stone walls keep the water from freezing. The park and tower were such a popular destination point that by May 1904 an average of 600 people a day climbed the stairs to the observation deck to enjoy a panoramic view of the city, as seen in the postcard below.

Birds Eye View Rockford Park, from Water Tower, WILMINGTON, Del.

1522

Bird's-eye View of Rockford Park from Water Tower, Wilmington, 1910s.

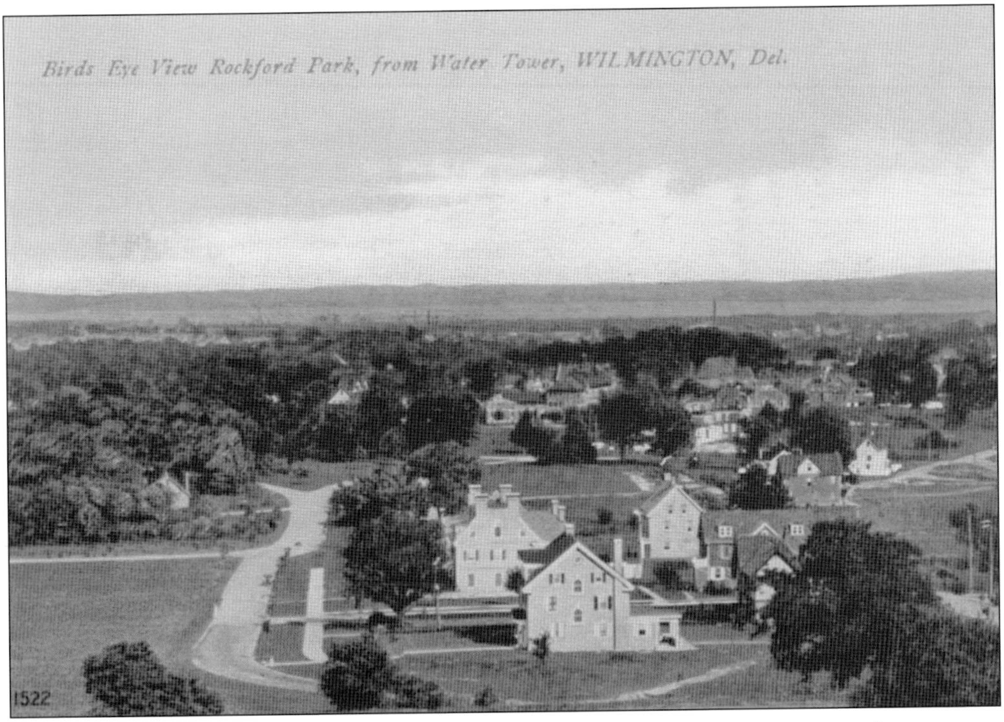

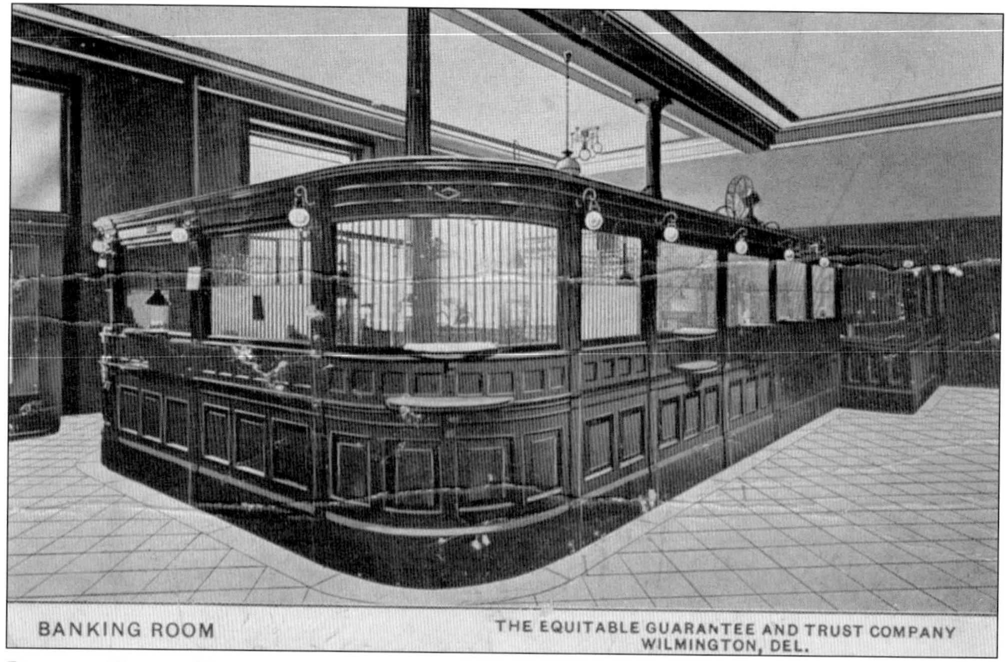

BANKING ROOM, THE EQUITABLE GUARANTEE AND TRUST COMPANY, WILMINGTON, 1900S. Historically, bank interiors were extravagant and were meant to provide customers with a sense of security in order to encourage them to deposit money. The Equitable Guarantee and Trust Company, seen here, was located in the Equitable Building on the northwest corner of Market and Ninth Streets and operated under this name from 1890 to 1916.

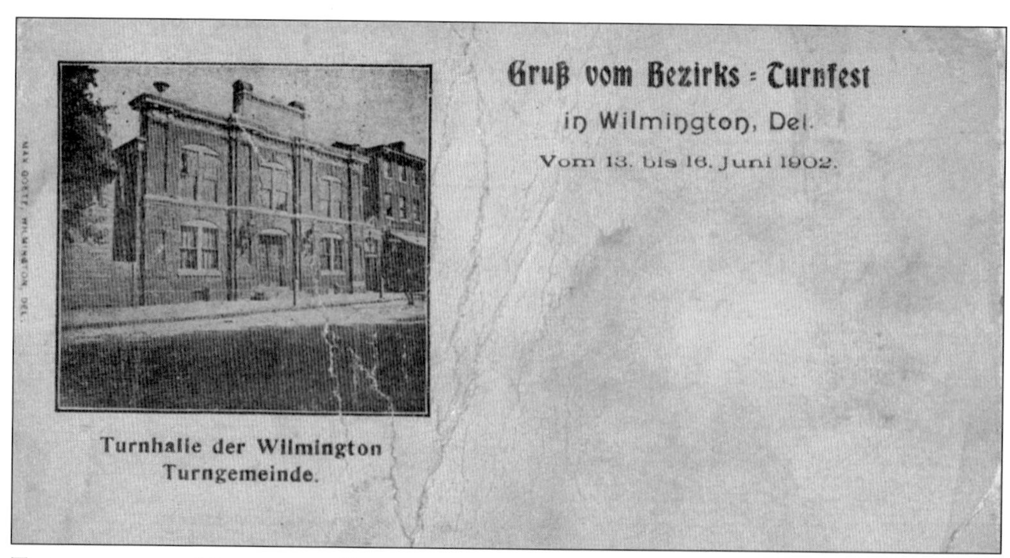

TURNHALLE DER WILMINGTON TURNGEMEINDE, 1902. In the early 20th century, Wilmington's Germans formed a close-knit community and were the only ethnic group to publish their own foreign-language newspaper, *Freie Press*. The Sangerbund, a club that is still active today, provided cohesiveness for the community. The Turn Hall, home of the Wilmington Turngemeinde, an athletic club, was built at Eight and French Streets in 1895. The club specialized in body-building gymnastics.

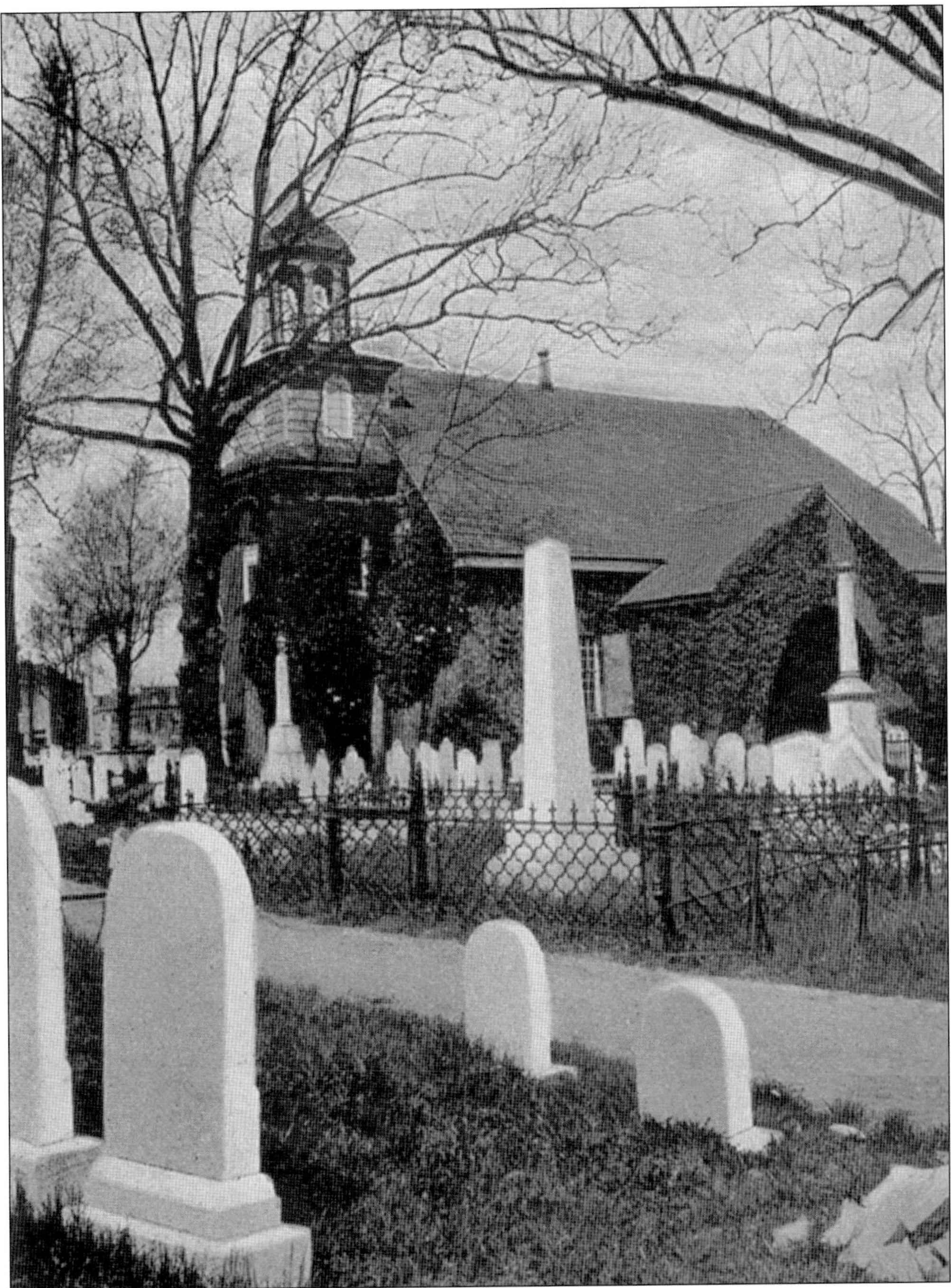

Old Swedes, 1906. Holy Trinity, or Old Swedes Church, has been the strongest visible link to Wilmington's first European settlers who arrived at Fort Christina in 1638. The foundation was laid on May 28, 1698, and the building consecrated on June 4, 1699. The brick tower, cupola, and bell were added in 1802. The church and graveyard remain a beloved spot that instantly transports visitors back in time.

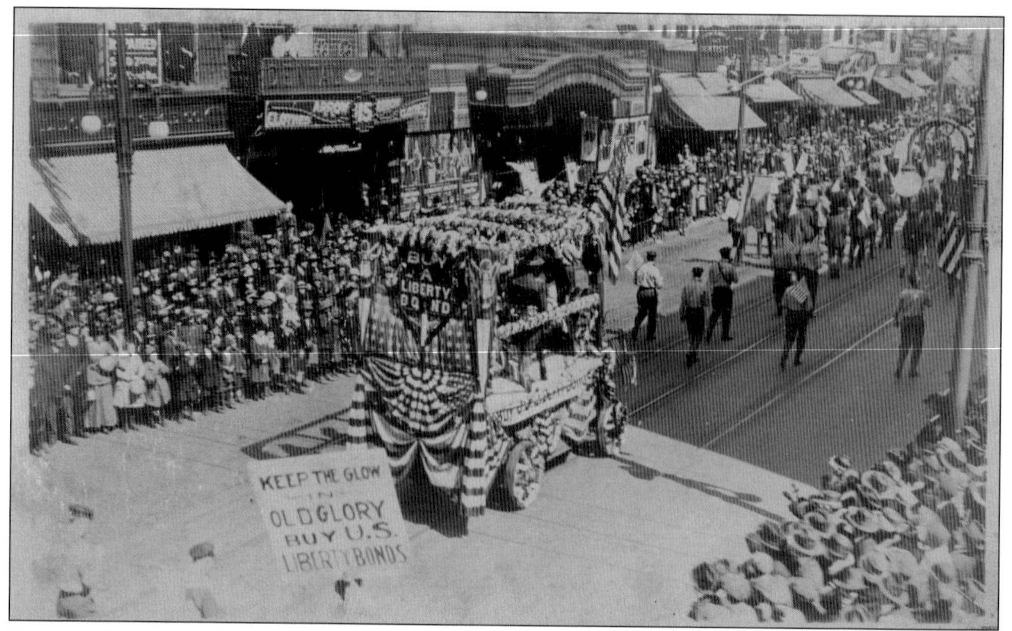

PARADE SCENE, *C.* 1917. During World War I, the tradesmen of the city put on this parade to boost morale, and this postcard is part of a series showing the parade route. Pictured here is the 700 block of Market Street including the New York Dental Parlor and the Majestic Theater in the center of the block.

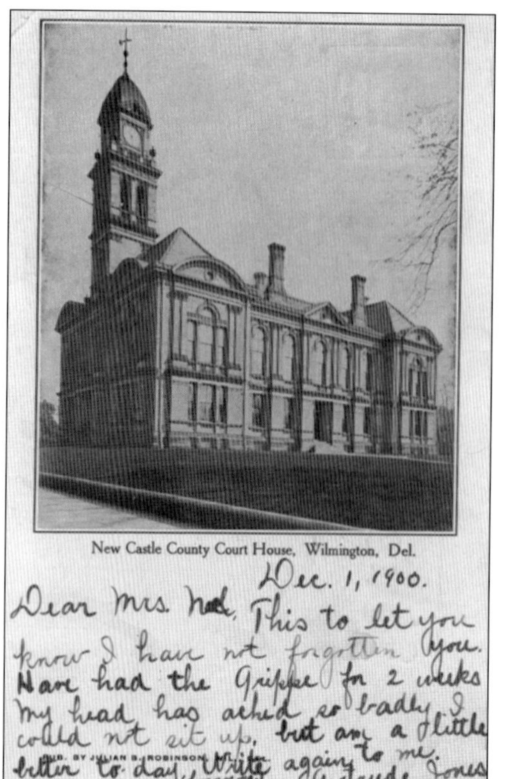

NEW CASTLE COUNTY COURTHOUSE, WILMINGTON, 1900. This courthouse was completed in 1881 when the county seat was moved from New Castle to Wilmington, but it was used only until the next city/county building, also known as the Public Building, was dedicated in 1917. Torn down in 1920, it fell victim to the city's plans to build Rodney Square—it had occupied the site of the grassy area in the square.

Soldiers and Sailors Monument, Wilmington, c. 1905. On the triangular piece of ground at Delaware Avenue, Broom, and Fourteenth Streets sits the state's first soldiers monument, built to honor those who died for the Union in the Civil War. It was dedicated on Memorial Day in 1871.

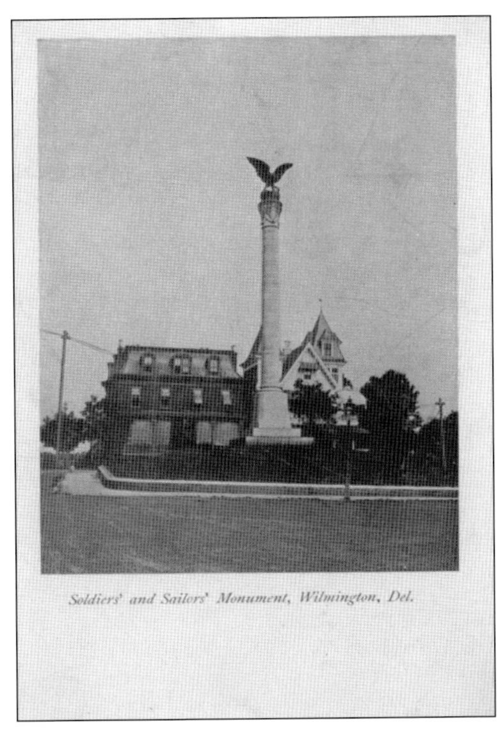

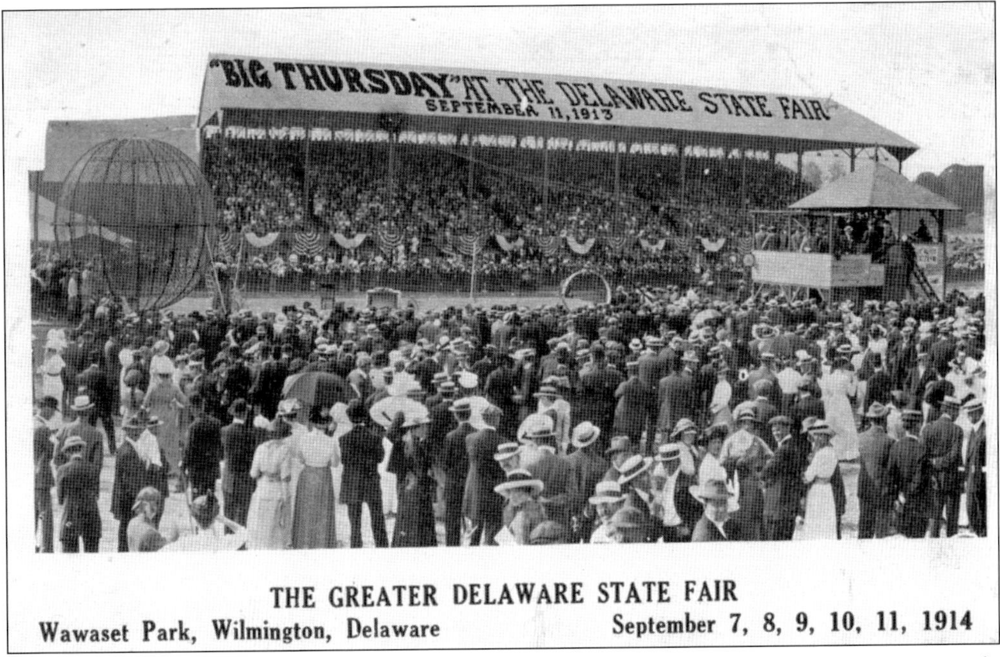

The Greater Delaware State Fair, 1911. The Delaware State Fair held at Wawaset Park, Wilmington, and later in Elsmere, began in 1901. Newspapers buzzed with daily news, estimating that Big Thursday, or Governor's Day, brought in about 20,000 people. Ten vaudeville acts and horse and dog shows kept visitors entertained. A Better Babies Contest helped to educate parents, and the suffragists had a tent, too.

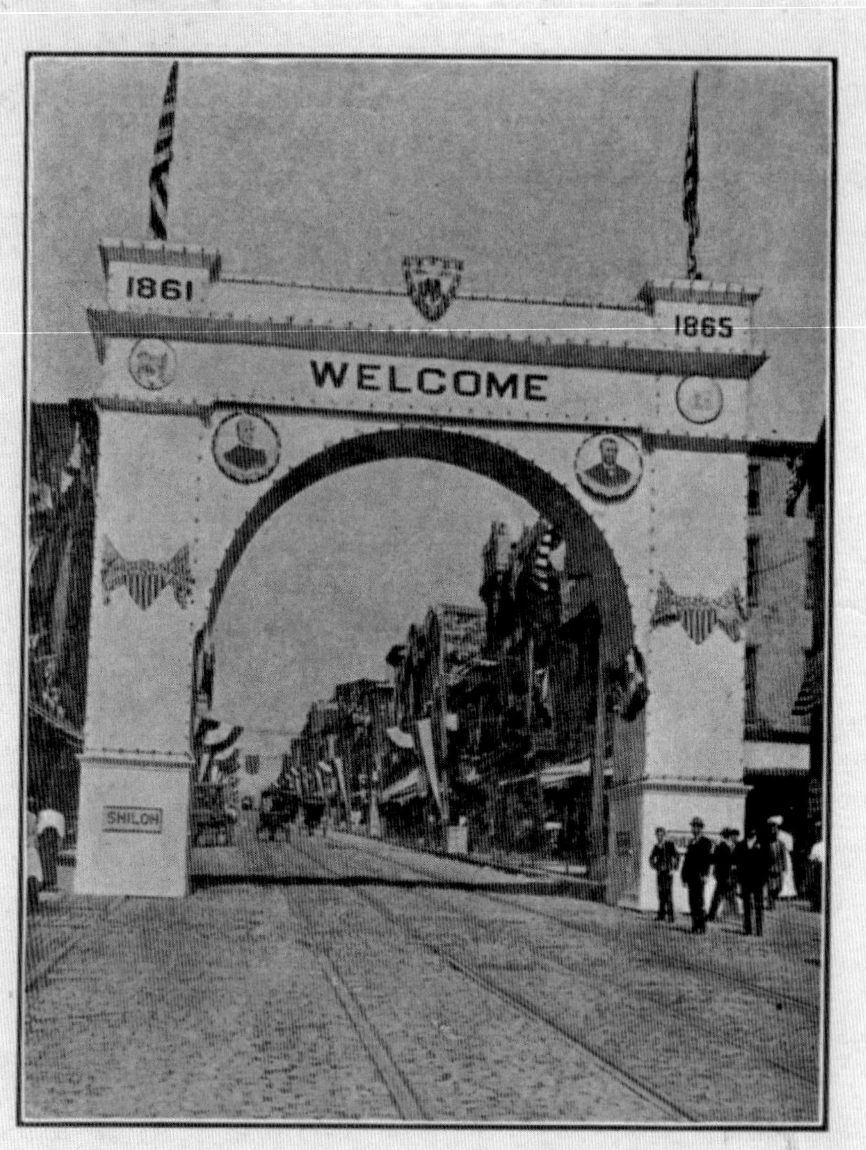

Triumphal Arch, Second and Market Street, Wilmington, 1905. This arch was the principal decoration in Wilmington when it hosted the 20th Annual National Encampment of the Union Veterans Legion on the 50th anniversary of the end of the Civil War. Designed by Howard D. Ross, who ran a clothing and dry goods store at 206–210 Market, the arch cost $500. Five hundred yards of muslin covered its frame, and it was decorated with flags, bunting, the dates of the war, major battle sites, and two large American flags atop six-foot-tall flag poles. One thousand electric lights lit the Union Veterans emblem and framed the arch. The word "Welcome," also lit, spanned 20 feet.

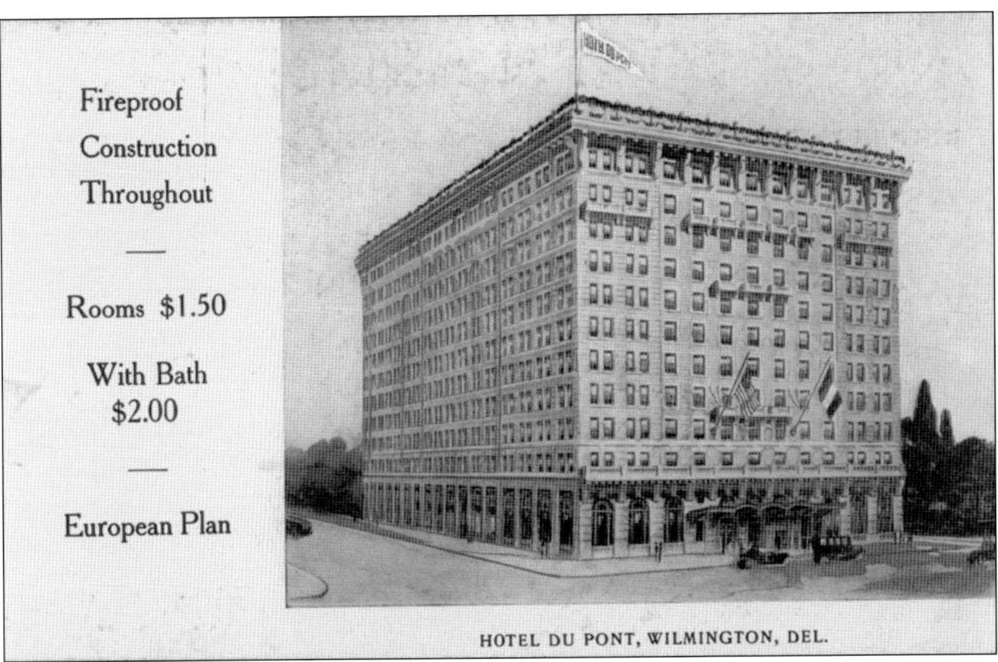

HOTEL DU PONT, 1911. Located in the heart of Wilmington, the hotel opened in January 1913. This is the architect's drawing, which was submitted for approval in 1911. When it opened, the hotel was considered a master achievement in hotel architecture and ingenuity both indoors and out. Downtown has changed dramatically in the 90 years since it opened, but the hotel serves the business, social, and civic needs of the community.

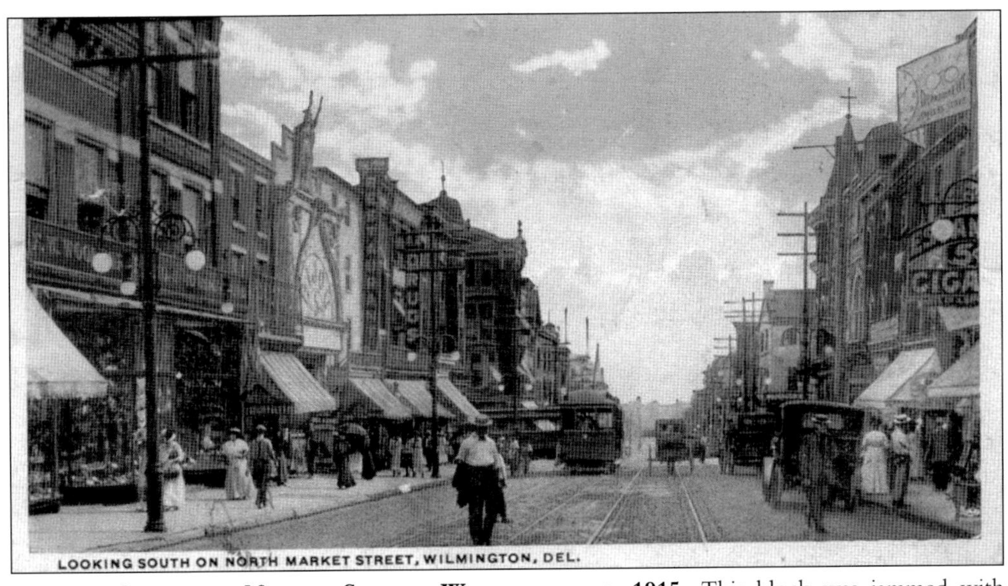

LOOKING SOUTH ON MARKET STREET, WILMINGTON, *c.* 1915. This block was jammed with activity; Woolworth's stands at 416 Market, at left, and the white building with the statue is the Bijou Theater, the third bearing that name, which operated from 1906 to about 1916. Also on this block were three of Wilmington's most important photographers: Adolph Markel, E.S.R. Butler, and Arthur N. Sanborn.

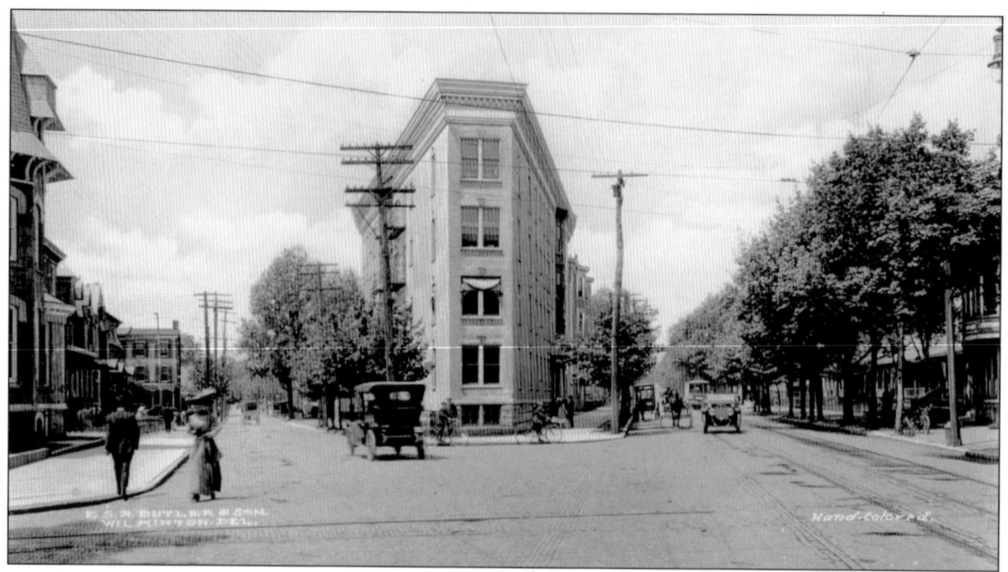

Delaware Avenue and Eleventh Street, Wilmington, 1905. Wilmington suffered a housing shortage in the early 1900s, due in part to the DuPont Company's decision to remain in the city. Many middle- and upper-income managers and scientists moved to Wilmington. Instead of living in boarding houses, singles and young couples lived in apartment buildings. The flatiron building, one of Wilmington's earliest apartment houses, stood near Trinity Episcopal Church.

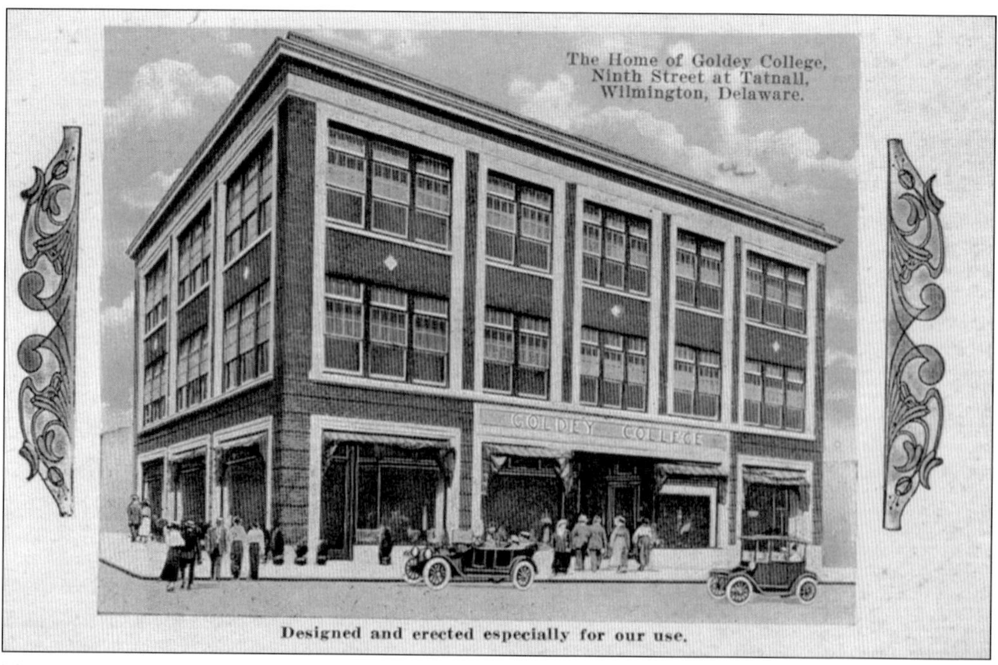

The Home of Goldey College, 1916. Goldey College, begun in 1886 by Harry Stuart Goldey, met in the Wilmington Institute Library until it leased this building at Ninth and Tatnall in 1916. Goldey trained students in business. One catalog described it as "a school that will teach that boy of yours, and that girl too, self-support . . . No theories, all the branches intensely practical." Goldey merged with Beacom College in 1951.

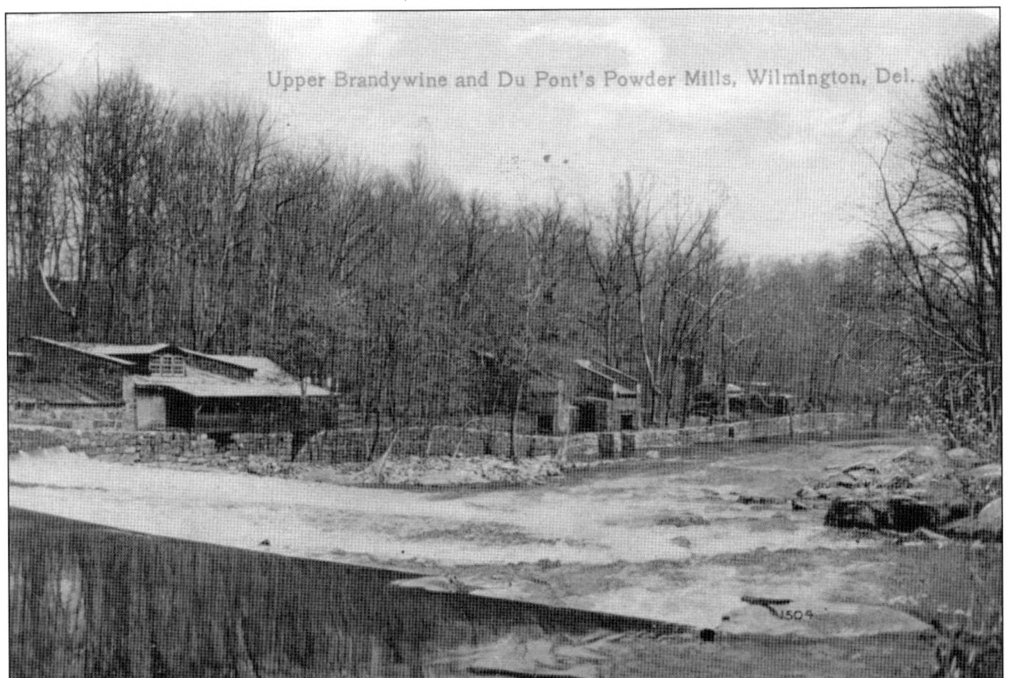

Upper Brandywine and Du Pont's Powder Mills, Wilmington, 1910. Founded near Wilmington on the Brandywine River in 1802, the DuPont Powder Mills sought to compete with the established powder manufacturers of England. The upper mills, seen here, were built in 1812. By 1834, when the lower mills were added, the DuPont Powder Company was the most extensive powder producer in the United States.

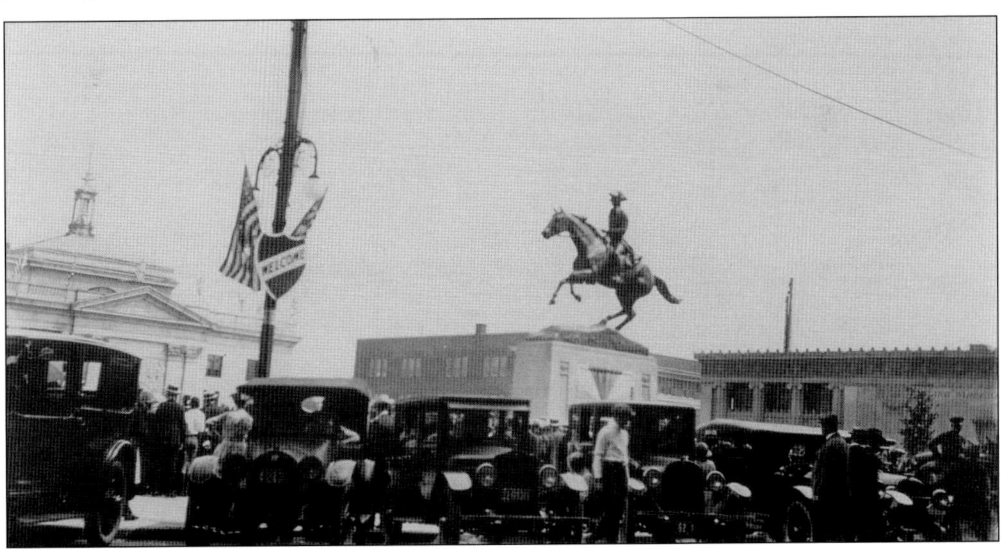

Unveiling of Caesar Rodney Monument, 1923. An estimated 10,000 people attended the unveiling of the statue designed by Edward Kelly on July 4, 1923. Six-year-old Eliza Rodney, a descendent of Caesar Rodney, unveiled the $35,000 statue and U.S. Senator Thomas F. Bayard was the guest orator. The bronze plaques for the sides were not yet completed, so the Caesar Rodney Equestrian Association placed red, white, and blue bunting over these spots.

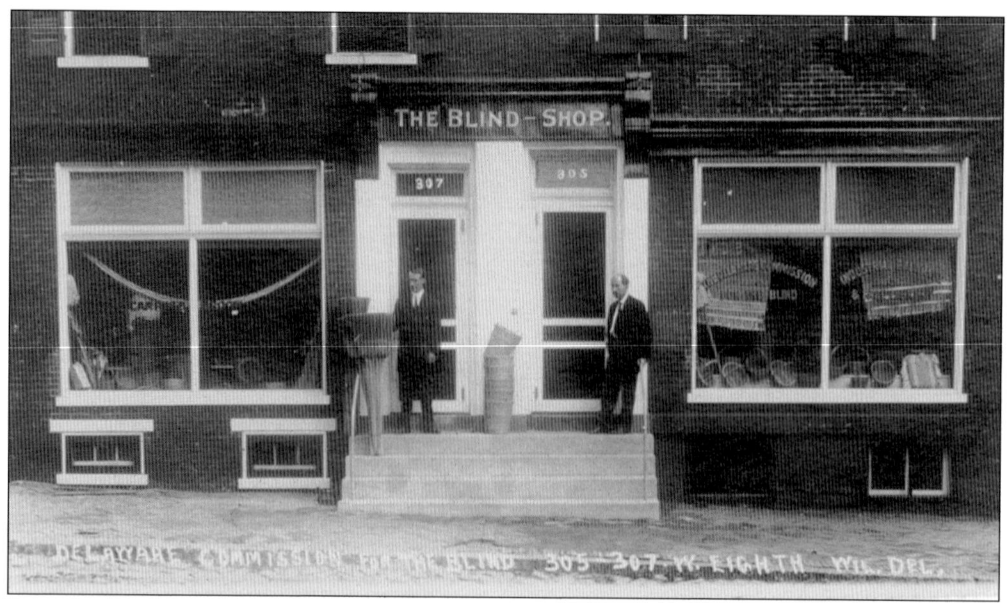

The Blind Shop, c. 1914. The Delaware Commission for the Blind first met on April 6, 1909, at the Wilmington Library. The commission, formed to provide gainful employment for those without sight, moved to its present headquarters, seen here at 305–307 West Eighth Street, in 1911. The building was completely remodeled in 1914. The two gentlemen pictured here are (left) W.H. Stephenson, activist for the blind, and (right) C. Reginald Van Kemp.

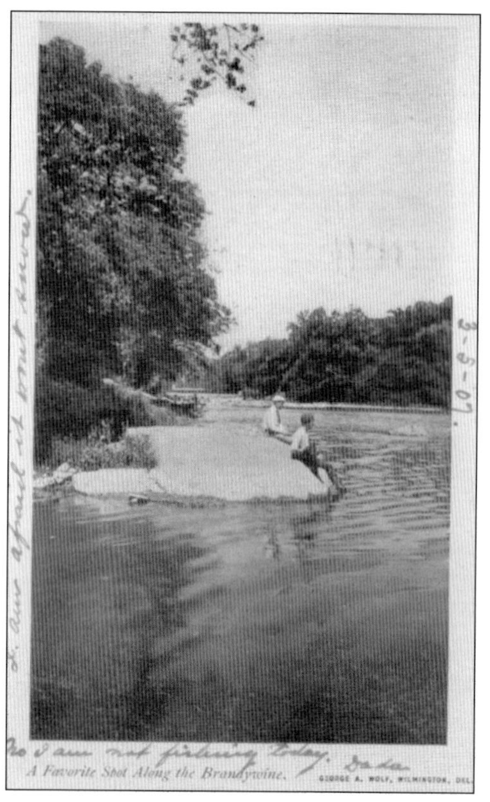

A Favorite Spot along the Brandywine, 1907. The Brandywine River has always been a favorite subject for artists and photographers alike.

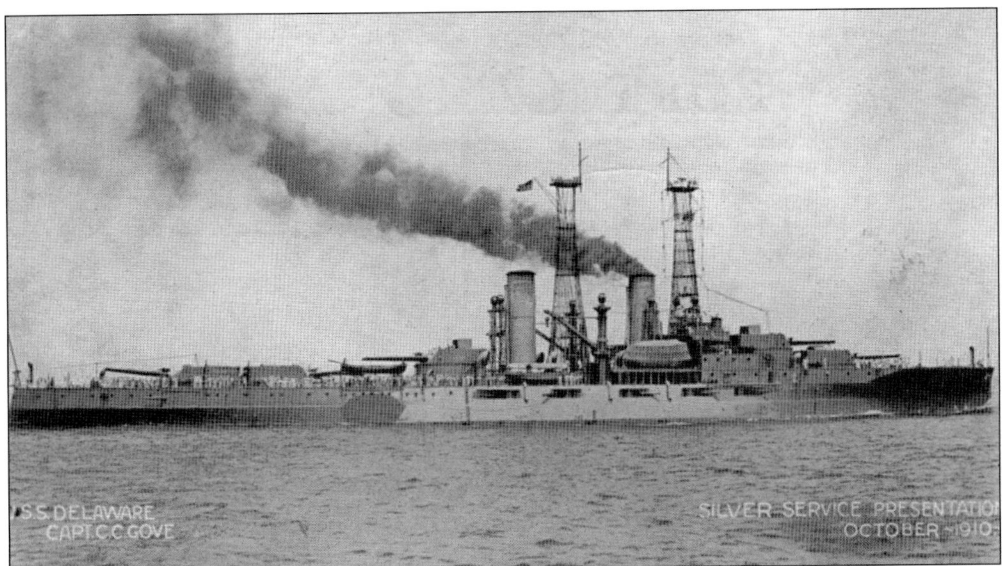

USS *DELAWARE*, 1910. The USS *Delaware*, the sixth to bear that name, was launched February 6, 1909, at Newport News, Virginia. For a time, it was America's largest warship. With its 25,000-horsepower engines and carrying 827 sailors and 55 officers, *Delaware* sailed into Wilmington on October 5, 1910. The images above and below come from a series of postcards commemorating the event. Delaware governor Simeon S. Pennewill presented gifts to Capt. Charles A. Gove, who had been "bestowed upon this monster of the seas which bears the name of the smallest but none the less brilliant in the diadem of states." In addition to a tea set, portraits of Delaware's naval heroes Comm. Thomas McDonough, Comm. Jacob Jones, and Adm. Samuel Francis Du Pont; flags; and colors were presented. The ship was decommissioned on November 10, 1923.

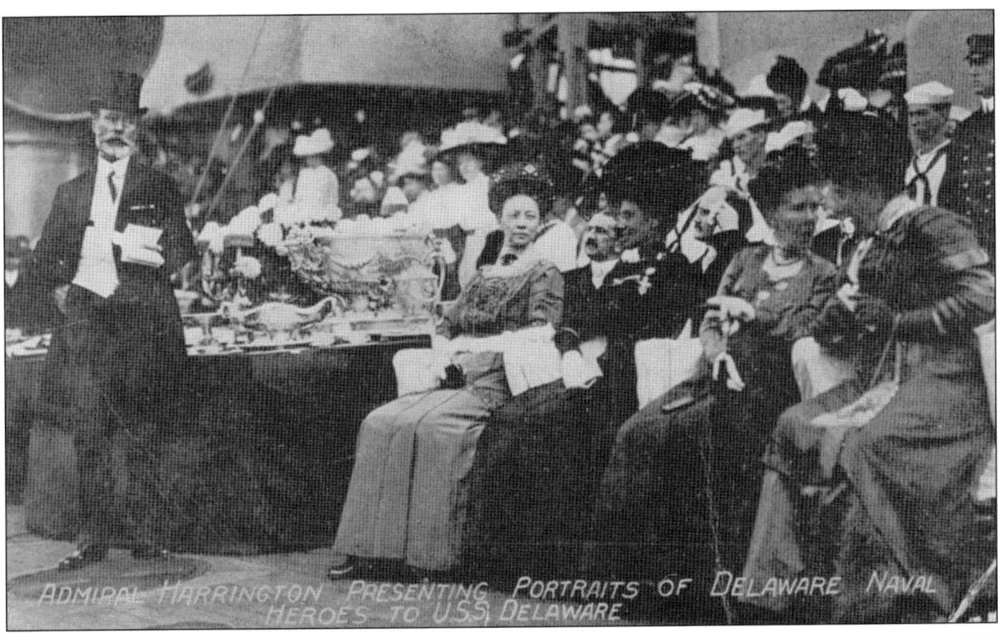

ADMIRAL HARRINGTON PRESENTING PORTRAITS OF DELAWARE NAVAL HEROES TO USS *DELAWARE*, 1910.

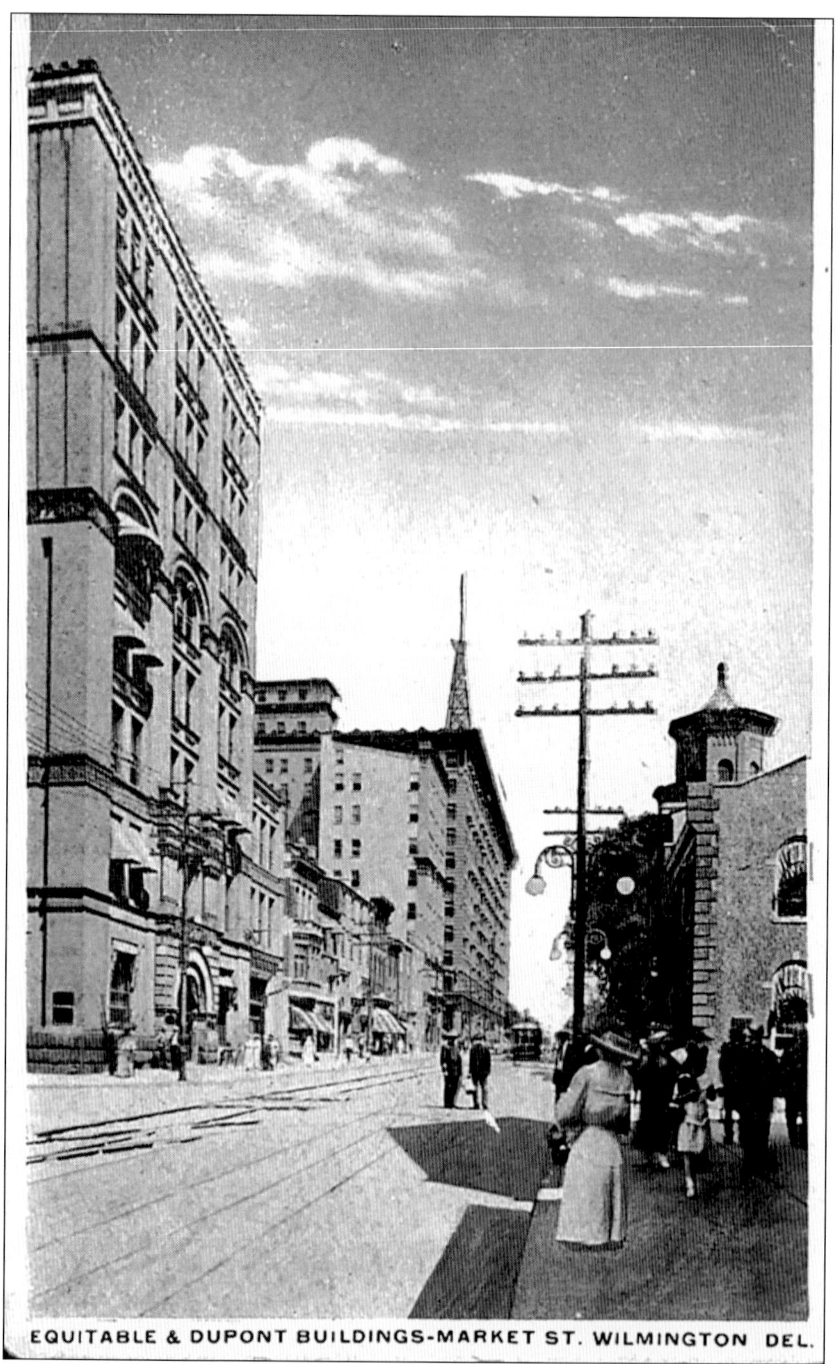

EQUITABLE AND DUPONT BUILDINGS, MARKET STREET, WILMINGTON, *C.* 1923. Looking north along Market Street, the Equitable Building (seen on the far left) is the city's first skyscraper. On the next block is the DuPont building with the WDEL radio tower sitting atop it. On the right is one of the twin steeples of the First Presbyterian Church, which was razed in the 1920s when Delaware Trust expanded its building.

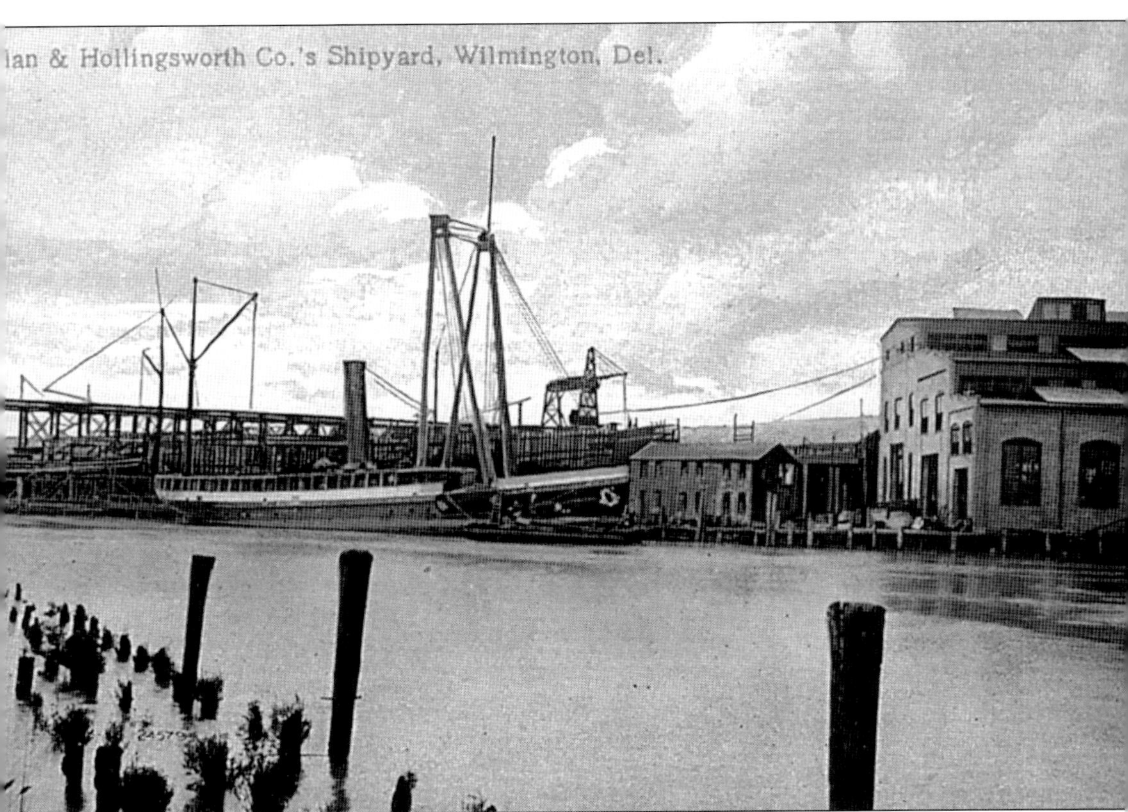

HARLAN AND HOLLINGSWORTH CO.'S SHIPYARD, WILMINGTON, *c.* 1910S. By the turn of the century, this manufacturer of ships and railroad cars was Wilmington's largest industrial firm. Founded in 1836, it was headquartered at the foot of West Street along the Christina River.